A History of
THE LEAGUE OF NATIONS

BY

JOHN I. KNUDSON, M. A., Dr. Sc. Pol.

Charles S. Baylis Professor of History and Economics
Polytechnic Institute of Brooklyn
Former Carnegie Teaching Fellow in International Law

☆ ☆
☆

TURNER E. SMITH & CO.
ATLANTA   GEORGIA

COPYRIGHT
IN THE UNITED STATES OF AMERICA, 1938
BY
TURNER E. SMITH & CO.

COPYRIGHT, 1938
IN GREAT BRITAIN, CANADA, IRELAND
AND IN ALL COUNTRIES SUBSCRIBING
TO THE BERN CONVENTION
BY
TURNER E. SMITH & CO.

Printed and Bound in the U. S. A. by
KINGSPORT PRESS, INC., KINGSPORT, TENNESSEE

CONTENTS

	PAGE
PREFACE	V
INTRODUCTION	3

PART ONE—INTERNATIONAL POLITICS

CHAPTER
I.	ORIGIN OF THE LEAGUE	19
II.	ORGANIZATION OF THE LEAGUE	42
III.	PACIFIC SETTLEMENT OF INTERNATIONAL DISPUTES	63
IV.	THE FORCE OF MORAL SANCTIONS	114
V.	REDUCTION AND LIMITATION OF ARMAMENTS	138
VI.	TECHNIQUE OF INTERNATIONAL ADMINISTRATION	157

PART TWO—INTERNATIONAL LEGISLATION

VII.	NON-POLITICAL ACTIVITIES OF THE LEAGUE	193
VIII.	THE ECONOMIC AND FINANCIAL ORGANIZATION	206
IX.	THE COMMUNICATIONS AND TRANSIT ORGANIZATION	225
X.	SOCIAL AND HEALTH QUESTIONS	244
XI.	INTELLECTUAL COOPERATION	272
XII.	THE UNITED STATES COOPERATES WITH THE LEAGUE	286

PART THREE—SEMI-LEAGUE ORGANIZATIONS

XIII.	THE INTERNATIONAL LABOR ORGANIZATION	315
XIV.	THE PERMANENT COURT OF INTERNATIONAL JUSTICE	333
XV.	EVALUATION AND FUTURE OF THE LEAGUE	355

PART FOUR—APPENDICES

I.	THE COVENANT OF THE LEAGUE OF NATIONS	373
II.	RULES OF PROCEDURE ADOPTED BY THE FIRST ASSEMBLY OF THE LEAGUE	390
III.	CONSTITUTION OF THE INTERNATIONAL LABOUR ORGANIZATION	401
IV.	THE STATUTE FOR THE PERMANENT COURT OF INTERNATIONAL JUSTICE	421
	BIBLIOGRAPHY	437
	INDEX	441

PREFACE

IN WRITING his *History of the League of Nations*, Professor Knudson has accomplished more than a work of excellent historical scholarship. Carried through during the lowest ebb of the League's affairs, his diligent interest and persistent researches are an expression of human faith needed for the long perspective and as a bit of home in a dark world.

Puny and ineffective as the work and influence of the League seem and, at critical times, are, the idea and achievements of the League in the far perspective of history have been tremendous in their implications. The tragic failures of the League in Manchuria and Ethiopia have been dramatic; its achievements and quiet work have been unheralded and taken for granted as a part of the work of the nations. With all its successes, the cruel fact remains that its responsibilities for keeping the peace far transcend any translation into effective international cooperation against war when decreed by the imperialistic interests of dictatorial powers. Geneva seems to be as yet only an international flag station on the world's road to war. Alternatives to the League—substitutes for international organization such as recourse to alliances and counter-alliances, reliance on isolation and neutrality, reliance on the prohibitive fears of scientific cruelties and technological destruction, on treaties and pacts, on international law without international organization—all these give less hope without Geneva. The mechanical inventions and the technological international framework encompassing the earth and holding up the economic structure of our modern world call for social inventions and mastery and an international political framework against drift toward war and the collapse of civilization.

Though such an international structure as has been erected by the nations seems to be tumbling in ruins, the flag of international organization for peace and cooperation must be kept flying at Geneva for the better day of our human hopes. The League, including the Assembly, the Council, the Secretariat, with their score of fields of international cooperation and their effective good offices in many international crises, the International Labor Office with its researches and conferences as a basis for the raising of international labor standards, and the Permanent Court of International Justice with its score and more of judgments in settlement of international disputes constitute an experience as the basis of the growth and improvement of a League progressively liberated from the injustices of the Treaty and as yet mainly in the prayers and aspirations of inarticulate people who fight the wars and do the work of the world.

Frank P. Graham

Jan. 20, 1938
CHAPEL HILL, N. C.

PART ONE
INTERNATIONAL POLITICS

INTRODUCTION

In view of transpired events in the world, it takes great courage to write an impartial history of the League of Nations. Its weakness is everywhere recognized, and many people hold that the inability of nations to cooperate effectively will inevitably lead to another major catastrophe. The forces working against successful collaboration have become stronger. A growing spirit of nationalism, accompanied by the world-wide economic depression is a contributing factor in weakening the existing peace machinery.

At present, the nations have reached a low ebb in their efforts to cooperate in solving their common problems. The depression was accompanied by high tariffs, trade and currency restrictions, nationalist rivalries culminating in competitive armaments, treaty violations, and actual warfare. The flaming hopes that characterized the first decade of post-war international relations have been dimmed. Nations are apprehensive of hostile neighbors and seek security not so much through the combined efforts of League members, as through the resort to armed strength.

A strange paradox exists in that every nation is assuming a defensive rôle that too often bespeaks the part of aggression. Nations are engaging in territorial conquests and under the guise of self-protection, are entering into "defensive" treaty arrangements. The present state of world chaos is surely not in keeping with the long development of nations toward their present achievements and greatness. The rich heritage of civilization has, in the broader sense, been procured as the result of international generosity and mutuality of interest in the common welfare of all nations.

Science and technology have made available vast resources that until recently were unknown, and the unlimited wealth of the world is now brought within the reach of all nations. Only shortsightedness can prevent the realization of national advancement, such as was never hoped for by the fondest dreamers of the ages. No nation need forego the things which nature and the skill of man have provided, if wise direction be given to their full utilization. The foremost task of the present generation is to rebuild a tottering world structure and provide not only a strong sense of security against aggressive warfare, but also free access to the world's resources. The path to a stable world order lies not merely in the repression of violence but in the achievement of political and economic justice through international planning. It is this task to which the League has set itself. The faltering, and too often hostile, attitudes of nations has, for the time being, materially weakened that institution.

There are basic principles upon which the League is founded that cannot be destroyed by recurring exigencies in world society. These are embodied in the League Covenant and are destined to outlive the forces which threaten to play havoc with an unstable world order. The underlying forces of peace and order are inherent in the hearts of men and will continue to exert themselves until an orderly world society is realized. The idea of the sanctity of human life has been developed in man over many centuries and is thus deeply imbedded in his nature. It is inevitable therefore, that man's efforts will ever be directed toward the preservation of life and not toward its destruction. It was on the basis of this deep-seated desire of the peoples of the world that the League was founded. Man is convinced of the horrors of war and the blessings of peace, but has not yet reached the stage of a tranquil world order. When intolerable conditions prevail, or when led astray by misconceptions of his own destiny, he engages in war. It is the primary purpose of the League to foster wholesome international relations and to keep ambitious nations from aggression.

Unfortunately, some people still accept the thesis that the institution of war, which dates back to the dawn of history, is so firmly established that its abolition is impossible. In answer to this, one should note that the history of man has been an effort to overcome the forces that are destructive to his existence. Numerous examples could be cited to show man's success in creating a better international society. If the nations of the world are able to cooperate in matters relating to human betterment, then the question arises as to why they are not able to unite in insuring world peace? This may be explained by the shortness of time during which the problem has been under serious examination. Great changes do not occur overnight. And if history serves as a guide, we will continue to grapple with this problem until a solution is found. It has been said that no problem is ultimately solved until it is solved correctly. Much encouragement may be found in the widespread interest now shown in world peace. Never before has so much study been given to this problem, which gives hope that some acceptable means will be found to create a warless world.

In a world threatened by war, one may ask, is national selfishness too strong to prevent the triumph of peace? Will national self-interest overcome international cooperation? Does morality exist as a force in international affairs? The pessimist, the prophet of doom, will find many arguments to bolster his views in the light of existing conditions, while the optimist has reason to expect continued improvement in international relations, when viewed in light of the longer historical perspective. Everyone will agree that a tremendous slump occurred in international morality in recent years. This was in sharp contrast with the idealism and unselfish service so much in evidence during and shortly after the war, when it was hoped that a better world order would emerge.

The later post-war years were marked by the upsurge of national interests to the detriment of all nations. One of the first manifestations of this was the United States Senate's rejection of American membership in the League of Nations. Other nations followed our example in selfish pursuits, with the resulting loss which comes from the lack of cooperation. The larger perspective in international planning would have prevented the threatening conditions that now confront us. It is unfortunately true that nations, like individuals, too often adopt policies of immediate expediency. National self-interest frequently dictates governmental policies, whereas international morality, as expressed in unselfish cooperation with other nations, would bring greater and more lasting benefits.

There comes a time in human affairs when nations cannot rely upon idealism and moral suasion to deter imperialistic nations. High sounding phrases that express a desire for peace may be regarded as a sign of weakness on the part of nations that sanctify war. Nor will a nation, bent upon aggression, be deterred by examples of sane international policy in other countries. This country has boasted of a righteous course in the conduct of foreign affairs, and we have held up our practises as a model for other nations to follow. But all nations do not follow our injunctions. The traditional policy of the United States was set forth by the Secretary of State, Cordell Hull, on July 16, 1937, shortly after the outbreak of hostilities in the Far East, when he issued a statement which is in part as follows:

> "This country constantly and consistently advocates maintenance of peace. We advocate national and international self-restraint. We advocate abstinence by all nations from use of force in pursuit of policy and from interference in the internal affairs of other nations. We advocate adjustment of problems in international relations by processes of peaceful negotiation and agreement. . . . We avoid entering into alliances or entangling commitments but we believe in cooperative effort by peaceful and practicable means in support of the principles hereinbefore stated."

This statement of American foreign policy was communicated by Mr. Hull to all foreign governments and to the League of Nations. Responses were made by more than fifty nations, in lip-service to these high sentiments. The effectiveness of this declaration was comparable to the "Outlawry of War" in which almost all nations agreed not to resort to armed conflict in the settlement of their differences, but to settle them only by pacific means. Declarations, such as the above, carry no weight if and when a nation desires to violate them. Pledges that are not backed up by enforcement machinery have thus far been of little value. Self-denying ordinances are basically sound if all nations would only adhere to then.

The Far Eastern conflict continued to grow in intensity following Mr. Hull's statement and our government became aroused, for Japanese aggression appeared to grow into vast proportions. If Japan succeeds in the subjugation of China, a condition will develop which, will in time, make Japan a powerful military empire with which this country may have to deal. If Japan is to be deterred from obtaining her objectives, some drastic steps will have to be taken immediately. The older policy of watchful waiting will not suffice if the future peace of this country is to be assured. President Franklin D. Roosevelt took cognizance of this change in the memorable speech he delivered in Chicago, October 5, 1937, repudiating our theory of isolationism, and setting forth a positive program calling for all peace-loving nations to check aggressors. Among other things, he stated:

"The political situation in the world, which of late has been growing progressively worse, is such as to cause grave concern and anxiety to all the peoples and nations who wish to live in peace and amity with their neighbors. . . . The present reign of terror and international lawlessness . . . has now reached a stage where the very foundations of civilization are seriously threatened. . . . Without a declaration of war and without warning or justification of any kind, civilians, including women and children, are being ruthlessly murdered with bombs from the air. . . . Let no one imagine that America will escape, that it may expect mercy, that this Western Hemisphere will not be attacked and that it will continue tranquilly and peacefully to carry on the ethics and the arts of civilization. . . The peace-loving nations must make a concerted effort in opposition to those violations of treaties and those ignorings of humane instincts which today are creating a state of international anarchy and instability from which there is no escape through mere isolation or neutrality. . . . It seems to be unfortunately true that the epidemic of world lawlessness is spreading. When an epidemic of physical disease starts to spread, the community joins in a 'quarantine' of the patients in order to protect the health of the community against the spread of disease. . . . Most important of all, the will for peace . . . must express itself to the end that nations that may be tempted to violate their agreements and the rights of others will desist from such a cause. There must be positive endeavors to preserve peace."

The public response to the abandonment of isolation was immediate. It electrified the democracies of the world and received the approval of eighty-five per cent of the newspapers of this country. The League Assembly took immediate note of the President's remarks, and on the following day invited the United States and the seventeen League members who had signed or adhered to the provisions of the "Nine-Power Treaty" (which guaranteed the independence of China) to meet, in an effort to end hostilities in the Far East. The Assembly declared that Japan had violated its treaty obligations by invading China and agreed that no steps should be taken which "might have the effect of weakening the power of China's resistance," and to "consider how far they can individually extend aid to China."

Secretary Hull immediately noted the Assembly's action and declared that, "The Government of the United States has been forced to the conclusion that the action of Japan and China is inconsistent with the principles which should govern the relationships between nations. . . . Thus the conclusions of this Government with respect to the foregoing are in general accord with those of the Assembly of the League of Nations." Mr. Hull subsequently announced that the United States would accept the Assembly's invitation to participate in the "Nine-Power" Conference to be held in Brussels. The Conference accordingly assembled, and an attempt was made to bring the disputants together to effect a settlement. Japan having already been condemned as the aggressor by the League Assembly and the United States, informed the Conference on November 12, 1937 of her refusal to attend.

The Conference proceeded to deliberate on possible steps that might be taken to check Japanese aggression. Proposals were made to lend aid to China by supplying her with the necessary war materials with which to continue the war against Japan. The Chinese contended that this was insufficient to combat the superior military forces of Japan. Steps should be taken, they said, to penalize Japan by denying her the necessary materials of war. This was a practical proposal. A major difficulty, however, lay in the inability of the powers to obtain the consent of the United States to discriminate against the aggressor, rather than treat both combatants on an equal footing. The delegates at the Conference, with the exception of the Italians, made it plain that they would go as far as the United States in taking effective measures to "quarantine" the Japanese. The people of this country are overwhelmingly in sympathy with China and do not wish Japan to gain her objectives. While we are opposed to Japanese aggression, the practical question arises as to how we may bring effective measures to bear against her, and at the same time avoid warfare. Practical steps must be taken if Japan is to be halted. Efforts of mediation at the Brussels Conference proved unsuccessful. A warlike nation does not hesitate to defy existing treaties nor will it listen to reason. Under such conditions it becomes necessary to resort to stringent measures if peace is to prevail.

Many may still insist that wars beyond our shores are of little or no concern to us. The fallacy of this viewpoint was clearly expressed in the speech by President Roosevelt when he indicated the nearness of such dangers. Japanese victory may, in time, lead to serious complications involving the United States. The time to check Japan is not at some future time, when she is better prepared, but at present, when she has already encountered stiff opposition in China and when her credit is seriously strained. This action need not be taken by the United States alone, but rather in conjunction with the member states of the League who have already condemned Japan's actions. Fifty or more states would unite effectively in this move if supported by the United States.

What effective measures, short of war, can be taken? Article XVI of the League Covenant provides for the application of economic sanctions against an aggressor, and by this means the preponderant majority of the nations may unite in denying a nation the necessary materials for the successful conduct of war. Some may counter that an embargo on goods to Japan means war. Sanctions do not mean war. What nation regardless of its military strength, would dare to wage war against the nations of the world. Fifty-five nations constitute the membership of the League and all but two denounced Japan by vote in the Assembly. If the United States, which has a greater stake in the Far East than most other nations, would unite with the League in applying effective sanctions against Japan, the conflict would be brought to a speedy end.

It is a lamentable fact that Japanese aggression is made possible by materials obtained in the very countries which now condemn her. Without this assistance, her war of aggression could not have been fought. She is not economically self-sufficient as regards raw materials such as oil, iron-ore, rubber, and cotton—all of which are essential in modern warfare. Prior to the war, Japan purchased seventy-five per cent of her oil, eighty per cent of her raw cotton, and fifty per cent of her iron from us, and the bulk of her rubber from Great Britain. The chief Japanese export is raw silk of which the United States purchases eighty per cent, while Great Britain imports almost the full remainder. If Great Britain and the United States should refuse to import silk, the Japanese farmers would face dire economic stress. Such a condition could not be ignored by the Japanese Government. On the other hand, if Great Britain and the United States were joined by the members of the League in denying Japan the essential commodities mentioned above, she would be rendered helpless in China. These are practical considerations, which, with good will, can be effectively applied. Japan has been aided by our supplying her with war materials, whereas China has been penalized, due to her inability to obtain them. This is not even neutrality.

The necessary machinery for bringing concerted action against Japan exists in the League of Nations. Inasmuch as she has been declared the aggressor, only active steps are needed to give effect to League condemnation. The possible course that the United States may pursue will depend upon the attitude of its citizens, since our Government can only act with popular approval. The people of this country should be ready to join with the League in applying effective economic and financial sanctions against Japan. The League Covenant distinguishes between right and wrong, which is also characteristic of the American people. And if we wish righteousness to triumph, it behooves us to unite with the recognized peace institution of the world in achieving it.

History will bear witness to the justice of League endeavors in achieveing peace and far-reaching international cooperation. The conference machinery has functioned smoothly and this, after all, is what the Geneva institution provides. The failures accompanying these efforts cannot be blamed upon the League, but rather upon the individual states that refuse to utilize present-day international means of collaboration.

The League, as an organization has no policy of its own, and is not a seat of government, except that it affords a convenient meeting place for the member states to gather and formulate programs of action. The League ideal represents certain high principles toward which the nations may strive. Through it ideas are promulgated, discussions are made possible and projects are initiated that lead to concerted international action. Tangible results are not always realized, but definite courses are charted, enabling nations to reach the haven of an orderly world society.

The standards set by League deliberation are sometimes more advanced than those of individual states, and conference discussions are thus devoid of results. Hence, there is at times the disposition to refer to specific League attempts as failures. This has been especially true in the formulation of plans for economic and political disarmament, and the insuring of world peace. Although these problems have not been adequately solved under the egis of the League, yet the endeavor to do so has been most genuine. A just indictment could be found against the League if it had made no attempts to solve embarrassing problems. All questions of international concern coming within the purview of the League are considered, regardless of the likelihood of agreements. To do otherwise would be to shirk the responsibility for which the League was created. Successes and failures have always accompanied international collaboration, and the history of the post-war era is no exception. It should also be remembered that the scope of international discussion has been greatly broadened and that the League has entered fields that did not permit of international discussion prior to its creation, let alone the successful solution of them.

While the League's activities have been accompanied by successes and failures, the fact remains that its record of achievements is unequaled in history. New forces have been set in motion which have made this possible. The amazing development of science and technology has brought about a unity of interests among nations, so much so, that a major disturbance in one part of the world has its repercussions in every other part. No single nation can live unto itself, for the well-being of one is bound up with those of others. Wars, or the threat of wars, have become the concern of all nations, and necessarily so, for while active participation may be avoided, no nation can escape the consequences resulting therefrom.

Normal peace-time activities in trade and finance are of international concern, and the dislocation resulting from the action of a single nation is felt in the far corners of the earth. These close relationships have materially enhanced human welfare. Markets are of world-wide import, as the daily needs of man are supplied from home and abroad. Stable world-markets lead to the enjoyment of higher standards of living and the evolution of a higher civilization. The benefits derived through international economic relations must be accompanied by increased national responsibilities, if they are to be fully realized. Thus, instead of greater independence among nations we find a high degree of interdependence. This function must be carried on through a central clearing agency which, today is the League of Nations. Not that this world institution is utilized in every way commensurate with international needs, but a marked beginning has been made and much encouragement may be derived from the multifarious activities of the League during the comparatively short period of its existence.

When the League was founded, many felt that it must be "all or nothing" and thus attempts were made to clothe it with prestige in one form or another. Liquidation of world war problems received much attention during the first few years of its history, but new questions arose in increasing numbers to claim attention at League meetings. These continued to grow in number and variety during the first decade, when it appeared that the goal of an orderly world-society had been reached. The world-wide depression followed and national ambitions were asserted to the distinct detriment of the League. The futility of international solidarity was made plain by isolationists, but growing dangers of war and national economic stress only served to reveal the weakness of their views. Thus serious thought is again given to the need for "concerted effort in opposition to those violations of treaties and those ignorings of human instincts which today are creating a state of international anarchy and instability from which there is no escape to mere isolation or neutrality." These bold words by President Roosevelt offer the only solution to future peace.

Future world security depends, to a large degree, upon the attitude of the United States. Aloofness has not brought the desired ends, and the future peace of this country is uncertain. The democracies that compose the membership of the League are denied the support of a foremost country in the world. The League's efforts to stem the onslaught of Fascist dictators is met with indifference here while we at the same time are seized with nervous "jitters." The United States is closely linked up with the members of the League in political, economic and cultural interests. Government by dictatorships has made inroads into free governments and, if democratic rule is to survive, a united front of free peoples becomes a vital concern. These are critical times and the United States is the essential link in establishing a preponderant influence on the side of world peace. The League has been greatly misrepresented before the American people and the possibility of uniting with League members against aggressor nations has received little support here. The growing danger of dictators should cause the American people to reconsider its attitude in the light of rapid world changes. Brazil has of late set up a dictatorship and this gives us a true sense of the urgency of the problem. The question of our relation to the League is of primary concern to every American.

There is urgent need for a re-interpretation of the League in view of the vast amount of criticism that has been directed against it, owing to its failures to cope effectively with recent crises. These failures have led many to look askance upon future collective efforts by nations. Few realize the long distance which nations have traveled in building the necessary institutions for permanent cooperation. As undue emphasis has been placed upon League failures, and very little upon its successes, this book seeks to set forth a more balanced perspective by emphasizing the history of its accomplishments, of which there are indeed many. The history of post-war international relations centers largely around the periodic meetings at Geneva. Many different view-points have been expressed in appraising the League as an institution to meet the collective needs of world society. While a degree of justification may be found in all of them, the viewpoint expressed throughout the following pages is definitely in defense of the League as an institution to promote the reign of law and order among nations, and that of a faith in the ultimate triumph of the League. These patterns and ideals are compelling. The League has championed the rule of moral principle as against world chaos.

Many books and treatises have been written on the subject of what the League *is* and *does* while this book attempts to set forth what the League has *done* and *how* it has done it. While a history of its achievements and failures is recounted yet the real interest in this study has been to emphasize League *methods*. This is not merely a history but a commentary upon it. Procedure in international conferences has of necessity been given much attention. Since the League, the Permanent Court of International Justice, and the International Labor Organization differ from one another in methods of procedure, they are fully discussed.

This book is planned for use in academic circles, clubs, forums and for general readers. It is intended to be suitable for both elementary and advanced students by giving an historical survey of the three foremost international institutions. Detailed study of specialized subjects may be continued by referring to books that are listed in the bibliography. The bibliography is by no means complete, as the literature on the League is very extensive. Only the more representative works are included. Footnote references would, of course, be useful as aids to further study, yet such references have purposely been omitted in order to simplify the subject and make it serviceable to a larger number of readers. In the absence of special references, the author wishes to acknowledge the ready availability of materials contained in Denys. P. Meyers, *Handbook of the League of Nations;* Manley O. Hudson, *The Permanent Court of International Justice;* and Ursula P. Hubbard, *The Cooperation of the United States with the League of Nations.*

My thanks are due to my students who have assisted in the detailed work necessary for the publication of the book; to my friend and colleague, Dr. Emil Lengyel, who read the entire manuscript and offered many helpful suggestions; and to President Frank P. Graham of the University of North Carolina for his genuine cooperation in writing the foreword.

It goes without saying that opinions will differ as regards many of the interpretations and conclusions contained in these pages. This must of necessity be so in dealing with a subject around which a great controversy has raged. While unanimity of agreement regarding an evaluation of the League is too much to expect, yet this book will have served its purpose if serious thought is provoked on the most effective means of building an orderly world society.

Brooklyn, New York   JOHN I. KNUDSON
November 15, 1937

CHAPTER I

Origin of the League

The birth of the League of Nations at the close of the World War marked a turning point in international relations. For the first time in history an institution was established to coordinate the interests the nations had in common. The continuing and systematic work as planned by the League was in sharp contrast with the older system of spasmodic cooperation among nations. The growing intricate nature of international relations led to greater frequency of contacts among nations, and in the course of time some such organization as planned by the founders of the League became an urgent necessity. The establishment of this world institution was hastened by the War, as at its close a state of flux existed that made great innovations possible.

Due to the growing need for a recognized clearing center, the desire to see it in operation was expressed by many leaders. More important than this was the hidden desires of the masses in all countries for some agency to fulfill the high aims for which the League stands. Therefore the basic ideas as embodied in the Covenant are not alone the aspirations of intellectual forerunners, but the product of the deeper hidden desires implanted in people everywhere. The more immediate urge that called for an organized international society grew out of the agony of the War and found expression in the deep yearning to prevent its reoccurrence. The desire for mutual protection led to the conviction that something must be invented to prevent another World War. The old "balance of power" in Europe was discredited, and armed forces offered no assurance of peace, hence a repetition of past experiences in international relations must needs be modified.

Similar attempts had been tried after great wars for a very long time. The most notable examples were the Quadruple Alliance supported by the Holy Alliance which existed from 1815 to 1823. They were formed following the French aggression in Europe and were intended to prevent future outbreaks. A similar condition gave immediate rise to the League in that the threat of German domination would, under its aegis, be checked. Although a similarity existed in the immediate desire to create a union of nations to ensure peace, yet the dissimilarities were extremely significant. The earlier "Concert of Europe" was created to maintain the status quo following territorial readjustments that disregarded national interests. The chief objective was to prevent change in any form which in the very nature of existing conditions was impossible and it was therefore destined to fail. On the other hand, while there was a strong urge on the part of many statesmen in 1919 to create a world order based on unchanging conditions, the Covenant was framed with the definite purpose of meeting new problems. In other words, the League was designed to be sufficiently flexible to meet varying conditions in a dynamic world. Other contributory factors to its formation were the increasing number of international conferences of one sort or another, and the organization of courts of arbitration to settle international disputes.

Proposals for an organized world society have been set forth by writers, poets, philosophers, jurists, and statesmen throughout medieval and modern times.

Pierre Dubois, a reformer during the reign of Philip the Fair of France, seems very modern, since he proposed a court of international arbitration, advocated outlawry of war, and held that the nations responsible for it should be starved out or "boycotted." About the same time Marsiglio of Padua attempted to analyze the causes of war and proposed remedies, some of which appear far in advance of his time. The poet, Dante advocated the unification of western Europe under one strong God-fearing ruler. Centuries later, in 1623, Emeric Crucé suggested a permanent council of ambassadors to settle disputes. Hugo Grotius, in 1625, published his plan of peaceful arbitration. About the same time the Duke of Sully wished to create a federation of European states. William Penn, a Quaker colonizer, wrote his "Essay toward the Present and Future Peace of Europe" (1693) in which he proposed periodic meetings of all the European princes for the purpose of creating rules of international law, and the adjustment of territorial and other disputes. If a sovereign refused to comply with the judgment of the princes the combined military forces of the others should be used against him. The Abbé de St. Pierre (1713) published his "Project of Perpetual Peace" in which he proposed a universal military alliance to guarantee territorial integrity and suppress revolutions. The Abbé proposed Utrecht as a center where the nations could collaborate in achieving the object of his plan. Jeremy Bentham, the English jurist and moral philosopher, wrote his "Principles of International Law" (1789) in which he denounced secret diplomacy, armaments and colonial imperialism. He also argued in favor of general defensive alliances and mutual guarantees if wars are to be abandoned. In 1795, Immanuel Kant proposed an international federation of states in an essay, "Toward Eternal Peace," and upheld the principle of non-intervention and the abolition of standing armies.

Numerous private peace organizations were established during the nineteenth century and the early part of the twentieth that prepared the soil for the founding of the League of Nations. The New York Peace Society was formed in 1815 and in the following year the Society of Friends founded the first European peace organization in London. The first peace society on the continent of Europe was formed at Geneva in 1830. The first International Peace Congress was held in Brussels in 1848 and a similar congress met in Paris the following year. In 1867 the International League for Peace and Freedom was formed by Victor Hugo, Giuseppe Garibaldi, and Antoine Lemonnier and is still a flourishing organization. In like manner the first International Women's Peace Society in Europe was formed in 1896, and from this grew several national women's peace organizations. The Nobel Peace Foundation was set up in the same year. In 1910 the World Peace Foundation was organized in Boston, and at the same time the Carnegie Endowment for International Peace was formed with an endowment of more than twelve million dollars to be used for the cause of peace. A large part of the fund from the Rockefeller Foundation, organized in 1913, has also been used for this purpose. The Union of Democratic Control was founded in London in 1914 to prepare a new policy to be pursued after the War in furtherance of peace. In the same year the Fellowship of Reconciliation was founded in Cambridge, England, to work out plans for a new social order in which war shall be excluded. Also in the next year the League of Nations' Society was organized in London and advocated "a treaty binding members to peaceful settlement of all disputes" and provide united action against an aggressor. These concepts were later enbodied in the League Covenant. In 1915 a Central Organization for a Durable Peace was created by the Dutch with members from most of the countries of Western Europe. The World Union of Women for International Concord was organized in Geneva in 1915 to study the causes of war and to seek if possible to prevent wars. These movements had as their aim the prospect of devising ways and means to bring about permanent peace. Many countries were included in the movement which indicated the wide spread interest in universal peace.

Sir Edward Grey and Prime Minister Asquith of England spoke in favor of the formation of a league of nations as the only alternative to the reoccurrence of another major war. Among other outstanding Englishmen who favored some form of a league of nations were Sir Henry Campbell Bannerman, Lord Bryce, W. B. Stead, Arthur J. Balfour, and Norman Angell. German political leaders began to take note of British and American suggestions for a league of nations late in 1916 and on numerous occasions voiced their approval. The French authorities began to consider plans for a proposed security of nations in July, 1917 and developed a definite scheme that provided for a tribunal, not only to decide international disputes, but what was more important, to ensure the execution of decisions regarding disputes.

Shortly before the United States entered the War, leaders of thought gave attention to the future prevention of war. The useless loss of life and property led thinking Americans to believe that isolation was not the highest goal to be sought but that steps should be taken to organize the nations against future aggression. The most notable move in this direction was the formation of the League to Enforce Peace in 1915 with ex-

President Taft as its president. The organizers included Theodore Marburg, Hamilton Holt, William Howland, and President A. Lawrence Lowell of Harvard. The object was to gain popular support in behalf of an attempt to organize a league of nations at the close of the War. The movement, as had been noted, was not altogether new, as numerous peace organizations had been formed earlier. But this was unique in that definite plans were formulated for the creation of an organized international society not far different from that now attempted by the League and the World Court. The plan provided for the formation of a world court to settle legal disputes, a commission of conciliation to solve non-justiciable disputes, and conferences to meet for the purpose of codifying international law. All disputants under this proposal would be required to submit questions to the proper body for peaceful settlement, and any nation refusing to do this and resorting to war would meet the combined resistance of all other League members. The plan was widely supported by leaders, including former President Theodore Roosevelt. His chief aim was to unite the nations through military force to prevent aggression, which he believed to be the basis of an effective peace. He and former President Taft spoke in favor of the League to Enforce Peace in various parts of the country and everywhere received enthusiastic responses. Unofficial polls were conducted which indicated an overwhelming majority in favor of concerted economic and military pressure against an aggressor nation. Conditions in Europe at the time clearly revealed the need for our active participation in the prevention of a similar catastrophe in the future. The program of the League to Enforce Peace influenced the British advocates of a league of nations and later helped to form the basis of official discussion in the framing of the Covenant.

Through the initiative of Lord Robert Cecil, who prepared a league memorandum, a Committee was appointed by the British Foreign Minister to elaborate a plan for a league of nations under the chairmanship of Sir Walter Phillimore. The proposal formulated by the Committee differed to some extent from that proposed by the League to Enforce Peace, especially as it did not provide for a permanent world court. Membership was to be limited to the Allied States in the War. It went beyond the immediate aims of war prevention by making the proposed league broaden its scope of activities. As means of preventing war the Phillimore plan provided for the pacific settlement of international disputes. A report based on this plan was submitted to President Wilson at the Peace Conference, and along with the American proposals, formed the basis of discussion in the framing of the Covenant.

President Wilson was not at first actively interested in the program of the League to Enforce Peace, but came out strongly in favor of it on May 27, 1916. Political differences were set aside and President Wilson stood shoulder to shoulder with ex-President Taft in endorsing a league of nations. Events moved rapidly and President Wilson took the opportunity on numerous occasions to speak in favor of a league. On December 18, 1916, the President addressed notes to the belligerent powers requesting "their respective views as to the terms upon which the War might be concluded and the arrangements which would be deemed satisfactory as a guarantee against its renewal or the kindling of any similar conflict in the future as would make it possible frankly to compare them." He voiced the hope that "a concert of nations" would be practicable when the War ended. On the basis of the replies the President addressed the Senate on January 22, 1917, at which time he remarked that "in every discussion of the peace that

Keystone View Company

WILLIAM H. TAFT, PRESIDENT OF THE LEAGUE TO ENFORCE PEACE

must end this War it is taken for granted that the peace must be followed by some definite concert of power which will make it virtually impossible that any such catastrophe should ever overwhelm us again."

The United States entered the War on the side of the Allies, April 6, 1917, and was designated as an "Associated Power." On January 8, 1918, President Wilson promulgated his famous Fourteen Points in which he set forth the conditions upon which peace must be based. The proposals were indeed searching and indicated the determination of the President to seek a peace based on justice and not on retribution. The last of the Fourteen Points stated that "a general association of nations must be formed under specific covenants for the purpose of affording mutual guarantees of political independence and territorial integrity to great and small states alike." This proposal significantly comes last for President Wilson recognized some such agency to be essential if conditions that lead to war should be remedied. Under an equitable peace settlement the proposed league should function effectively. Later addresses by the President enlarged upon this concept and he pointed out more specifically the nature of the proposed league. President Wilson's pronouncements were referred to by Germany on October 4, 1918, when she made them the basis of overtures for peace. After a protracted exchange of notes between Germany and the United States on tentative proposals to draw up a peace treaty based on Wilson's Fourteen Points and subsequent public utterances, the correspondence was transmitted to the Allied governments and accepted by them with certain reservations. The War ended soon thereafter and preparations were made for the Peace Conference which met in Paris January, 1919.

To the Conference came plenipotentiaries of twenty-seven nations which had either declared war against

Germany or had severed diplomatic relations with her. This was the greatest diplomatic gathering in history. Delegates from war-torn countries were ready to present exorbitant demands, and it seemed as if all of them were determined to procure the greatest possible benefits for their countries. The one exception was the delegation headed by President Wilson, for the United States had no self-seeking interests to serve. Our delegates were thus placed in a favorable position to work for an equitable peace settlement. The work of the Peace Conference was done through a Supreme Council and commissions. Numerous experts served in an advisory capacity. The Supreme Council itself consisted of the two ranking delegates from each of the five Principal Allied and Associated Powers, known as the "Big Ten." While much of the work was done by the commissions, the ultimate decisions rested with the Supreme Council representing the United States, Great Britain, France, Italy, and Japan. This procedure was much criticized, as it was felt that the destinies of millions of persons should not be placed in this small body. Newspaper reporters were especially incensed because of the secrecy of the deliberations, but news of the work of the "Big Ten" leaked out and it was decided to reduce the number to five. This change was also deemed expedient in order to hasten the work. In due course the Supreme Council began meeting in unannounced hotel rooms, offices, and private flats as it was desired to avoid having a fixed time and place of meeting where numerous other delegates could come and press their demands. It was also believed that the unscheduled meetings were held to prevent the leading Japanese delegate from attending for Japan had few interests in the outcome of the deliberations, and to have the delegate present only complicated the already existing language difficulties.

The Council was therefore automatically reduced to the "Big Four" with the Japanese delegate officially a member but never quite able to determine the time and place of the meeting. Yet the Japanese by no means left the Conference empty-handed. President Wilson in time opposed Signor Orlando, the Italian Premier, in his demand for Italian annexation of Fiume and Dalmatia, and the seriousness of the controversy led to the temporary withdrawal of the Italian delegation from the Conference. With the dropping out of Japan and Italy, the Supreme Council included President Wilson, and Premiers Lloyd George and Clemenceau as the "Big Three" who assumed the responsibility of making momentous decisions relating to the post-War Settlement.

The smaller, intimate body of the "Big Three" decided many ponderous questions relating to the final peace settlement. The President of the Peace Conference and the Supreme Council was Georges Clemenceau, the seventy-seven year old Premier of France, who was popularly nicknamed the "Tiger." He seldom spoke in the meetings of the Council except when the interests of France were at stake, and otherwise rested contentedly under a black skull-cap in apparent sleep. He was short and sturdy and spoke with great energy when he wished to carry a point. He manifested an uncompromising attitude and expressed the very epitome of pre-War statesmanship. Clemenceau desired, above all else, to cripple Germany permanently, and to do this, he wanted the Central Powers totally disarmed and the frontiers of France extended to the Rhine River. The idea of organizing the world on the basis of mutual cooperation made little appeal to the President of the Conference.

Lloyd George was dynamic, shrewd, nimble-minded, and extremely popular with the masses of England for he spoke the language of the common people. He was a very successful Prime Minister in the latter stages of the War and won a general election by an overwhelming majority prior to the opening of the Peace Conference on the very shallow issue of "hanging the Kaiser" and making Germany pay for the War. Lloyd George was both severe and moderate in his demands; he wanted the German colonies, merchant fleet, navy, huge reparations, and curiously enough, had a great desire to destroy the overseas markets of Germany and to write a clause into the Treaty placing responsibility for the War on her. The Article saddling the War guilt on Germany caused more bitterness than any other part of the Treaty. He was also anxious to see the Kaiser and the other war lords brought to public trial in England as criminals, for he had promised this to the voters in a previous election. On the other hand, his conciliatory attitude was manifested on questions not affecting the immediate interests of Great Britain. In general, he wished to treat the Germans less severely than did the French. By and large, the record of Lloyd George at the Peace Conference was less important than the "Tiger's."

The third member of the triumvirate was President Wilson, the spokesman of the moral and idealistic forces of the world, who desired nothing at the Conference except an equitable settlement and an orderly world society living in peace. Born in Virginia, of Scotch and Scotch-Irish descent, his parents moved to Georgia, the heart of the Old South, while he was a child. There, during his impressionable years, a vivid picture of the Civil War and its aftermath was deeply implanted in his mind. Popular sovereignty and self-determination of peoples became the warp and woof of his mental processes. As the son of a Presbyterian clergyman he could readily conceive of the nations united by a "solemn league and covenant." Wilson was clear-minded, tenacious, and a tireless worker. The unpublished deliberations of the "Big Three" reveal him in the rôle of dominating the discussions, although in the final decisions the other conferees too often gained their ends. During the last weeks of the discussions, which coincided with the absence of the Italian delegate, decisions of far-reaching importance were reached rapidly. The fifty-two commissions that had been appointed by the Council of Ten reported their findings to the "Big Three," and the ultimate decisions were made by them. The full sessions of the Conference merely met to give formal approval of decisions already reached.

In the second plenary session of the Conference on January 25, 1919, a unanimous resolution was adopted which provided that the Covenant of the League should be an integral part of the Peace Treaty, and that its drafting should be delegated to a special Commission representing fourteen states with President Wilson as Chairman. The first meeting of the Commission was held on February 3, when a composite plan was submitted. Suggestions were welcomed from neutral countries as their contemplated membership in the League made it necessary that they have a voice in its organization, and some valuable proposals made in an unofficial meeting on March 20, were received from these sources. Daily sessions were continued for some time when many suggestions were offered in addition to the several plans already submitted. Anglo-American drafts were presented early, and it remained for the delegates from other nations to offer suggestions to be embodied in the Covenant that would best serve their national interests. As an example of this, the Japanese made an effort to amend the preamble of the Covenant so as to endorse "the principle of the equality of nations and the just treatment of their nationals." The Italians submitted a project containing some unique features for the settlement of disputes by an "International Court of Justice." Stress was placed upon international equity by changing international law to meet new conditions. Their plan even envisaged the creation of an international legislature. The later proposals were unfortunately not given sufficient consideration by the Commission. The French scheme did not differ widely from the Italian, as both made elaborate provisions for coercion against a guilty state, but it was more rigid and legalistic, hence not adaptable to changing conditions. Probably the most distinctive suggestion related to the creation of an international military force to be supplied by the member states under league jurisdiction. The British and American delegations strongly opposed this.

Some unique features were contained in a plan for a league submitted by General Smuts of South Africa in which he urged nationalization of munitions trade under international inspection, the abolition of conscription, a system of mandates, and a council of the great powers. He argued that "the real work of the league will be done by its council," and this would necessarily "be a comparatively small body as it is not possible to have executive action taken and more difficult contentious administrative work done through a larger body." He showed foresight in anticipating the Council, and he contemplated numerous technical committees to take up the functions which the league would perform. Lord Robert Cecil had summarized the various British proposals in the form of a draft including his own observations. He was the first to suggest Geneva as the seat of the league, although this matter was left in abeyance until the end of the Conference. This draft was transmitted to President Wilson who gave it, with a plan worked out by himself and his colleagues, to David Hunter Miller, an American legal advisor, and Sir Cecil

Hurst, a British legal advisor, who formulated a draft which President Wilson presented to the Commission on February 3, 1919. The Miller-Hurst draft was discussed at length, and, with some modifications, became the Covenant's final accepted form.

While the framers were discussing the Covenant, it was necessary for President Wilson to return to the United States for the adjournment of Congress on March 4, 1919. While in Washington, he met with the Senate Committee on Foreign Relations to discuss the Covenant. Sufficient progress had been made so that it was only a question of the kind of league that would set up. Opposition was already beginning to crystallize in the Senate, led by Senator H. C. Lodge, the newly-chosen Republican Chairman of the Committee. Outside of Congress active discussions centered on the proposed league with some supporters proposing amendments to protect American interests more adequately. President Wilson took these suggestions back to Paris and, in addition to other proposals cabled from this country, was able to get them accepted before the Covenant was finally drafted. The proposals came from Republican leaders such as former President Taft, Charles Evans Hughes, and Elihu Root, and it was believed by the President that if their suggestions were embodied in the Covenant, the Senate, which now had a Republican majority, would not refuse ratification. The substance of Taft's proposals were: the right of withdrawal from the League on two years notice; periodic reexamination of armaments limitations agreements by the Council; the unanimity rule in voting by the Council and Assembly; the reserving of the Monroe Doctrine from interference by the League; and the exclusion of all domestic questions from League jurisdiction. These eleventh-hour proposals by the Republican leaders were of far-reaching moment, and to get them accepted by the delegations at the Peace Conference was indeed a diplomatic maneuver of the first order. President Wilson was later able to report the following to the Senate Committee on Foreign Relations: "On my return to Paris, all these matters were taken up by the Commission on the League of Nations, and every suggestion of the United States was adopted." The acceptance seemed necessary at the time in order to avert serious opposition in the Senate.

Meanwhile a minority of the Senators had already signed a resolution opposing the proposed Covenant. This included more than one-third of the membership, sufficient to kill both the Treaty and the Covenant. Some of these Senators were opposed to a league in any form. They were known as the "irreconcilables," destined to play political havoc with the League.

Upon returning to Paris on March 14, President Wilson learned that in his absence a strong sentiment had developed among the delegates to set aside the League and proceed at once to frame a punitive treaty for Germany. The President strongly opposed this move and succeeded in his earlier aims of making the Covenant a part and parcel of the Treaty. He well understood that if the organization of the League and its acceptance were left to a later date there would be little likelihood of a League at all. It might appear that the most propitious time to attempt this great task would surely not be when the shadow of war was still hanging over Europe like a great cataclysm, yet this, like other great historic institutions, could only originate under the most unseemly conditions. President Wilson was beset by many obstacles through growing political antagonism at home and a general attitude of indifference abroad, where the atmosphere of war could not readily be harmonized with the concept of peace. To create a permanent peace organization in an atmosphere still dominated by the military spirit was of course paradoxical and only an idealist, such as Wilson, could see beyond the immediate horizon and contemplate once more normal conditions. For four years the nations had built up a war psychology of hatred fed by a vivid realization of the great loss of life and property defying human imagination. To change this war-psychosis in the course of three months at a peace conference was to anticipate the impossible. Neither President Wilson nor the American people were war-minded as yet due to their brief participation in it. Hence it was reasonable to suppose that America's position at the Conference would differ from those more deeply involved. Thus the President did not immediately gain the support of the other delegations to a program of permanent peace. The absence of a strong belligerent attitude by the American people also helps to explain their hearty support of the League in its early stages.

The difficult task of the President at the Peace Conference was enchanced by his efforts to frame a Covenant that would meet the arguments of the "irreconcilables," as well as of delegates who might regard some parts of it as contrary to their interests. Leading Americans insisted upon a clause safeguarding the Monroe Doctrine, although it was unnecessary, as any attempt by European nations to seize the territory of American republics would be contrary to other provisions of the Covenant. Since the delegations did not wish to place a stumbling block in the way of America's entrance into the League, they agreed to the inclusion of Article 21 which states that "nothing in this Covenant shall be deemed to affect the validity of international engagements, such as treaties of arbitration or regional understandings like the Monroe Doctrine, for securing the maintenance of peace." The President argued that the Covenant was in substance a world-wide application of the Monroe Doctrine in so far as both were directed against aggression. Nevertheless there were many who did not share this interpretation. Despite the inclusion of Article 21, the seeming conflict between the Covenant and the Monroe Doctrine later became the subject of heated debates in and out of the Senate.

Article 10 of the Covenant obligates the members "to respect and preserve as against external aggression the territorial integrity and existing political independence of all members of the League. . . ." This was a distinct American contribution and was referred to by the President as the very heart of the Covenant. The obligation herein embodied was in keeping with the stand taken by the League to Enforce Peace and found no serious opponents when it was first advanced. Americans looked upon forceful measures as practical means of restraining an aggressor. Relying upon this generally accepted view, President Wilson succeeded in getting this principle written into the Covenant. Later opposition to American membership in the League centered largely around the nature of this commitment. This, like other provisions of American origin in the Covenant, was destined to create the strongest objections to our membership in the League. While framing the Covenant the President had overcome the foremost objections, but could not anticipate the later criticisms.

Although many proposals were made for a League that might satisfy the particular needs of the many countries represented at the Conference, there was a remarkable willingness on the part of the delegations to make concessions in order that a general agreement might be reached. It is safe to say that the American delegates made fewer concessions in the creation of the League than any other country.

With the completion of the draft of the Covenant, the report was made to the plenary Conference and not to the "Big Three" as in the case of reports from other commissions. The League Covenant was submitted to the full Conference on April 28, 1919, and was unanimously adopted with only a single change, as proposed by the President. This acceptance was tentative, however, as the Covenant was yet to form a part of the Peace Treaty and to be formally accepted. In order that preparations might be made for the creation of the League as a going concern, President Wilson moved at the same time "that the first Secretary-General of the Council shall be the Honorable Sir James Eric Drummond." He also requested that the powers permanently on the Council, in addition to four temporary representatives from other states, should meet to prepare plans for the organization of the League, the establishment of the seat of the League, and the preparation of the agenda for the first meeting of the Assembly. The Committee arranged temporary headquarters in London and agreed upon Geneva as the permanent seat of the League.

Meanwhile preparations were made to bring the Peace Conference to an end, the German delegates presented their credentials to the Allies on May 1, 1919, and a week later received the Treaty of Peace. This was not a negotiated Treaty giving both sides an equal voice in determining its provisions. The one-sided deliberations did not accord with the wishes of President Wilson, as he did not want a dictated treaty imposed on the vanquished. His famous "fourteen points" anticipated a Treaty that would be freely agreed upon by all parties. Such negotiations had taken place at other great war conferences, including the Congress of Vienna, where Talleyrand, representing defeated France, had played a prominent rôle in formulating the decisions. As Germany had no part in framing the Treaty, nor in the organization of the League, it was agreed that she and her allies would not immediately become eligible for membership. This discrimination would naturally tend to prejudice Germany against the new peace organization. The Treaty presented to the German delegates was the longest ever drafted, containing 440 Articles, besides numerous Annexes. The final provision stipulated that it would enter into force as soon as it had been ratified by "Germany on the one hand and by three of the Principal Allied and Associated Powers on the other hand." This condition was fulfilled on January 10, 1920, and it marks the origin of the League. Two days later, President Wilson, in compliance with Article 5 of the Covenant, issued a call for the first meeting of the Council to be held in Paris on January 16. The meeting was held with representatives from Great Britain, France, Japan, Spain, Belgium, Brazil, and Greece. The United States as the prime mover in the creation of the League did not participate in this meeting called by the President. Although the League had not yet been rejected by the Senate, it was evident at the first meeting of the Council that the growing political antagonism in this county was making American membership increasingly doubtful. This condition caused the members of the newly-created Organization to speculate as to its effectiveness. It had been taken for granted that the United States would become a member. Great Britain had joined the League after debating the issue for two days in the House of Commons, but the United States Senate took months to discuss it, only in the end to reject membership.

The Treaty of Versailles, including the Covenant, was submitted by the President to the Senate on July 10, 1919. From that time until the elections in November 1920, the Treaty and more especially the Covenant, were the major subject of discussion in this country. The issue to be decided was whether this nation should depart from the time honored policy of isolation, clinging to the counsel contained in Washington's Farewell Address of remaining aloof from the embroilments of the Old World. It was evident that the conditions of the twentieth century were not the same as those of Washington's day and hence his injunction could not justly serve as a guide for twentieth century foreign policies. American markets and financial interests were now world-wide, and our prosperity depended in a large measure upon the maintenance of universal peace. Thus a disinterested view of conditions in parts of the world was impossible. These questions loomed large in the minds of the American people, and tended more and more to be decided by political and emotional factors than by dispassionate reasoning. In addressing the Democratic National Committee in February 1919, President Wilson stated that, "We ought not even to create the appearance of trying to make that [The League] a party issue." The Republican National Committee agreed to consider the Treaty as non-partisan and adhered to this position until it was formally submitted to the Senate. The Republican leaders then saw an opportunity to make political capital out of the League by arousing popular prejudice against the dangers of foreign entanglements. The election of November in 1918, had returned a Republican majority to the Senate and if the President had belonged to that party, he would undoubtedly have secured Senate approval of the Treaty. Such is the fate of political fortune.

The high ideals that pervaded America during the War, when it was believed that the conflict was waged to end war, to make the world safe for democracy, had materially cooled. This slump of the emotions found ready expression in a desire to withdraw from European political disturbances. Senators Henry Cabot Lodge,

Philander C. Knox, and Warren G. Harding had lauded the work of the League to Enforce Peace in 1916, but opposed the League of Nations in 1919. The vote in the Senate at first showed a majority in favor of the League, with mild reservations, but with the passing of time more members turned against it. The Treaty including the Covenant was finally rejected by a vote of 49 to 35 with some twenty of the former favoring the League but voting in the negative on the advice of the President, who felt that the whole Treaty or none should be accepted and that reservations proposed by the Senate would materially weaken the League. He stated that "We ought either to go in or stay out." The President was justly criticized by many of his friends for taking this uncompromising stand, as other countries had entered the League with reservations, and the value of their membership was not thereby lessened. Another just criticism of the President may be found in his failure to name one or two prominent Republicans as delegates to the Peace Conference. Men of the caliber of ex-President Taft or Elihu Root would have done much to win the confidence of the Republican majority in the Senate as they could have more justly maintained that America's part in the creation of the League was not to be construed as a democratic triumph.

Not to be deterred by the adverse vote in the Senate, the President decided to appeal to the country in an effort to rally public opinion in favor of an unamended Treaty. He toured the middle and far West from September 3 to 27, 1919. In the tenseness of the campaign he collapsed, never to regain his health. Senators Wm. E. Borah, Hiram W. Johnson, and Jas. A. Reed trailed him and made speeches in opposition to the League. Due to prolonged illness, the President was unable to assume active leadership in the fight for Treaty ratification, but later relied upon Governor

James M. Cox, the Democratic nominee for President, to carry the fight before the people. He opposed Senator Warren G. Harding, the Republican nominee, who spoke in favor of some form of an "association of nations" and thus confused the issue in the minds of the voters. The election gave the Republicans an overwhelming victory. Since, however, many other issues were involved in the campaign, a popular referendum on American membership in the League was not held. President Wilson was bitterly disappointed. He had courageously championed the League from its inception until his strength failed him. He died February 3, 1924 in the realization that those seeking political capital had defeated his purposes. Thus ended the work of a man who had assumed moral leadership of the world by creating an institution designed to preserve peace and strangely enough failed to have the United States back him up. The League was duly organized and began to function in the absence of this country. It appeared now as if the victory that the United States had won in the War had been lost. Subsequent world history has no doubt been materially altered as a result of such slogans as "America must not be drawn into the maelstrom of European diplomacy and intrigue."

CHAPTER II

Organization of the League

We have noted the various forces that operated in the framing of the Covenant, and have found that the League of Nations is the product of several concepts focused in the direction of maintaining an orderly international society. The victors in the War were also in favor of an organization that would ensure the permanent fulfillment of the Peace Treaties. They succeeded in writing provisions into the Treaty of Versailles and the other Peace Treaties that placed the responsibility of their execution upon the League, thus closely uniting it with the Treaties. This was in some respects unfortunate, as the Treaties were by their very nature punitive and unjust, whereas the League was set up to promote peaceful relations among nations. President Wilson fully realized this strange contradiction and sought to harmonize the dual purposes of the League by the inclusion of Article 19 which provides for the reconsideration of treaties which have become inapplicable by "conditions whose continuance might endanger the peace of the world." The Treaties pointed to the past and the Covenant to the future in the hope of rectifying existing injustices. Thus President Wilson was compelled to consent to what he regarded as many injustices in the Treaties.

The history of the League has been the struggle of these two forces: the one favoring the maintenance of the status quo, and the other striving to make the League serve the needs of a changing world order.

The former has too often controlled the formulation of international policies to the detriment of the peace machinery, and a tendency has prevailed to rely upon treaty commitments, thus disregarding needed changes. Examples of the failure by the League to cope with international problems have been due in a large measure to provisions contained in the Treaties and not to the machinery of the League. President Wilson conceived of an organization that would operate as an instrumentality of change. He did not desire to see the League made an agency to stabilize War gains. Yet the League was so firmly woven into the very fabric of the Treaties that opportunities for effective operation too often crippled its work. This was not a weakness of the Covenant, but of the Treaties and more especially the unwise use of League agencies to deal with unworkable situations. The successes of the League are to be found in its adjustments of post-War problems not linked to Treaty commitments. The organization and authority of the League were concentrated in the hands of the Allied and Associated Powers with countries such as Germany, Austria, and Russia excluded and ineligible for membership. This was no doubt inevitable at the time, but it militated against the concept of universality which was its final goal. Nevertheless, an attempt was made to get away from the old "balance of power" of pre-War Europe.

The membership is divided by the Covenant into three categories. The first comprises the original or "charter" members who were signatories to the Treaty of Versailles, and are named in the Annex to the Covenant. The second includes those "invited" states that were neutral and hence not parties to the Treaty but were mentioned in the Annex. They were allowed two months to signify their intentions to become members after the Covenant became operative. Thirteen states thus invited did become members. Other fully self-governing states, dominions, or colonies, not named in the Annex, were eligible for admission if agreed to by a two-thirds vote of the Assembly, but only if effective guarantees are given to observe international obligations. The membership grew from twenty-four at the first meeting of the Council to fifty-eight at the present time. The admission to League membership was purposely made difficult in that a two-thirds majority vote of the Assembly is required to admit a state, and election is contingent upon promise of the scrupulous fulfillment of treaty obligations. Although the Central Powers were barred from membership, the framers envisaged a condition where not only they but all states would seek admission. There has been an insistent desire not only to enlarge the membership, but also to retain some states whose practices should have made them subject to expulsion. Article 16 provides that "any member of the League which has violated any covenant of the League may be declared to be no longer a Member of the League by a vote of the Council concurred in by the Representatives of all the other Members of the League represented thereon." Italy was singled out as a violator of the Covenant in 1935, but was not expelled. Hence a certain leniency prevails that may give rise to a feeling on the part of individual states that their membership is greatly desired. It may be said however, that by and large, membership is highly valued, and participation in League functions is taken seriously. Provision is made in Article 1 for the withdrawal of any member from the League after two years' notice has been given. The important states that have withdrawn under this provision are Japan, Germany, and Brazil. The more recent admission of Russia has partly overcome this loss.

The League is composed of self-governing states and dominions which have voluntarily accepted membership and are free to withdraw of their own volition. There is nothing in the Covenant that suggests a super-state on the one hand, or a mere alliance or concert of states on the other. The framers of the Covenant were con-

THE COUNCIL OF THE LEAGUE OF NATIONS

fronted with the task of setting up an institution with sufficient independence to make it effective, while at the same time reserving to the member states their cherished sovereign power. The members are to a certain degree limited in their freedom of action, to which they agreed voluntarily. The traditional fear of infringement upon sovereignty has not given concern to the member states, although it loomed large in the discussions of the American Senate when the Treaty was under discussion. While the member states have reserved to themselves almost complete independence of action, the League may exercise jurisdiction over various matters. This is done through its three principal organs, the Assembly, Council, and Secretariat. Each of these bodies has special duties to perform, although in some instances their jurisdictions overlap. It might appear from a study of the Covenant that the League exercises extended jurisdiction, but in actual practice this is not the case. The Assembly and Council initiate many movements, carry on investigations, freely discuss them, and decide upon a course of action, but the binding force of these decisions is left to the member states and it is they who give validity to such decisions. It is not the League that makes laws, but the member states. This initial work may be undertaken by the Council, the Assembly, the International Labor Office (an autonomous Institution but closely associated with the League), and international conferences initiated by the Council.

The Assembly consists of not more than three delegates from each member state, but substitute delegates are admitted, hence some of the great powers frequently send large delegations to the meetings. Each state has one vote in the meetings which are held annually in Geneva beginning the first or second Monday in September. Special sessions may be summoned at the request of any member if the majority agree, and several such meetings have been called. The President of the Council presides over the Assembly until a President and six vice-Presidents are chosen, which is the first order of business. The elected officials constitute the Executive Committee and supervise the deliberations. Six standing Committees are appointed by the Assembly, and on each may sit a representative from every member state. They deal with: 1. constitutional questions; 2. technical organizations; 3. armaments; 4. budget administration; 5. social problems; and 6. political questions. The work of each Committee is referred by a rapporteur to the Assembly where action may be taken in the form of a resolution, recommendation, or agreement to be submitted to the member states for acceptance. The delegates are accredited plenipotentiaries, and are thus in a position to bind their respective countries to a definite course of action. But official steps are not often taken in the Assembly, the function of which is mainly to influence world opinion, through debates. It was assumed when the League was organized that the Assembly would act more as a diplomatic conference binding the member states to numerous commitments, but the practice has developed of calling special conferences when occasion requires to deal with international matters. The Assembly has to some extent the semblance of a legislative body in composition and deliberation, but here the resemblance ends. Independent action is taken by the Assembly mostly on such questions relating to the operation of the League, as the control of the budget, selection of non-permanent members on the Council, admission of states to League membership, and the election of judges to the Permanent Court of International Justice. Article 3 of the Covenant gives the Assembly somewhat vague but wide competence to "deal at the meetings with any matter within the sphere of action of the League or affecting the peace of the world." The Assembly may also consider the revision of treaties and must ratify amendments to the Covenant. A unanimous vote is often required to reach decisions, with questions of procedure as an outstanding exception to the rule as indicated in Article 5 of the Covenant. Procedure in the matter of voting was given great weight by the United States Senate in discussing League membership. The question of voting in international conferences has for a very long time given rise to serious objections on the part of large and small governments alike. The same difficulty arose in the framing of the United States Constitution, as the large States did not wish to be checked by the smaller ones, while the small States insisted upon equality in the affairs of the Government. The small states of the League jealously guard the principle of unanimity in Assembly meetings, but by the growth of numerous precedents the majority or two-thirds rule has now come into wide use. The meetings are always interesting as visitors assemble at Geneva from various parts of the world to follow the discussions, and journalists come in large numbers to report on the deliberations. The exchange of views by the delegates and the informal meetings among responsible officials lasting for almost a month can do much to develop cordial relations.

The second deliberative body is the Council which is composed of one delegate from each state composing its membership. The Covenant provided for five permanent and four non-permanent members. The former were to be the British Empire, France, Italy, Japan, and the United States, and the other members were to be elected periodically by the Assembly. As the United States did not join the League, the permanent members were reduced to four, but increased to five with the admission of Germany in 1926. Russia was given a permanent seat on the Council upon becoming a member in 1934, but Japan and Germany withdrew in 1935, thus leaving four permanent members. In 1922 the Assembly increased the non-permanent members from four to six, and in 1926 this number was increased to nine. Under this arrangement the Assembly elects three members each year for a term of three years, and a plan has been devised whereby a system of rotation operates to exclude the re-election of members until all other states have been represented. The Covenant states that the Council shall meet at least once a year, but the practice began very early of meeting four times yearly in addition to extraordinary sessions, as occasion requires. The President is chosen in rotation by alphabetical order of the member states. Article 4 provides, in substance, that any representative of the League not a member on the Council may, by invitation, sit with it during discussions affecting that member. Non-members are not accorded this privilege, although the United States accepted an invitation by the Council to attend a few sessions of the Council during the Sino-Japanese dispute. The Council, like the Assembly, may deal with any matter coming within the sphere of action of the League or affecting the peace of the world. Unanimity prevails in voting, although exceptions are also to be noted, more especially when dealing with procedural matters. The Council has often been referred to as the executive organ of the League, and due to the many duties placed upon it by the Treaty of Versailles, this designation may well apply.

The specific duties of the Council are enumerated in the Covenant and include: the approval of staff appointments of the Secretariat; the formulation of plans for the reduction of armaments. If arms agreements are reached, the limit cannot be exceeded without the Council's consent; and it must advise on the prevention of the evil effects attendant upon the manufacture of munitions and implements of war by private concerns. Under Article 10 the Council alone has the duty of advising upon the means by which League members are to preserve the independence of the members; it acts as conciliator in the case of a threat of war, and proposes steps to be taken in making an arbitral award. The Council alone was given the right to formulate plans for the establishment of the Permanent Court of International Justice. Under Article 16 it recommends the military, naval, or other measures that members are to contribute in defeating an aggressor, and can expel any member which has violated the Covenant. It receives annual reports from the mandatory powers; consents to the action of the Secretariat on matters of international interest; and finally, under Article 26, must give unanimous approval if the Covenant is to be amended.

The Treaties of Peace place certain duties upon the Council, such as the modification of the limitation of armaments fixed for Germany; a degree of control over the tariffs of the defeated powers; extended authority to revise clauses of the Treaty relating to ports, waterways and railways; modification of various economic clauses in the Treaty of Versailles; supervision over the public debt of Turkey assigned to her detached territories; appointment of arbitrators to settle disputes relating to waterpower in certain former Austro-Hungarian territories; appointment of mixed arbitral tribunals to settle boundary and other disputes; the choice of governing commissions of the Saar; and, the appointment of the High Commissioner of Danzig. These powers have been expressly conferred upon the Council. The exercise of jurisdiction by the Council without any stipulated authority is far more important as is indicated by the long record of decisions contained in the official publications of the League. Here it may be seen that the Council has assumed extensive jurisdiction beyond the power expressly delegated to it. There is nothing in the Covenant to prohibit this and indeed certain Articles, such as the first and fourth, imply the exercise of wide latitude as regards jurisdiction. A typical example will suffice to illustrate this assumption of power. On February 19, 1920, the Council resolved to convene an International Financial Conference to be held at Brussels in the autumn of the same year. This authority was not granted in the Covenant, but was held to come within the spirit of Article 24, and the precedent was established, whereby the Council issues invitation for international conferences. The Council may thus act independently of any stated authority.

A new technique is found in the frequent calling of conferences which meet under League auspices at the invitation of the Council. As this body meets four times each year, there is no delay in calling conferences or in dealing with other problems. Before the War the governments were without any central agency for calling them together. The League changed this, so that instead of accidental meetings, such as were held before the War, periodic gatherings are now planned as an established practice in the international order. The regularity of the meetings of the Assembly and Council are as important as any of the powers the League possesses. The jurisdiction of the two bodies is difficult to determine, as the competence of each is not always clearly defined in the Covenant. In many respects the functions are the same, as numerous questions may be referred to either body or questions may be passed from one to the other. The Assembly went on record at the outset in opposing any precise definition relating to the functions of the Assembly and Council. This allows for a wide latitude of powers by the two bodies. The Assembly also decided that it could not reverse the action of the Council, nor the Council that of the Assembly. In a study of the Covenant and the Treaties of Peace, it is found that the Council is given a larger measure of power to act than the Assembly. Not only does the Council exercise wider power to initiate measures, but it is also the executive organ of the League. The deliberations of the Council are more informal than those of the Assembly, as this is a small body and its meetings are conducted much like that of a board of directors. The Covenant provides definite procedure, to be followed in discussions relating to international disputes, but in the discussion of other matters the Council has evolved its own rules of procedure. The Assembly has printed rules to guide its deliberations, and these have been worked out in great detail.

The question of the scope of League authority has received the attention of both the Assembly and the Council. The subject was discussed in the Assembly, in 1926, when the British delegation requested "the appointment of a committee to consider and report what questions are, and what are not, within the sphere of League action . . . ," for the British delegate stated that "where the League had been formed to insure peace it was gradually entering more and more into the life of nations and the more it did this the more likely it was of encountering opposition." The British Government later insisted upon restricting the League's "sphere of action" in a communiqué addressed to all the members pointing out two possible dangers: first, the obscuring of the first and highest purpose of the League, namely the preservation of peace, and second, that the League not being a super-State but an association of sovereign states, individual states might resent anything which bore the appearance of an infringement of their national independence or an interference in their municipal affairs." This statement seems strange in view of oft-repeated expressions that the League is a weak institution and cannot serve the needs of international society. The British suggestion was not favorably received because of the general desire to enlarge its scope of work. Following this proposal a committee report was submitted to the Assembly favoring the avoidance of subjects that "would detract from the real mission of promoting peace in the world and of facilitating cooperation between nations for the peaceful progress of mankind." The wording of this resolution was sufficiently broad to permit League action in all international matters.

The Assembly and Council are sometimes referred to as the initiating organs to bring about international agreements, but it must be said that a great part of the initial effort takes place even before these bodies assemble, so that often they merely study and give approval to projects already launched. Initial effort originates with governmental proposals to the Secretariat, with committees engaged in various studies, and with representatives of the Secretariat. The latter organization performs very useful service in preparing records, reports, and documents for the Assembly and Council. This feature of the League is new to international life. The Covenant merely states that there shall be a permanent Secretariat established at the seat of the League to comprise a Secretary-General and such secretaries and staff as may be required. The staff of the Secretariat numbers some six hundred men and women selected from more than fifty countries. They comprise the international civil service branch of the League and are continually on duty to initiate projects, assist in conferences, and after the diplomatic gatherings, to perform the duties relating to the execution of official decisions. A large number of experts are connected with the Secretariat and it is their task to prepare the groundwork for the Assembly, Council, Conferences, and Commissions. Rapporteurs are chosen at League meetings to report upon special subjects, and they receive much assistance from the experts. The international servants at Geneva do not lose their national identity or interest, but their chief concern is directed toward the building up of the work of the League, and in this capacity they enjoy diplomatic immunity as international officials, provided for in Article 7 of the Covenant. The Article places men and women on the same footing in seeking employment in the Secretariat. The officials may not engage in any occupation which is incompatible with the proper discharge of their regular duties, may not be candidates for political office in their countries, and must avoid any action by word or deed which might affect their position as international officials. The rules governing the conduct of members of the Secretariat are laid down in the Staff Regulations which are enforced by an Administrative Tribunal consisting of three judges and three deputy judges meeting in January of each year. This is unique, but when it is recalled that the officials are under no national jurisdiction it is essential that the League officials live under a miniature form of government of their own creation.

 The first Secretary General was named in the Annex of the Covenant, and those following him are appointed by the Council with the approval of the Assembly. The present Secretary-General is M. Joseph Avenol who was appointed in 1932 to succeed Sir Eric Drummond. Article 6 of the Covenant makes it incumbent upon him to act in the capacity of Secretary of the Assembly and Council, although his duties reach far beyond the provisions thus mentioned. He is in close touch with the committees and conferences meeting under League auspices and is responsible for keeping their records. He acts as a liaison officer between different organs of the League, and is in constant touch with the member states. His office collects and distributes all relevant information of international interest that may be required by conferences, commissions, etc. He appoints, and may remove, officials of the Secretariat subject to the approval of the Council and not of least importance is his duty of general direction over the policies of the fourteen Sections of the Secretariat.

The first duty of the Secretary-General is in connection with the action that may be taken by the League in case of war, as Article 11 confers upon him the task of summoning a meeting of the Council if requested to do so by a member. He makes all arrangements for investigations and the consideration of disputes between members. He is also required to communicate with disputants for the purpose of obtaining accurate information relating thereto, and submit it to the Council. His duties call him to various capitals of the world on special missions regarding League matters. Much of his time is occupied in attendance at various conferences, and more especially at the sessions of the Assembly and Council. The presiding officers at these gatherings are often not conversant with the procedure that has grown up over a period of years, and hence the Secretary-General may be found sitting beside them as an adviser. The prominence of the office makes him widely known throughout the diplomatic world. Under his direction the members of the Secretariat prepare provisional reports for the League assemblies, and they act as secretaries at these meetings. The agenda for each session of the Assembly are prepared by the Secretary-General with the approval of the President of the Council and are distributed to the members of the League "as nearly as possible four months before the date fixed for the opening of the session." Included in the agenda is a report on the work of the Council and Secretariat since the last session of the Assembly, and the measures taken to execute its decisions, all items which the Assembly ordered to be included in the previous session, all items prepared by the Council and by the League members, the budget for the next fiscal year, and the report on the accounts for the previous year. The early distribution makes it possible for each member to study the agenda carefully, and if need be, make suggestions before the Assembly meets. The delegates are also able to deliberate wisely if they are conversant with the subject matter to be discussed.

Each day during the sessions of the Assembly and of diplomatic conferences, the Secretariat publishes the "Journal" which is a summary of the proceedings of plenary and committee meetings, the verbatim records of the proceedings of the plenary meetings, and the Procès Verbaux of the proceedings of the committees. The "Official Journal" is published monthly and contains the minutes, text of reports, and resolutions of the Council and official documents sent or received by the Secretariat. The Secretariat also publishes the "Monthly Summary" in six languages which contains a record of all League meetings and a concise analysis of important events relating to the League. The services of the Secretariat are utilized in translating, interpreting and publishing documents (in two languages) and clerical services. The difficulties generally encountered in international gatherings due to the multiplicity of languages, have been greatly limited by League procedure. The official languages are French and English, and speeches delivered in the one are immediately translated into the other. To do this requires an experienced staff and the Secretariat fulfills this need. When members of the Assembly, Council, or League conferences speak in other than an official language, it is required of them that they provide for the translation.

The administrative officers of the Secretariat consist of the Secretary-General, two Deputy Secretaries-General, and three Under-Secretaries-General. These officials, together with the Chief of the Legal Section, frequently meet as a central committee to formulate policies for the betterment of the service. The Secretariat is divided into fourteen Sections, with a Director or Chief over each. They assume control over the internal organization of their respective departments, and are responsible for making the necessary preparations for, and organizing of, all meetings and conferences relating to their particular sections. The first is the Internal Administration that has charge of the services in the Secretariat, such as distribution of documents, accounting, and direction of the library, the latter having become a leading research center with gift of two million dollars by John D. Rockefeller, Jr., in 1927. The Political Section is closely allied with the Assembly and Council in presenting data on political questions affecting international relations. The Chief of the Section closely follows all disputes that come before the Assembly and Council, and must be thoroughly conversant with the circumstances surrounding such questions. The Legal Section is more directly associated with the Secretary-General and his subordinates by giving them legal advice on various matters relating to the internal organization, but are also occupied in the interpretation of international law and treaties as they relate to work of the League. This Section supervises the registration and publication of treaties in accordance with Article 18 of the Covenant which provides that "every treaty or international engagement entered into hereafter by any Member of the League shall be forthwith registered with the Secretariat and shall as soon as possible be published by it. No such treaty or international engagement shall be binding until so registered." By May, 1937, there were 4,120 treaties and international engagements registered and published in 170 volumes in the two official languages, as well as their original language if this is not French or English.

The Information Section fills an important place in the Secretariat, as through it are issued numerous communiqués, special pamphlets concerning League activities, and reports that are broadcast bi-weekly over the League radio station. Contacts with foreign offices and newspapers are maintained to disseminate and receive information relating to the League and more especially as regards popular reaction toward it. In brief, it attends to all League publicity and seeks to create favorable opinion toward it. The Minorities Section, as its name implies, supervises the work in connection with League activities in the exchange of populations and interests itself in the enforcement of the Minorities Treaties. Administrative problems concerning Danzig are under the jurisdiction of this Section. The Mandates Section assists the Mandates Commission, the Assembly and Council in questions concerning mandates and slavery. This work is largely clerical, as the technical work is done by the Commission which is composed of experts. The Disarmament Section has been prominently engaged in collecting information and performing secretarial tasks to facilitate the work of various commissions, and the World Disarmament Conference which met in Geneva in 1932. The Section publishes a vast amount of material relating to all phases of armaments. These publications are valuable as sources of information. The Financial

Section is, with an assisting body, known as the Economic Intelligence Service, the largest of them all and performs secretarial and research duties for the Financial Organization and its subsidiaries, such as the Fiscal, Statistical, and other financial expert groups connected with the League. The Section of Economic Relations performs a similar task on questions relating to economics.

The Section on Communications and Transit serves as Secretariat for the Communications and Transit Organization, and assists in the compilation of data for the periodic conferences in this field. The Health Section, with a Medical Director, assists the Health Organization in committees or conferences, and publishes periodicals and studies relating to this phase of the League's work. Intellectual Cooperation and International Bureaus are combined in one Section, its members performing the usual duties in connection with both. Article 24 of the League places new Bureaus under the League, and also the older ones with their consent. Some important Public Unions are outside the League but cooperate with it through this Section. Publications are issued, including the Handbook of International Organizations, which contains particulars of more than six-hundred organizations. The Section on Social Questions and Opium Traffic has a wide scope of duties to perform in connection with Child Welfare, Traffic in Women and Children, and Opium Traffic. Preparatory work for the Council, Assembly, Commissions, and Conferences occupy the attention of those connected with this Section. The Treasury Section is the custodian of League funds, and their disburser to the League branches, including the International Labor Organization, and the World Court. The Assembly allocates the funds on a pro rata basis that are received from the members of the League, with the Secretary-General as "the Chief Financial Agent for the League as a whole."

The League budget for the year 1937, including the Labor Organization and the World Court, was almost twenty-nine million Swiss francs, or roughly $6,670,000. A Supervisory Commission of five members, appointed by the Assembly, directs the economical operation of the League bodies, examines the budgets proposed by the Secretary-General, and audits the League accounts. The finances are continued on a sound basis, and large accumulated surpluses made the erection of the new League buildings possible.

In addition to the Assembly, Council, and Secretariat, there exist a number of auxiliary organs connected with the League that are more or less autonomous as regards their own work, but are at the same time subject to the control of the Assembly and Council which created them. The Treaties of Peace provided for the creation of some, and the Covenant anticipated others. They assist the Assembly and Council in the capacity of experts in specialized fields that require action by these bodies. The many intricate problems with which the League has to deal require the services of specialists able to consider impartially problems in order to reach dispassionate solutions. Some are permanent organizations, others temporary, and they are so numerous that hardly a week goes by without the holding of a meeting by one of them at Geneva. All are connected with the Secretariat which acts also for them, as it does for other League bodies. The auxiliary organizations are as follows: 1. Economic and Financial Organization; 2. Communications and Transit Organization; 3. Health Organization; 4. Intellectual Cooperation Organization; 5. Permanent Advisory Commission for Military, Naval, and Air Questions;

6. Permanent Mandates Commission; 7. Commission of Enquiry for European Union; 8. Advisory Commission for the Protection and Welfare of Children and Young People; 9. (a) Advisory Committee on Traffic in Opium and Other Dangerous Drugs; (b) Permanent Central Opium Board, (c) Supervisory Body; 10. Supervisory Commission; 11. Committee on the Allocation of Expenses; and 12. Advisory Committees of Experts on Slavery. The work of these auxiliary organizations is extensive and will subsequently be discussed in detail.

The members of the Secretariat, including the auxiliary organizations, explore fields that are ripe for official action by the Assembly, Council, and League conferences. They assist in advising these bodies on technical and procedural matters and when they adjourn, after meeting in short sessions, the Secretariat remains to supervise and assist in the administration of the decisions. This work could not be performed without a continuing staff such as the Secretariat. Conferences that have met outside League jurisdiction have often agreed upon measures that were subsequently not carried out, as no central agency existed that was comparable to the Secretariat. This follow-up work is extremely important, and has added greatly to the effectiveness of the League in the consummation of its work. The seat of the League serves as the center for watching over the effective fulfillment of international commitments, and all official documents relating to League decision are kept there. The Secretariat cooperates with the member states in the execution of decisions where the latter are called upon to act. League decisions are ratified and executed by the governments concerned, and others by the administrative branch of the League. Where the governments have this responsibility, unnecessary delay is often occasioned, and it falls on the officials of the Secretariat to urge more immediate action. Not only are governments spurred to action by the Secretariat, but pressure is sometimes brought to bear upon them by publishing notices of unfulfilled obligations in the "Official Journal." The Council is thus in a position to reinforce the Secretariat by urging upon the governments to cooperate wholeheartedly with the League. Far-reaching steps have been taken to effect an efficient organization for the transaction of business among nations, and the League organs promise to continue the fulfillment of this necessary task.

CHAPTER III

Pacific Settlement of International Disputes

International relations have become vitally important in this twentieth century world. Nations carry on extensive trade relations with one another, nationals of one country travel in other countries, and we commonly say that the world has become a unit. Where complex relations exist among nations there are bound to arise numerous disputes of one sort or another, and such disputes are always likely to lead to war. To guard against this eventuality, the nations have attempted to set up machinery for the settlement of international differences.

The most common method of settling disputes arising between two nations is by diplomatic means. Direct negotiations take place between the contending parties through the efforts of diplomatic representatives, which usually result in peaceful settlements. Other methods of adjusting international differences are through arbitration and mediation. Through mediation a solution is proposed by a state other than the two disputing states. The primary effort of the mediator is to find a basis for compromise where the parties to a dispute have been unable to do this. Such intervention is regarded as a friendly act but the deliberations in no way bind the disputants.

Arbitration, on the other hand, means that the disputants select a tribunal of impartial judges to hear the facts and render a decision. A distinction between mediation and arbitration has been succinctly made by an American jurist, John Basset Moore, who said: "Mediation is an advisory, arbitration a judicial, function. Mediation recommends, arbitration decides." These methods have long been employed, and numerous controversies have been settled which otherwise would have led to grave international complications.

Disputes between nations are ordinarily of two kinds: legal and political. Legal controversies are, as a rule, more easily settled than political ones, as they do not affect a nation's sovereignty, nor threaten its "national honor." Many legal disputes have been settled by arbitration through the Permanent Court of Arbitration established at the First Hague Peace Conference in 1899. Since the World War, the Permanent Court of International Justice at the Hague has become the recognized body for the settlement of international legal disputes. The record of settlements in the field of arbitration has been most encouraging. This phase of international relationships has been adequately handled.

Political disputes between nations arise from time to time but do not lend themselves to ready adjustment, as in the case of legal controversies. If a nation's honor is threatened, or if a dispute relating to territorial questions arises, serious complications may result. Nations have too often in the past been unwilling to submit matters affecting "national honor" or "vital interests" to peaceful settlement. These exceptions are sufficiently broad to make it possible for a nation to decline pacific settlement of disputes. In the past, nations were reluctant to permit any encroachments upon their freedom of action by outside powers. Now some nations are willing to yield a point in this rigid exercise of national sovereignty.

Legal disputes are ordinarily so classified when based on established facts, while in political disputes the determination of facts in the merits of the controversy may not be easy. Conditions arise which cause bitter feeling between two nations where each blames the other and if such disputes are to be settled, concessions must be made by both sides, national pride must be allayed, and a genuine desire to maintain peaceful relations between the disputing nations must be paramount. Since the war, the settlement of political disputes has been of major concern to the Council of the League, the chief purpose of which is the maintenance of peace. The Covenant provides various methods of settlement for disputes among nations. The first method is provided in Article 11 which states: "That any war or threat of war whether immediately affecting any members of the League or not, is hereby declared a matter of concern to the whole League, and the League shall take any action that may be deemed wise and effectual to safeguard the peace of nations." This Article gives the League bodies blanket power to deal with disputes in any part of the world, if such occurrences are likely to threaten peace. No definite machinery is here provided, but the intent is to leave the way open to deal with each case as it arises.

This Article is designed to provide the procedure to be followed in terminating disputes, which may lead to war. Where "such emergency shall arise, the Secretary-General shall, on the request of any member of the League, forthwith summon a meeting of the Council." The Council when assembled acts as a conciliating body, discussing the problem with the two parties and thus attempting to make them accept a settlement. It is the task of the Council to forestall wars, and if hostilities break out, to put an end to them. The disputing states occupy seats in the Council on an equal footing with the other members, and are assured a full hearing. When Article 11 is invoked, both parties to a dispute give their consent to the efforts of the Council. A solution must meet the approval of both parties, and all members of the Council. The broad scope of Article 11 permits the Council freedom of deliberation in all phases of a dispute without restricting it to a prescribed course of action. This is the procedure usually followed in the early stages of an international controversy. This informal approach to the settlement of a controversy opens effective avenues of procedure, and it takes for granted the genuine desire by two nations, engaged in the dispute, to arrive at a peaceful settlement. If this inclination is not present, little can be hoped from discussions.

The Council may attempt to conciliate two disputing parties under Article 11 of the Covenant without serious threat to the League's prestige, since, even if its efforts fail, no legal obligation devolves upon the members to act. It is only when other and more stringent efforts are made to force recalcitrant parties to adjust their differences, that the obligations of the League members under the Covenant are invoked. This preliminary exploration by the Council may, of course, result in harsher measures. If this is attempted, the Council is required first to name the aggressor, and second to adopt one of several forms of procedure to check him. There is always the danger that the League may adopt stringent measures against an aggressor and fail to carry them out. To call the bluff of a disturber of world peace, and later back down, would materially weaken the League. Therefore, it would be unwise for the Council to undertake any move that could not be fulfilled. The present weakness of the League has caused the Council to hesitate in bringing pressure upon an offender, since such attempts have failed, and only a few have succeeded. However, as a result of the uncertain power of the League, the Council has in most disputes confined its efforts to conciliation, as provided for under Article 11.

It should not be inferred that the broad provisions contained in Article 11 lessens its importance. So far some forty disputes have been brought before the Council under this Article, and most of these disputes have been settled. Extensive jurisdiction of the Council is enhanced by the provision in Article 11 which states: "It is also declared to be the friendly right of each member of the League to bring to the attention of the Assembly or the Council any circumstance whatever affecting international relations which threatens to disturb international peace, or the good understanding between nations upon which peace depends." Thus the League is empowered to attempt the settlement of a dispute when requested to do so by a member. It should be noted that this procedure does not admit single members to intervene, but it is the League as a whole that assumes responsibility. No provision is made whereby a member state may call upon the League to refrain from such interference. An interpretation of the Covenant implies that it is the task of the League to act as the stabilizer of world peace. Its authority is further enhanced by the ability of the Council to intervene in the early stages of a controversy. Too often in the past, no machinery has been set in motion to deal with disputes until conditions have become most serious. There is of course the danger that the Council may concern itself with petty quarrels of no great significance. While this may be possible under the provisions of Article 11 it is hardly probable that the Council would lessen its prestige by seeking to intervene in local quarrels of limited significance.

The wide latitude of powers exercised by the Council and Assembly under Article 11 may be seen by the large number and variety of disputes which have come before these bodies. The following is a résumé of the more important political disputes that have been dealt with by the League.

1. Conflict between Persia and Soviet Russia (*the Enzeli Affair*)

This case was an appeal by the Persian Government on May 19, 1920 and was dealt with by the Council on June 16, 1920. Persia, a member of the League, appealed to the Council for help in repelling a Soviet force that had bombarded and occupied the town of Enzeli and other Persian towns on the Caspian Sea. Persia received telegrams from the Soviet Government giving assurances that the Russian forces would be withdrawn from the territory, which led the Council to await the outcome of these promises. The dispute was satisfactorily settled by the withdrawal of Russian troops.

2. The Aaland Islands Controversy between FINLAND and SWEDEN

In accordance with the rights conferred upon it by Article 11 of the Covenant, as a third, non-interested party, Great Britain brought before the League Council on July 11, 1920, a dispute between Sweden and Finland, relating to the Aaland Islands in the Baltic Sea, mid-way between the two countries. Finland gained her independence from Russia in 1918, and the Aaland Islands, which had, for more than a century, formed part of Finland, and therefore belonged to Russia likewise became independent. The islanders were for the most part of Swedish origin, and hence wished to be annexed to Sweden. Finland was not yet a member of the League, and protested against this interference by the Council on the ground that the matter was wholly domestic and therefore beyond the jurisdiction of the League. A bitter dispute ensued between Sweden and

Finland, but the Council prevailed upon the two countries to take no hostile action during the period of the League's investigation. A Commission was sent to the two countries, as well as to the islands to report its findings to the Council. After extended hearings, by representatives from Finland and Sweden, as well as the islanders, the Council decided that the Islands should remain under Finnish sovereignty, subject to certain new guarantees whereby the preservation of the Swedish character of the islanders would be maintained. The proposal of the Council was loyally accepted by the two countries on June 24, 1921. This settlement led to a broader international agreement for the permanent demilitarization of the whole archipelago. A bitter controversy was thus brought to an end through mediation by the League.

3. The Conflict between Poland and Lithuania

When the World War ended, Poland and Lithuania were left facing one another along undefined frontiers, with hostile armies on both sides, ready to occupy disputed territories. Intermittent warfare followed and conditions became menacing when the Polish Government brought the dispute to the attention of the Council on September 5, 1920. The League machinery was set in motion to avert hostilities, followed by years of patient negotiations, in an attempt to settle this controversy. The means employed by both the League Council and Assembly failed to effect a satisfactory settlement, but the intervention served to put an end to the fighting. This dispute which may be regarded as a partial success for the League, was one of the most serious with which the League has had to deal. The continuous conference method served to keep the dispute before the bar of world opinion which did much to prevent the disputants from renewing hostilities. It was on October 5, 1927, that the Lithuanian Government appealed to the Council under the provisions of Article 11. The Council succeeded in obtaining the consent of the two governments to end the state of war, and was able to adopt a resolution on December 15, 1927, which noted that peace existed between the two countries, recommending that the two governments should undertake direct negotiations for the establishment of an enduring peace. While the disputants agreed to respect one another's rights, there was continued delay in carrying out these commitments. The Council again took a hand in the matter on September 8, 1928, and the result was another provisional agreement. Finally, on May 21, 1931, the Council obtained assurances from both parties that frontier incidents no longer gave rise to hostilities. Economic and political problems had been adjusted without formal agreements. Nevertheless, it must be said that the prestige of the League was in no way enhanced by this long-drawn out dispute.

4. The Tacna-Arica Dispute (*Bolivia, Peru, and Chile*)

A dispute between Chile on the one hand and Bolivia and Peru on the other over the desert wastes of Tacna-Arica came before the League soon after it was organized. This territorial dispute, based on a Treaty of 1884, aroused bitter controversy among the interested states with the discovery of valuable nitrate deposits in the region. Long years of negotiations failed to effect a settlement, although the United States and other American republics had attempted conciliation. With the organization of the League, Bolivia on November 1, 1920, invoked Article 19 of the Covenant with the object of receiving assistance from the Assembly in the reconsideration of the older treaties. Peru joined in a similar demand by invoking Articles 15 and 19 of the Covenant, as she contended former treaties respecting Tacna-Arica were no longer applicable. The protests were directed against Chile who contended that the League was not competent to act, as Article 19 merely provided that "the Assembly . . . may advise the reconsideration . . . of treaties. . ." The Assembly agreed to postpone action while a Committee of jurists should study the legal questions involved. The contention of Chile was upheld by the Committee and the rule established that the Assembly can only act under Article 19 when a treaty is no longer in force, or if conditions threaten the peace of the world. This report led to the withdrawal of the protests by Bolivia and Peru.

Negotiations were transferred to Washington with repeated efforts at arbitration and the supervision of a plebiscite in the disputed area by the United States. These efforts at first came to naught, but after repeated delays, the Treaty of Santiago, July 28, 1929, was signed. Tacna was granted to Peru, and Arica to Chile, while Bolivian claims were dismissed. The intervention by the United States brought an end to League efforts and robbed it of any claim to credit for final adjustment. This was not serious, however, as League intervention in a dispute is not undertaken for the purpose of recording successes, but rather to preserve peace. Agencies other than the League which may accomplish this end have been welcomed by that body.

5a. The Albanian Boundary Dispute

This vexatious problem was typical of the numerous post-war quarrels because of undefined boundaries. Albania was admitted to League membership at the first Assembly, and a movement was immediately inaugurated to get her frontiers defined. However, certain delays occurred resulting in frontier skirmishes, whereupon a Commission of the League was sent to the disputed area to investigate. The hostilities involved Albania, Greece, and Jugoslavia, over territories contiguous to Albania. The Albanian Government appealed to the Council for assistance against the aggressors on April 29, and again on June 15, 1921. The provisions of Article 11 of the Covenant gave Albania the right to call upon the Council for assistance in such an emergency. The matter was discussed in six sessions of the Council, and one session of the Assembly. The former urged that the boundaries in question be determined by the Conference of Ambassadors which had the matter under consideration. The armies of Jugoslavia continued their advance into Albania, whereupon the British Government moved to invoke Article 11 anew, by requesting the Council to meet and "consider the situation, and to agree upon measures to be taken under Article 16 in the event of the Jugoslavian Government's refusal or delaying to execute their obligations under the Covenant." The Council met in a special public session on November 16, 1921, and for the first time in the history of the League, the economic boycott as a weapon to check an aggressor was discussed. The deliberations of this session of the Council proved effective, and the Conference of Ambassadors almost immediately determined the boundary lines of Albania which were "acceptable" to her neighbors. It was largely as a result of Italy's sudden interest in protecting Albania's rights that Jugoslavia was forced to give up her aggressive designs. Prior to the boundary settlement, the Council of the League had succeeded in establishing a neutral zone which was respected by the disputing states. The alertness of the Council, backed by strong sentiment against war in the Balkans, as well as the possibility of instituting an economic blockade against Jugoslavia, were sufficient to solve one of the most acute, early post-war crises of the League.

5b. Evacuation of Koritza

Later frontier disturbances caused Albania to appeal to the Council on September 27, 1924, by invoking Article 11 of the Covenant. In this instance Albania pressed for the evacuation of fourteen villages held by Greece in the Koritza zone. This zone had, by treaty, been allotted to Albania. On October 3, the Greek representative gave assurance to the Council that his government would carry out the earlier boundary provisions.

6. The Upper-Silesian Question

The territory known as Upper-Silesia is rich in coal and iron deposits, and is a valuable industrial area. It belonged to Germany before the signing of the Treaty of Versailles. Article 88 of this Treaty stipulated that a portion of Upper-Silesia was to be governed by an Inter-allied Commission until such a time as the inhabitants should, by plebiscite, determine their future allegiance. The plebiscite took place on March 20, 1921, but did not settle the matter, as the Allied Powers with whom the decision rested, were divided on the question of the boundary to be fixed. A majority of the inhabitants of the plebiscite area expressed themselves in favor of Germany. Confronted with this expression of popular sentiment, the Supreme Council of the Allied Powers turned to the Council of the League on August 12, 1921, for assistance in settling the frontier between Germany and Poland. Because of the mixed population the problem was indeed a difficult one. On September 1, 1921, the Council selected representatives of several disinterested governments to make an impartial study of the problem based on first-hand observations, and to report to the Council. On the basis of these findings, the Council recommended on October 12, 1921, the drawing of a definite frontier line, and the conclusion of a treaty between Germany and Poland to this effect. The Conference of Ambassadors accepted the Council's recommendations which led to a final agreement between the two countries on May 15, 1922. The Council went beyond the immediate frontier problem, and obtained the consent of Germany and Poland to the adjustment of certain economic and social conditions to prevent future uprisings in this territory. This dispute which had failed of solution in the hands of the Supreme Council, was thus amicably settled through League agencies.

7. Dispute between Finland and Soviet Russia over Eastern Carelia

In November, 1921, disorder broke out among the inhabitants of Eastern Carelia who had been granted autonomy at the close of the World War. This territory between Finland and Soviet Russia brought the two interested countries into the dispute and Finland quickly appealed to the Council under the provisions of Article 11 of the Covenant, to effect a settlement. The matter was discussed in four separate sessions of the Council, after which it was referred to the Permanent Court of International Justice at The Hague for an advisory opinion because the Soviet Union challenged the jurisdiction of the League over her, since she was not a member of that body. She asserted this was a domestic matter and did not appear before the Court to argue the case and the Court refused to express an opinion on it. The Council did not pursue the matter further, as Finland no longer pressed for settlement. It is safe to say that the active interference by the Council in the dispute of Eastern Carelia had a deterrent effect on Russia's aggressive designs in this territory. Full discussion under Article 11 greatly aided in bringing about an amicable settlement between the two disputing parties.

8a. Bulgarian Armed Bands on the Frontier

On June 14, 1922, the governments of Greece, Rumania, and Serbia addressed a joint protest to the Bulgarian Government because large bands from that country raided their territories. Following the World War, some 500,000 refugees from the neighboring countries were stranded in Bulgaria and their presence constituted a menacing problem. Bulgaria regarded the joint note as a serious threat and appealed to the Council of the League, under Article 11 of the Covenant, in a communication dated June 17, 1922. This thorny problem was fully argued before the Council where all agreed to settle the dispute by negotiation. It was further agreed that if negotiations failed, to re-submit the case to the Council. The dispute was settled in the manner proposed, and the Council was relieved of any further interference.

8b. Hungarian-Czechoslovak Frontier

The Council acted to conciliate a dispute between Hungary and Czechoslovakia over a frontier region between the two countries known as the Salgó-Tarján coal basin. Hungary brought the matter before the Council on November 16, 1922, whereupon plans for settlement were worked out. A member of the Council, aided by experts from the Secretariat, drew up a report which was agreed to by the Council on April 23, 1923. Both parties accepted the report which brought a solution to this frontier incident.

9. Hungarian Property in Rumania

An involved controversy between Hungary and Rumania was taken up by the Council of the League as a result of an appeal by the Hungarian Government on March 15, 1923, to settle a dispute involving the expropriation by the Rumanian Government of lands belonging to Hungarians. With the transfer of new territories to Rumania at the close of the war, many Hungarians found themselves under alien rule. Some left Rumania and the Rumanian Legislature decreed that their property should belong to the state. Hungary asserted that this was contrary to an earlier treaty arrangement. She brought the case before the Council for settlement under the provisions of Article 11 of the Covenant. The Council attempted various methods to effect a settlement but at first met with little success. Negotiations were kept open, however, until the dispute was merged into another controversy and a general settlement was reached on April 28, 1930. Hungary declared her claims were satisfied and she requested the Council to withdraw the matter from the agenda of the League.

10. Dispute between Greece and Italy (*The Corfu Incident*)

An Italian delegation under the Conference of Ambassadors was engaged in delimiting the boundary between Albania and Greece in August, 1923, when they were murdered on Greek territory. Italy immediately dispatched a harsh ultimatum to Greece, some terms of which were quite unacceptable. The Conference of Ambassadors took a hand in the matter and made certain demands upon Greece, but before receiving a reply, the Italian forces occupied the Greek island of Corfu, following the bombardment in which a number of Greeks and Armenians were killed and wounded.

On September 1, Greece appealed to the Council under Articles 12 and 15 of the Covenant with the declaration that its proposals would be acceptable. The Italian representative on the Council challenged the jurisdiction of the League, particularly since the Conference of Ambassadors was considering the dispute. The unwillingness of the Italian delegate to admit League jurisdiction caused general resentment in the Assembly then meeting in regular session.

In a meeting of the Council on September 6, eight proposals were submitted as the basis of settlement. The final resolution was not wholly acceptable to the Italian representative, whereupon it was agreed that the proceedings should be sent to the Conference of Ambassadors for its information. On the basis of the Council's resolution the Conference of Ambassadors fixed the penalty against Greece, which was promptly accepted by both Greece and Italy. Although the penalty was harsh, peace was preserved. Here the slower conciliation procedure under Article 11 was not applicable in view of the serious crisis which had arisen. Drastic action was required of the Council, with Italian forces occupying Greek territory. Although severe measures were undertaken by invoking Article 15, League success was not assured. Nevertheless, Italy evacuated Corfu, but practically all her demands were met. This was the first instance in which a great Power defied the authority of the League, and the new peace institution was not yet strong enough to meet the challenge. Divided responsibility, due to the consideration of the dispute by both the Council and the Conference of Ambassadors, made the League bodies extremely timid in assuming responsibility for a settlement of the dispute. While the League is not credited with the settlement of the Greco-Italian dispute, nevertheless valuable precedents were established in its procedure, and strong opinion was created in its favor as an institution serving world society in times of stress.

11. The Polish Czechoslovakian Frontier (*Jaworzina Question*)

Following the World War, a special Commission was appointed under the terms of the Treaty of St. Germain to adjust the boundary lines in the Jaworzina district between Poland and Czechoslovakia. The Commission was instructed to determine the boundary in case the two countries failed to accept within the stated time the frontier fixed by the Treaty of St. Germain. The time specified for the settlement elapsed before an agreement was reached, and a deadlook resulted.

Czechoslovakia contended that the frontier described by the Peace Treaty should be retained, as no new agreement had been reached while Poland insisted that new negotiations were necessary. The Conference of Ambassadors, which supervised the enforcement of the Treaty of St. Germain, appealed to the Council under Article 11 of the Covenant, on September 20, 1923, in an effort to affect a final settlement. The Council in turn referred the dispute to the Permanent Court of International Justice for an advisory opinion to determine whether the dispute was already settled, as claimed by Czechoslovakia. The Court held that the original boundary settlement was to be retained with minor adjustments as embodied in the original settlement, subject to changes by the Council. The two disputants accepted the opinion of the Court when the matter was discussed by the Council on December 13, 1923. The Council continued to deal with this boundary question and was able on March 12, 1924, to recommend to the Conference of Ambassadors a complete settlement, which the Conference accepted, thus bringing to a satisfactory conclusion one more of the acute boundary problems arising from the World War.

12. The Memel Dispute

The port of Memel on the Baltic Sea, with adjacent territory including the mouth of the Niemen River, was taken from Germany at the close of the War, and intrusted to the Conference of Ambassadors for final disposition. The Conference transferred the territory to Lithuania in the summer of 1923. The terms of the transfer were wholly unacceptable to Lithuania as she considered the privileges granted Poland in the use of the seaport far too favorable to the latter country. Following this refusal, the Governments represented by the Conference of Ambassadors referred the matter to the Council on September 25, 1923, and asked that Article 11 be invoked in the settlement of the Memel dispute. The Council set up a special Commission with Mr. Norman Davis of the United States as the Chairman to investigate the situation on the spot. The Commissioners produced an admirable report which was approved by the Council, and accepted by Lithuania and Poland in an agreement signed on May 8, 1924. The Treaty granted Lithuania full sovereignty over Memel, but gave to this province a certain amount of autonomy in local matters, while the Port was internationalized and made free to world commerce. From time to time disputes arose in this area between Lithuania and Germany which charged the former with violations of international agreements. The Council dealt with these problems, but did not change the status of this territory.

13. The Mosul Boundary Dispute

In a Treaty of peace between Turkey and the Allied Powers signed at Lausanne, July 24, 1923, a clause called upon Great Britain and Turkey to settle the boundary lines in the territory of Mosul. Provision was made that in case of failure to arrive at a settlement within nine months, the matter should be referred to the Council for settlement. Failing to reach an agreement, the British Government on August 6, 1924, requested the Council to settle the dispute. The Turkish Government accepted the Council's invitation to participate in the discussions. The question arose as to the jurisdiction of the Council to act as a body to execute the Treaty of Lausanne, and whether the interested parties could vote. The matter was referred to the World Court for an advisory opinion, which held that the Council was free to make final disposition of this controversy, in accordance with the procedure described in the League Covenant. The principle was also set forth by the Court that in such agreements Article 5 of the Covenant called for unanimity by the Council but that the votes of the parties to a dispute would not be counted. (The Court held that the Council must proceed under Article 15 of the Covenant in the settlement of this quarrel). This opinion by the Court is important in that the Council has since adhered to this practice in dealing with international disputes. On the basis of these developments, the Council rendered a decision fixing the boundary line through the Mosul district. The frontier traced by the Council was slightly modified by the United Kingdom and Turkey, and a Treaty was signed at Angora, June 5, 1926, which finally disposed of this frontier problem.

14. The Expulsion of the Oecumenical Patriarch

The Lausanne Treaty of 1923 provided for the exchange of Greek and Turkish populations. While going forward with this, the Turkish authorities expelled the Greek Oecumenical Patriarch from Constantinople. The Greek Government protested against this, and appealed to the Council on February 11, 1925, under Article 11 of the Covenant. The Turkish Government requested the Council to disregard the appeal of Greece, contending that the matter was purely domestic, and should be settled by the two Governments directly. The Greek representative argued that the question was an international one, as it involved the application of the Treaty of Lausanne. The Council asked the Permanent Court for an opinion to determine whether the Council was competent to deal with this dispute. In the meantime, the President of the Council urged the disputants to find a basis of agreement. This appeal proved successful, and on June 1, 1925, the Greek Government requested the Council to be permitted to withdraw its appeal as the matter had been amicably settled. The Council informed the Permanent Court that an advisory opinion was not desired.

15a. The Greco-Bulgarian Incident

On October 19, 1925, a Greek soldier crossed the border into Bulgaria, and fired on a Bulgarian sentry, who returned fire and killed the Greek. This incident led to general firing, whereupon Greek soldiers advanced some five miles into Bulgaria and were ordered to launch a general offensive on October 24. In the meantime, the Bulgarian Government appealed to the League under Articles 10, and 11 of the Covenant. As Bulgaria appealed to the League, it was incumbent upon the Secretary-General to, "forthwith summon a meeting of the Council" and an extraordinary session of that body immediately met in Paris. The President of the Council telegraphed the Greek and Bulgarian Governments, reminding them of their obligations under Article 12 of the Covenant, and at the same time requesting the withdrawal of their troops behind their frontiers. At the first meeting it was decided to request the two Governments to notify the Council within twenty-four hours that orders had been given for the withdrawal of all troops behind their frontiers, and that within sixty hours all troops had actually been withdrawn. While the case was argued before the Council by representatives of the Greek and Bulgarian Governments, firing ceased, and the troops evacuated the occupied areas, complying with the time limit fixed. The Council proceeded to set up a Commission of Inquiry which was sent to the scene of hostilities in order to determine the causes of the conflict and fix responsibility as well as to recommend measures which would prevent the recurrence of similar outbreaks. A month later the Commission submitted its report to the Council fixing the blame upon Greece, whereupon the Greek Government was asked to pay an indemnity of $210,000 within two months, with which it complied.

This incident was unique in the history of the League in that the intervention by the Council came at a time when fighting was actually going on. Prompt action resulted in the triumph of sanity and reason over passion and violence. Although the Council dealt with an outbreak between two smaller countries, the test of the League machinery was effective, and a precedent was established to guide the Council in dealing with future disturbances.

15b. Greco-Turkish Frontier

On February 24, 1926, the Greek Government invoked Articles 11 and 14 in an appeal to the Council requesting it to seek an advisory opinion of the Permanent Court on a question relating to the interpretation of the Treaty of Lausanne in respect to a boundary in the district of the Maritza. The representative of Turkey argued that the Council lacked jurisdiction but it appointed a Committee of jurists which held that the boundary should be determined by a commission as provided for in the Treaty of Lausanne. The decision of the Council was accepted by the two Governments, which resulted in the establishment of a definite boundary.

16. Moslems of Albanian Origin in Greece

This dispute grew out of the enforcement of a provision in the Treaty of Lausanne, 1923, which required Greece and Turkey to exchange large numbers of their peoples. Many of the Moslems living in Greece were of Albanian origin, and the Greek Government was accused by Albania of transporting them to Turkey. The Albanian Government brought the matter before the Council under Article 11 of the Covenant, on August 11, 1924, demanding that Moslems of Albanian origin in Greece, should not be exchanged under the Lausanne Treaty. The Greek representative stated that his Government did not wish to force the Moslems of Albanian origin to leave. The Council voted to refer the matter to the Mixed Commission which had been set up to supervise this work with the understanding that the Albanian views in the matter should be respected. The Commission was instructed to keep the Council informed of any matters of special importance which might arise. On December 11, 1924, the Council appointed permanent representatives to remain in Greece in order to supervise the enforcement of treaties relating to the protection of minorities. The representatives submitted their final report to the Council on September 16, 1926. Another appeal was made by the Albanian Government to the Council on May 10, 1928 when Article 11 was again invoked in an effort to enlist the aid of the Council to prevent discrimination against Albanian minorities in Greece. The Council was inclined to hold that the matter should be settled under existing minority treaties, and it agreed that Article 11 of the Covenant should only be invoked in grave cases.

17. The Chaco Dispute between Bolivia and Paraguay

Bolivia and Paraguay waged a deadly war against each other almost continuously from 1928 to 1935. The war, which was historic in origin, resulted from rival claims to the territory known as the Gran Chaco. This territory, which lies between the two countries, involves a vast area of swampy plains and jungle lands, which are largely uninhabited. The League was helpless to put an end to the war, although it was up for discussion in several sessions of the Council and Assembly. The remoteness of the two countries and their unwillingness to accept outside interference handicapped the League. Other attempts equally unfruitful, were made by the neighboring powers, by the Pan-American Conferences at Washington in 1928, and at Montevideo in 1934. Sheer exhaustion did more to end the war than the collective conference systems.

The efforts by the League in this crisis enable us to understand its technique in the handling of a thorny problem. As Bolivia and Paraguay were both members of the League, the Council took the initiative on December 11, 1928, in reminding both contestants of their obligations under the Covenant to settle disputes by peaceful means. The rôle of the Council was made difficult by the interference of the Pan-American Conference, which at the same time was attempting to effect a settlement. Out of deference to the United States and Argentina (not members of the League) the Council hesitated to take steps which might conflict with the efforts of these two members of the Pan-American Conference to mediate in the dispute. The Council approved the efforts of the Conference to work out a settlement, but the methods employed to end hostilities proved to be fruitless. The Council was an onlooker while the American Republics vainly attempted to terminate the war.

After the renewal of hostilities on a large scale by Bolivia in July, 1932, the League's system was again set in motion. Paraguay appealed to the League under Articles 10 and 11 of the Covenant. The Council still hesitated to interfere with the efforts of the American States, preferring to await the outcome of concerted action on this side of the Atlantic. The League Powers in time became impatient with the lack of progress and consequently inquired of the United States whether she would object to vigorous action by the Council to uphold the Covenant. This Government did not favor the move, but wished to continue the peaceful efforts already attempted. Nevertheless, in the fall of 1933, a League Commission of Enquiry was sent to South America, where for a time its efforts to settle the crisis seemed promising. In cooperation with the Montevideo Conference a truce was arranged but proved to be of short duration. The truce ended in January 1934, and in May, Bolivia invoked Article 15, and the dispute was transferred to the Assembly. The active interference by the Assembly led ultimately to the announcement by Paraguay of her intention to withdraw from the League. An embargo on munitions against the two warring countries was agreed to by the League Powers, but with the withdrawal of Paraguay, some nations lifted the embargo against Bolivia, thus plainly indicating League sympathies for a member. The Assembly considered the matter in September, 1934, whereupon a Committee of twenty-two members was set up to explore the possibilities of conciliation under Article 15, of the Covenant. A special session of the Assembly was held in November to consider the report of the special Committee, and, if possible, to find some basis for settlement of the controversy at this late date. The Committee of Twenty-Two drew up the most comprehensive peace plan in the history of the League, which was considered by the special session of the Assembly. Continued fighting made further efforts at conciliation impracticable. The scene shifted to Bolivia and Paraguay and a new peace Conference met at Buenos Aires with the approval of the Special Committee of the Assembly. Argentina, Brazil, Chile, Peru, the United States, and Uruguay eventually induced Bolivia and Paraguay in January 1936, to resume diplomatic relations, exchange of prisoners of war, and consent to the peaceful settlement of territorial differences. The prospects for permanent peace in the Gran Chaco seemed more promising at that date than at any previous period in the long conflict, but the willingness of the two powers to end war was due not so much to the efforts of the League, nor to the American Republics, as to the sheer exhaustion of the two countries involved.

18. The Sino-Japanese Conflict

The first ten years of the League's history was marked by numerous successes in settling international disputes and the League as a peace institution had become well established. The members had over and over again invoked Article 11 as the accepted method of League procedure in adjusting international quarrels. However, an incident occurred in September, 1931, which was destined to shake the peace machinery at Geneva to its very foundations. The League members were called upon to check a major power which, under the

Covenant, was clearly regarded as an aggressor in a conflict.

The underlying causes of the dispute between China and Japan need not detain us here. The Japanese troops occupied Mukden, the capital of Manchuria, in retaliation for the alleged destruction of Japanese railroad properties near that city by the Chinese. On September 21, the Chinese Government submitted the matter to the Council under Article 11 of the Covenant. The Japanese continued their invasion of Manchuria under the guise of protecting their national interests, and with the assurance that they had no territorial ambitions. With the appeal of China, the Council cabled Nanking and Tokyo, asking them to refrain from any action that might aggravate the situation, and requesting them to withdraw their troops from the critical areas. The Council at the same time submitted the matter to the government of the United States for its information and possible cooperation, in view of special American interests in the Pacific.

At China's request, the Council met in special session in October. Much time was wasted over the question of American participation in the Council meetings. The United States had declared its willingness to "reinforce what the League does" and authorized its consul at Geneva to sit as the first official American representative with the Council. A decision was reached to invoke the Kellogg-Briand Pact to which the United States is a party, calling the attention of China and Japan to their obligations under Article 2 of that Treaty. The weakness under this procedure was that this Treaty contained no provisions for organized opposition against an aggressor, since it is merely a solemn promise on the part of the signatories to settle conflicts by pacific means. American participation in League sessions under these conditions could carry no weight except insofar as moral pressure on a warring power was concerned.

On October 24 the Council unanimously voted to ask the Japanese Government to withdraw all troops "into the railway zone" before November 16, and requested China to insure the safety of the Japanese in her country. Then the Council adjourned until November 16, when it met in Paris. Prior to this meeting, the government at Washington modified its position in regard to official cooperation with the Council. The American consul at Geneva remained at his post, while the Ambassador to England was commissioned to go to Paris to confer with representatives of the Council, but not to sit with that body. After our sudden withdrawal, the prestige of the previous session of the Council suffered considerably. Certainly the dignity of America was in no way enhanced by requiring the Ambassador to remain away from League sessions.

While the Council was deliberating in Paris, the Japanese forces were advancing into north Manchuria. With the failure of the Council to check Japan, the deliberations took a different turn when on December 10, 1931, the Council unanimously decided to send a Commission of Inquiry of five members to Manchuria to obtain first-hand information of all the facts relating to the dispute with the view to guiding the Council in its deliberations. The Commission was duly appointed and arrived in the far East late in February. It undertook an impartial study relating to all phases of the controversy. The summary of the findings, known as the Lytton Report, was submitted to the Council in September, 1932. It is a comprehensive document setting forth recommendations, which if followed, would have been fair to both China and Japan. During the long period of investigation Japan proceeded to organize Manchuria into an allegedly independent state of "Manchukuo." On January 7, 1932, the American Government notified Japan and China that it would not recognize "any situation, treaty or agreement which may be brought about by means contrary to the covenants and obligations of the Pact of Paris." This definition of policy which became known as the "Stimson Doctrine" was applied by practically all the governments of the world, and up to the present this new state has not generally been recognized either "de jure" or "de facto."

The Assembly of the League took a hand in the matter March 1932, as a result of an appeal by China under Articles 12 and 15 of the Covenant. The special Assembly created a committee representing nineteen States, which was to study developments and investigate possible developments which might lead to a peaceful settlement. The Committee of Nineteen failed in its efforts at conciliation, but submitted a significant report to the special Assembly on February 24, 1933, in which Japan stood condemned before the world. Following this report Japan announced her intention to withdraw from the League.

No one will deny the failures of the League in the months of its efforts to settle the Sino-Japanese conflict when every phase of peace machinery was tried short of military and economic pressure. The remoteness of the conflict and the severity of the world depression did much to weaken collective action against an aggressor state. The United States had vital interests in the far East and was desirous of preventing Japanese aggression, but failed to cooperate effectively with the League. The danger of actual warfare made the League powers hesitant to do more than merely attempt a negotiated settlement. This instance of dealing with a major power found the League machinery inadequate, and its failure in the Far East has often been cited by critics of the collective system. Although the League failed in this test, there is little justification to anticipate similar failures in all future disputes. World opinion may yet be centered more than ever upon the system of collective action and instead of a breakdown in the peace structure at Geneva, peoples everywhere may realize more and more the need of an international agency to insure world order.

19. The Anglo-Persian Oil Dispute

In November, 1932, the Persian Government announced the cancellation of a concession which had been granted in 1901 to the Anglo-Persian Oil Company. The drop in oil prices during the depression caused the Persian revenue from this source to decrease. Persian officials were convinced that the Anglo-Persian Oil Company acted in bad faith by failing to pay the sums agreed to under the terms of the existing concession. The British Government took a strong stand against the cancellation of the leases, as more than half of the stock was owned by the British Government, and large supplies of oil for her navy were obtained from this area. The vital interests of Great Britain were seriously affected, and might have resulted in direct pressure by a major power against a weak state. Instead, the British Government submitted the dispute to the Council on December 14, which discussed the question, appointed a rapporteur, and brought about a settlement. A new agreement between Persia and the Anglo-Persian Oil Company was signed April 29, 1933, which granted the Company the exploitation of oil deposits of an area of more than 100,000 square miles, and fixed Persia's royalties at a minimum of $3,800,000 per year. The invocation of Article 15 in this dispute was indicative of its seriousness. Had the League not existed, a strong power would in all likelihood have imposed its will on a weaker one. In this case, too, the just methods of free discussion by disinterested parties resulted in an equitable solution.

20. Conflict between Columbia and Peru (*Leticia*)

On August 31, 1932, Peruvian armed bands occupied the small town of Leticia, and later extended their occupation to the surrounding territory. Leticia was the chief town in a region of the upper Amazon, transferred from Peru to Columbia by a Treaty which went into effect in 1930. Although Peru disclaimed all responsibility for the seizure of Leticia, her officials did not interfere. The move proved to be very popular among the Peruvians. Columbia sent an expedition of 1500 men up the Amazon which was regarded by Peru as an act of aggression. Disinterested states made attempts at conciliation, and discussions took place in the Council. On February 16, Peru officially reported the "matter to the League of Nations for necessary action under the Covenant" and on the following day Columbia invoked Article 15 of the Covenant. A Committee of Three, already appointed by the Council, proposed that a League Commission take an active hand in settling the dispute, but the suggested procedure was unacceptable to the two parties. The Council noted its failure to effect arbitration and recommended that the Peruvian forces evacuate Leticia, to be followed by negotiations between the parties in order to bring about a permanent settlement. On the same day, March 18, the Council announced the principle of non-recognition of territorial changes contrary to the League Covenant or the Kellogg-Briand Pact. An Advisory Committee was set up to watch the situation and it invited the Governments of the United States and Brazil to collaborate. It held frequent meetings and succeeded in obtaining the consent of the disputing parties to stop hostilities. The Council was informed on May 25 that an agreement had been signed providing for the appointment of an international Commission to take charge of Leticia until a final settlement had been reached. The armed Peruvians transferred the rule over this territory to the Commission which governed this area with the assistance of a small group of Columbian soldiers. This League rule continued while Treaty negotiations took place at Rio de Janiero and a final settlement was reached. The territory was handed back to the Columbian Government as provided for in a Treaty between Columbia and Peru signed at Rio de Janiero, May 24, 1934. The Treaty contained a protocol of peace, friendship, and cooperation together with a provision relating to special agreements which would later be concluded respecting customs, trade, policing of frontier, etc. The settlement of the Leticia incident proved to be one of the high points in League conciliation efforts. The Council took vigorous hold of the matter and moved with unusual dispatch. To be sure, the parties concerned were not major powers, but their remoteness from Geneva, and the seriousness of the crisis, made the successful conciliation efforts of the League noteworthy.

21. The Hungarian-Yugoslav Frontier Incidents

On May 12, 1934, Hungary, under Article 11 of the Covenant, requested the Secretary-General to place on the agenda of the Council, the question of certain frontier incidents, which had arisen between Hungary and Yugoslavia. The frontier area, over 600 kilometres long, and 20 kilometres wide, was created by an earlier treaty as a neutral zone between the two countries. The Hungarian representative cited numerous cases of unjust use of firearms and interruption of frontier traffic by Yugoslav officials. It was pointed out that great hardships to the Hungarian land owners along the frontier had resulted from these restrictive measures. An appeal to the Council was held by Hungary to be preferable to reprisals but the representative of Yugoslavia expressed surprise at this appeal as he maintained that direct negotiations were proceeding satisfactorily between the two Governments. He accused Hungary of acting in bad faith by invoking Article 11. While admitting that border incidents had occurred, he stated that they were due to terrorists who sought refuge in Hungary where they continued to plot against the Yugoslav state. This he held was with the knowledge and often with the assistance of Hungarian authorities. He contended that strict frontier regulations were made necessary because of the failure of the Hungarian Government to suppress the terrorists. With both countries suffering as a result of the frontier incidents, they expressed their willingness to settle the matter by direct negotiations. The Council considered the mutual grievances on June 5, and expressed the hope that a direct settlement would be reached. The successful termination of this matter was endangered by another crisis between the two countries of greater political importance.

22. Continued Hungarian-Yugoslav Frontier Incidents

The situation on the Hungarian-Yugoslav Frontier was still tense when on October 9, 1934, news was received that King Alexander I of Yugoslavia, and Foreign Minister Louis Barthou of France were assassinated at Marseilles in France. The Yugoslav Government appealed to the Council on November 22, by virtue of Article 11 of the Covenant to determine "certain very serious aspects of the Marseilles outrage which were of a nature to disturb good understanding and peace between Yugoslavia and Hungary." Its investigation showed that the outrage was abetted by terrorist elements in Hungary of which the Yugoslav representative had previously complained to the Council. The case was argued before an extraordinary session of the Council on December 7, when both sides were fully presented. On December 10, the Council's unanimous resolution brought the controversy to an end. It condemned the Marseilles outrage, and declared that it was "the duty of every state neither to encourage nor tolerate on its territory any terrorist activity with a political purpose." The Council also held that the negligence of certain Hungarian authorities was partly responsible for events in connection with the preparation of the crime and the Government was requested to find and punish these officials. The Council likewise appointed a committee of experts to draw up a preliminary draft of an international convention for the "Repression of conspiracies or crimes committed with a political or terrorist purpose." On January 16, 1935, Hungary submitted a report to the League disclaiming the government's responsibility for the outrage. It admitted, however, that some officials had been guilty of negligence and stated that they had been punished, and more stringent rules governing political refugees had been put into force. Both Yugoslavia and Hungary accepted the settlement which was made possible through the efforts of the Council. Where the threat of war was sounded after the Marseilles tragedy, the dispassionate conversations at Geneva cooled the passions; violence gave way to reason, and the League's prestige was materially enhanced.

23. The War Losses of Swiss Nationals

The question of compensation for damages suffered during the World War by Swiss nationals in France, the United Kingdom, Italy, and Germany, was brought before the Council on September 27, 1934. Having failed to obtain reparations through diplomatic channels, the Swiss representative requested the Council to ask the Permanent Court for an advisory opinion to determine whether the claims were well founded in international law. The Council, meeting in January, 1935, accepted a report which denied the legality of the claim, but on the grounds of equity upheld the application of Article 11 of the Covenant as valid. The matter was referred to a Committee which recommended on May 23, that the Council withdraw this item from its agenda. The absence of a threat to peace, made it unnecessary for the Council to proceed under the provisions of Article 11 of the Covenant.

24. Claims of Finland against the United Kingdom

On July 30, 1931, Finland brought before the Council a claim against the United Kingdom to secure remuneration to the Finnish owners of vessels which England had used during the World War. Great Britain had earlier denied the claim and had refused to arbitrate the matter. Diplomatic negotiations between the two countries proved unsuccessful, whereupon Finland appealed to the Council to intervene. The British argued that the jurisdiction of the Council did not extend to cases which had been settled under British law, and the dispute could not properly come under the provisions of Article 11 of the Covenant. On January 30, 1932, the Council decided that it possessed the power under Article 11 of the Covenant to deal with the dispute. It was still unsettled on January 18, 1935, when the Council appointed a Committee of jurists to study the data which had been presented by the two governments, and thus determine the relevancy of Article 11. The Committee submitted its report to the September, 1935, session of the Council.

25. The Italo-Ethiopian Conflict

The immediate cause of this serious conflict was an alleged clash between troops of Ethiopia and Italian Somaliland on December 5, 1934. Both governments reported the incident to the Secretary-General of the League. The Ethiopian Government made a formal appeal to the Council on January 15, 1935, requesting the matter be taken up under Article 11 of the Covenant. Direct negotiations between the two governments having failed, Ethiopia appealed to the League on March 17 under Article 15, as the "continued dispatch of troops and war material to the Italo-Ethiopian frontier" by Italy seemed "likely to lead to a rupture." However, the deliberations of the Council on January 19, April 13, May 25, July 31, and August 3, were carried on under the provisions of an Italo-Ethiopian Arbitration Treaty of 1928, instead of Article 15 of the Covenant. Under this procedure a Committee of Arbitration was chosen which met several times during the summer of 1935 in an effort to conciliate the two parties. The arbitrators submitted a report to the Powers on September 3 which contained the interesting provision that neither Italy nor Ethiopia was responsible for the so-called "Walwal incident." This was of little significance, however, as the Italian Government was bent on going forward with her plans without outside interference.

The Council met on the following day at Geneva and agreed to the previous Ethiopian request for the application of Article 15. On September 6 the Council appointed a Committee of Five which was to seek a settlement by conciliation. These efforts were again in vain as Italy refused all proposals for a negotiated settlement. The dispute was discussed in the September session of the Assembly, with no tangible accomplishments. On the basis of the efforts of the Committee of Five, the Council decided to draw up a report under Article 15 to include "a statement of the facts of the dispute and the recommendations which are deemed just and proper in regard thereto."

The background of this conflict is found in a move by Great Britain and Italy near the close of 1925 when these two countries entered into an agreement recognizing each other's influence in certain areas of Ethiopia. British interests centered largely around Lake Tana, while the Italians looked forward to the building of a railroad through Ethiopia. The agreement to divide Ethiopia into spheres of economic interests was reached without the consent of the Government involved. A protest was lodged with the Secretary-General of the League on June 19, 1926, which resulted in elaborate explanations by Great Britain and Italy. The British Government maintained that it had no intention to put pressure upon the Ethiopian Government, while Italy held that the agreement "would naturally be subject to the decisions of the Abyssinian Government." With the matter thus seemingly cleared up, Ethiopia merely registered an official protest. The League served to bring the discussions into the open and compel two major powers to relinquish well-laid plans for the partitioning of this backward Empire. The British continued to forego their Ethiopian designs, but Italy turned her attention once more to East Africa as a field of exploitation. The next encounter was between the forces of Italy and those of Ethiopia. At this time the Council unanimously decided (in the absence of the Italian delegate) to constitute itself a Committee of Thirteen to carry out the provisions of Article 15, of the Covenant. If Ethiopia accepted the report of the

Council, and Italy refused to do so, a condition would prevail in which Italy could not, under the Covenant, go to war with Ethiopia. Italy was now in great danger of being found a violator of the Covenant. She hurriedly informed the League of her intention to advance the Italian forces into Ethiopia as a "measure of defense," which she did on October 3. Four days later, the Council decided that the Italian Government had violated Article 12 of the Covenant. A special session of the Assembly convened on October 9, and two days later, the delegates from fifty-one countries declared Italy to be the aggressor in disregard of her treaty obligations. With this indictment of Italy, Article 16, automatically came into force calling for the enforcement of sanctions against Italy. This was the first instance in League history where such measures had been undertaken. The League machinery, which so often proved cumbersome, was able to function with unusual swiftness. The members of the League, excepting three, undertook to apply economic and financial pressure against Italy. This new test of League power was adopted not as a penalty, but as a means of rendering Italy's military efforts ineffective.

With the coming into force of Article 16, the Assembly proceeded to appoint a Committee of Eighteen to coöperate with the member states in devising plans to make sanctions effective. This committee took up the work in earnest by agreeing to impose an arms embargo on Italy, and lift a provisional arms embargo from Ethiopia. All loans and credits were to be withheld from Italy. It was agreed to prohibit importation of goods from Italy to member countries of the League. By this move it was expected that Italian exports would be decreased by some seventy per cent. Italy was still permitted, however, to purchase many of the goods she needed, with the exception of certain key raw materials, but it was expected that the credit embargo and her inability to pay for imports with exports, would make further aggression impossible. The Committee of Eighteen likewise devised a plan for the mutual support of those League members which would suffer most from the loss of trade with Italy.

The Committee of Eighteen set November 18, 1935, as the date for the application of sanctions and the head of the Italian State protested vehemently to the League Powers against these stringent measures, declaring at the same time that Italy would oppose sanctions with "implacable resistance." The replies to this protest offered little encouragement to Italy, as the member states regarded their obligations under the Covenant as mandatory. The League members accepted these measures with marked promptness and the economic effects were soon felt in the form of higher prices in Italy, and strict governmental supervision to effect the greatest possible economy. On January 29, 1936, reports showed that fifty-two nations had accepted the application of sanctions on arms embargo and the severance of financial relations with Italy, while fifty had agreed to prohibit imports from Italy, fifty-one had agreed to place an embargo on key raw materials, and forty-six had agreed to mutual financial support in the application of sanctions.

The effectiveness of these sanctions was lessened by the ability of Italy to increase her trade with the United States. The Department of State Press Releases showed that American exports to Italy greatly increased after sanctions were applied. The exportation of arms, ammunition, and implements of war were prohibited by law, but materials such as scrap iron, oil, copper, trucks, and steel were legally permitted. Secretary of State Cordell Hull issued a statement on November 15, 1935, in which he decried the practice of American shippers in supplying these essential war materials to Italy. In spite of this and other official pronouncements, American exporters continued to benefit by the increased trade with Italy, while the League states were attempting to cut off many supplies from that country. It goes without saying that these trade practices did much to render the League sanctions nugatory.

The combined efforts of the League against Italy were interrupted by an Anglo-French agreement for a settlement of the conflict. The terms of the agreement made public on December 13, 1935, provided for the ceding of extensive Ethiopian territory to Italy, and reserving other areas for Italian expansion and colonization. This agreement was universally condemned. Due to public indignation, Sir Samual Hoare, one of its authors, was forced to resign as British Secretary of Foreign Affairs. Although Premier Pierre Laval of France, the other author, retained his post, he was nevertheless criticized because of his part in yielding to Italian ambitions. The Hoare-Laval agreement was presented to the League Council and after a brief discussion was buried.

The Committee of Thirteen, (the Council minus Italy) held a meeting in London on March 3, 1936, to discuss a report of its Chairman concerning previous negotiations with Italy and Ethiopia to terminate the war in East Africa. Italian insistence upon the lifting of financial and economic sanctions before negotiations could proceed, made the efforts of the League ineffective up to this time in putting an end to the conflict.

After continued fruitless efforts by the Committee to terminate the war in Africa, the Council again met on April 20 to consider possible steps in the light of the rapid Italian conquest. The Council urged the "prompt cessation of hostilities and restoration of peace in the framework of the League." Ethiopia accepted this appeal while Italy refused and under these conditions, the Council decided to continue the enforcement of sanctions against Italy. A strong appeal was made to Rome to make peace in view of the danger arising from German military occupation of the Rhineland, but instead the Italians went so far as to hint at the complete subjugation of Ethiopia as a condition of peace.

With marked swiftness the Italian armies finally succeeded in conquering Ethiopia, and Ethiopia's last hope ended with the fall of her Capital. The rapidity with which the Italian armies overran Ethiopia was a surprise to the member states of the League, as it was expected that a prolonged struggle would occur in the conquest of such a vast country, during which time the economic sanctions would prove effective. This plan failed of fulfillment, and since the war was over, it was necessary for the Assembly to meet in July, 1936, to take steps to end sanctions. At the meeting of the Assembly on July 4, it was decided to do so thus admitting defeat in the first effort by the League to apply economic pressure against an aggressor country. While admitting failure, the Assembly at the same time voted to invite "League members to submit to the Secretary-General before September 21 any proposals they think necessary to perfect the application of the principles of the Covenant in the spirit of the limitations indicated above."

The League members adopted the same procedure in this instance as in the Japanese aggression against China in 1931, namely, non-recognition of territorial conquest in violation of treaty obligations. This attitude infuriated Mussolini and made Italian membership in that body of doubtful value. Much speculation was rife as to whether Italy would withdraw from League membership—a move, which curiously enough she did not undertake. An additional blow to Italian prestige was witnessed in the fall meeting of the Assembly when the delegates voted to seat Ethiopia's representatives. As a result of this step the Italian Government refused to attend the session of the Assembly, but she did not go so far as to withdraw from membership. The step taken at the Assembly was a moral victory for the League in that almost unanimous assent was expressed in upholding the principles of the Covenant. This was a splendid example of an almost universal desire on the part of the member states to uphold the principles of law and justice.

The combined efforts of the League powers in checking Italy was seriously interrupted by the marching of German troops into the Rhineland on March 7. This move by Germany greatly perturbed France, and caused her to favor a policy of lifting sanctions against Italy, and applying them against Germany. Great Britain adhered to her former sanctionist policy, which caused a threatened rift between herself and France. As a member state of the League, the support of Italy to check Germany as a violator of treaty obligations was not forthcoming so long as sanctions were still in force against her. A paradoxical condition existed where Italian assistance was needed against Germany at the time economic and financial pressure was directed against Italy herself.

26. Germany Defies the Peace Treaties

A. The Rearmament of Germany

Under the provisions of the Treaty of Versailles German armaments were limited. One of the aims of National Socialist Party under the leadership of Adolph Hitler was the remilitarization of Germany. The diplomatic excuse for this move was Germany's contention that other major powers had failed to live up to their commitments to reduce armaments. Giving as a reason the failure of other countries to fulfill their obligations, the German Government seized the opportunity to rearm in violation of the Treaty of Versailles. On March 9, 1935, the Berlin Government announced the establishment of military air force and on March 16 a decree was issued increasing the Army. As a result of these treaty violations, France invoked Article 11 and condemned the Reich before the Council. In a meeting of the Council on April 17 a draft resolution was unanimously adopted reading in part that it is the "essential principle of the law of nations that no power can liberate itself from the engagements of a treaty nor modify the stipulations thereof unless with the consent of the other contracting parties . . . Germany has failed in the duty which lies upon all members of the international community to respect the undertakings which they have contracted." This was a direct condemnation of Germany. However, the Council invited the United Kingdom, France, and Italy to continue the negotiations with Germany, begun prior to her open defiance of the Treaty, and to seek a general agreement within the framework of the League. These efforts came to naught when, on April 20, the Reich in a note to the members of the Council, challenged their right "to set themselves up as judges of Germany."

B. Remilitarization of the Rhineland

Germany's bold move of rearmament continued in the face of opposition by the Council. She had succeeded in defying the powers, as no definite action was taken to enforce treaty commitments, which Germany had so flagrantly defied. Flushed with success, the German Government was ready to undertake a second drastic step in defiance of the Treaty of Versailles as announced on March 7, 1936, in a formal statement to the Locarno signatories. Coincident with this, more than 20,000 German troops marched into the Rhineland in violation of Article 43 of the Treaty of Versailles and Article 1 of the Locarno agreement. A German declaration sought to justify the step with a recent Franco-Soviet Pact, which it held was directed "exclusively against Germany," and constituted a violation of the Locarno Pact of 1925. The following day France and Belgium laid the matter before the Council, whereupon the Secretary-General of the League invited the German Government to send a representative to attend the Council which, however, she refused to do. This meeting took place in London on March 14 when a decision was reached to renew the invitation. Germany accepted it this time on condition that she be received as an equal in the negotiations, and that proposals submitted by the German Government to safeguard the peace of Europe be considered. The Council replied that Germany may meet on terms of equality in the discussions, but it would not consent to a discussion of the German peace proposals designed to supplant the Locarno Treaty. A German delegation arrived in London on March 18, and on the following day it presented Germany's case to the Council. This was the first instance in over two years that Germany officially participated at a League Council meeting. The Council adjourned after having invited the Locarno powers to keep it informed about future negotiations with Germany. All proposals for agreement between the Reich and the powers had failed up to this time.

A significant aspect of the crisis was the willingness of all parties to continue negotiations. A tense situation prevailed with war a strong possibility as Europe reached the darkest period since 1914. If the League had not existed as a natural clearing system the offended countries, France and Belgium, might have resorted to military means. A most significant fact was the spontaneous turning to Geneva by France upon receiving information of Germany's intention to remilitarize the Rhineland,—a provocation for war of the first order. Many wars have been fought over less serious causes. The all-important factor of time served to allay military excitement. Where freedom of discussion was possible, the earlier likelihood of rash judgment gave way to reasoned consideration. At such times the League is an invaluable institution for the prevention of war.

27. Uruguay Severs Diplomatic Relations with Russia

On December 27, 1935, Uruguay announced the severance of diplomatic relations with Russia, because of her alleged subversive activities throughout South America. The Soviet officials denied this charge and on December 31 lodged a protest with the League under Article 11 of the Covenant. While the Soviet officials could not bring pressure to bear on Uruguay to restore diplomatic relations, they no doubt felt that a full discussion before the Council might keep other states from following a similar course. In a discussion of the matter, before the Council, the Russian representative demanded proof of the charge, which was withheld on the ground that it was confidential. The Russians took the position that any dispute likely to lead to a rupture should come before the League. Uruguay contended, on the other hand, that this was a domestic question which did not come under League jurisdiction and that states maintain their sovereign right to establish and break off diplomatic relations of their own accord. The Council appointed a Committee to investigate the dispute, which avoided mention of most points involved, and directed its efforts toward conciliation. This effort was successful, as the two countries agreed to refrain from action which might interfere with the resumption of normal relations, and let world opinion judge the merits of the dispute.

28. Dispute Concerning Alexandretta

On December 9, 1936, Turkey appealed to the Council under Article 11 of the Covenant requesting that protective measures be taken "to ensure the safety of the Turkish people of Alexandretta, Syria, whose lives and liberties are endangered." The district of Alexandretta is situated in the northwest of the Mandated Syrian territory granted to France at the Paris Peace Conference. This territory, in addition to the whole of Syria, had been taken away from Turkey. Under an agreement reached in 1936, Syria was promised independence in 1939. The dispute grew out of the degree of autonomy that the Turks in Alexandretta should receive when Syria is made a sovereign state. Turkey demanded the immediate independence of the district, possibly to be annexed by her at a later date, as the population is predominantly Turkish. The League dispatched a Commission to investigate the conditions, which, upon arrival, witnessed a hostile demonstration that was met by thirty thousand French troops. The findings of the neutral Commission were reported to the Council, and on their basis a peaceful settlement was reached on January 27, 1937. This was in the nature of a compromise, as the Alexandretta district is to constitute a "separate entity" of internal independence, with Syria to control its foreign affairs, subject to supervision by the Council. Once more this was a typical League endeavor to bring recalcitrant states to terms where they showed a willingness to accept a compromise.

29. The Civil War in Spain and International Rivalry

The deadly civil war in Spain, based largely upon conflicting theories of government, could not fail to arrest the interest of European governments, and especially the non-democratic countries. Sensing the danger of foreign intervention, the French Government took the initiative on August 1, 1936, in sounding out the Mediterranean powers as to an agreement against various forms of intervention. In response to this invitation, Great Britain joined with France in seeking adherents to the plan, whereupon some eighteen other countries agreed to it. This was later increased to a total of twenty-seven countries that united in an effort to make foreign non-intervention in Spain effective. A Non-Intervention Committee was chosen for the purpose of preventing the shipment of arms to Spain. The Committee met frequently and listened to complaints of violations by the signatory powers in the sending of soldiers and war materials to aid one side or the other. Flagrant violations of non-intervention were widespread, and the Non-Intervention Committee was helpless to cope with the situation, notwithstanding the oft repeated intention of the signatories to remain neutral.

As Germany and Italy favored the rebels and had formally recognized the de facto Government of the rebel leader, General Francisco Franco the regularly constituted government of Madrid was led to appeal to the League against the foreign connivances with the insurgents. Under date of November 27, 1936, the Spanish Government notified the Secretary-General of the unneutral acts on the part of Germany and Italy. In conjunction with this notification, the Spanish Government invoked Article 11 of the Covenant, called upon the Council to examine the situation, but did not request intervention by the League. The Council met in an extraordinary session on December 10, and two days later recommended, among other things, that League members on the Non-Intervention Committee should spare no pains in taking measures to ensure non-intervention. The obligations of League members to respect the territorial integrity and political independence of Spain was stressed by the Council, but responsibility for the actual fulfillment of this was left to the Non-Intervention Committee. The Committee held its meetings in London, and at a session in February, 1937 decided that the six most interested Powers represented on the Committee, namely France, Germany, Great Britain, Italy, Portugal, and the Soviet Union, should take part in a naval patrol of Spanish waters, and assigned each to a specific zone. Serious incidents occurred in the bombing of vessels, and retaliation that followed heightened international tension in Europe and led to the termination of the international patrol in the early part of the summer of 1937. The negligible part played by the League in the Spanish revolt, including its international implications, was due, first, to the weakened position of the world peace machinery following the breakdown of sanctions against Italy, and second, to the nature of the struggle in Spain which was primarily domestic, and did not involve an open breach of the Covenant. Inaction by the League cannot therefore be condemned. The war in Spain seriously threatened the peace of Europe and revealed above all else the need for a strongly organized institution for the maintenance of peace.

A summary of the foregoing disputes reveals that the League has been markedly successful in settling disputes by conciliation. This success hinges upon the willingness of the contending parties to seek solutions by peaceful means. In some instances, where Article 11 was invoked, the dispute passed from the stage of conciliation to pressure against countries which assumed the rôle of aggressor. In such cases the League bodies deliberated, first under Article 11, and later under other articles of the Covenant, as those articles outlined the procedure against a recalcitrant state. In passing from Article 11 to other articles, the League bodies have thus far not met with marked success. Although Article 11 provides for great flexibility, the procedure under it has at times been faulty. The Council operating under this authority has not at all times pursued a wise and just course. Settlements may be reached with great injustice to a party in a dispute by the domineering influence of the powers. On the other hand, even a bad settlement is better than a resort to arms.

When considering this problem, it appears obvious that a serious weakness exists in Article 11 which requires unanimous consent to reach an agreement. While the Sino-Japanese dispute was discussed, Japan exercised a veto on practically all proposals. This delayed the Council and rendered void a long series of negotiations. Under such circumstances Article 11 may be used only as a gateway to the employment of other articles where such veto is not possible. Some consideration has been given to the need for a revision of present practice requiring unanimity. Good faith on the part of each member of the family of nations could, of course, lead to a wider application to the unanimity rule. Free negotiations and consent on the part of the nations would have a more lasting effect than force.

The framers of the Covenant envisaged conditions where states would refuse to yield freely in all disputes. To meet such exigencies the procedure under Articles 12, 15, 16, and 10 were adopted as stages of increasing pressure. Some appeals were made to the League by invoking one or more of these articles without any attempt to effect conciliation under Article 11. Such procedure is likely to be followed if a sudden crisis arises which forestalls the slower methods of conciliation.

The procedure is very definite in the settlement of international disputes if Article 12 is invoked by the Council. By this Article the members of the League agree, in case of dispute likely to lead to a rupture, to "submit the matter either to arbitration or judicial settlement or to enquiry by the Council." A definite committment is made by each member of the League to submit disputes to some form of pacific settlement. Provision is made for the settlement of legal disputes by arbitration or judicial processes and of political disputes by the Council. The seriousness of disputes is contained in the phrase "likely to lead to rupture," which calls for League action differing from that contained in Article 11 which refers to the "threat of disturbing the good understanding between nations upon which peace depends." The logical procedure followed by the Council in the settlement of disputes is first to invoke Article 11, and if this fails, due to a serious threat of war, to bring more definite pressure upon the Covenant-breaking state. Fortunately, most disputes are settled in their earlier stages. Otherwise, the parties to a dispute assume definite commitments not to resort to armed force during the "reasonable time" when such dispute is under consideration.

The two important principles contained in Article 12 are, first, that of delay, and second, the obligation to enter into negotiation. The disputants agree in no case to resort to war until three months after the award has been handed down. The obligation imposed upon the parties to a dispute to refrain from going to war for a period of three months after such award, was intended as a "cooling off" period. This provision may be tremendously important if the nations live up to it. Wars sometime break out as a result of heated controversies and aroused passions in the absence of reason. If time is given for reflection, nations may very well adopt some course other than war. The rapid turn of events during the outbreak of the World War offers a splendid example of the very thing which the framers of the Covenant attempted to prevent in the future. A glaring example of the failure by a League member to fulfill this provision of the Covenant was found in the invasion of Ethiopia by the Italian armies on October 2, 1935. The members of the Council, with the exception of Italy, declared on October 7, that the Italian Government had resorted to war in disregard of its obligations under Article 12 of the League Covenant. In the early stages of the dispute between Italy and Ethiopia no decision was reached by the Council, which made it illegal for Italy to resort to war. Later, because of an overt act by the Italian Government, the Council declared that Article 12 had been violated and proceeded to impose sanctions against Italy, as provided for under Article 16 of the League Covenant. There is serious doubt as to the ability of the League to successfully employ harsh measures in checking aggression by a major power. The few failures, however, do not serve to guide one in evaluating the enforcement machinery.

During the years of the League's history, many examples are recorded of its successful effort in preventing war, and the list of achievements warrants the continuance of the collective system. These political efforts have been notably successful in Europe, while in Asia, Africa, and South America, the League has met with failures. It is not strange that this should be so as the immediate interests of a larger number of countries were not affected in those far-away continents. While each nation acts in its own interest, the best interests of one nation coincide with those of all others.

Unfortunately, members of the League have not at all times acted on this premise, and a few failures loom as conspicuous results of League weaknesses. But it is hardly fair to take them as standards of judgment, as the value of an institution must be measured by comparing all results.

Nevertheless the general opinion prevails that the League is still weak, but it is often forgotten that compared with other world institutions, the League is still in its infancy, and perfection is hardly to be expected during the earlier stages of trial and error. This Organization must be strengthened and in time no doubt will be. Certain glaring weaknesses now manifest themselves particularly in the machinery to carry out League decisions. Unanimity rule as practiced under Article 11 of the Covenant reveals marked shortcomings. Some steps have already been taken to overcome this weakness, and insistence upon effective operation will, no doubt, remedy this.

The chief weakness of the League as a peace organ is to be found not in its technique, but in the lukewarm support which world opinion has been ready to furnish it. We have in this new world-institution the expression of the highest ideals of peace. These ideals have not universally manifested themselves among the nations, hence no machinery can effectively cope with every phase of international disorder.

The League has often been criticized for its slowness of action and it is true its efforts to find peaceful solutions of international disputes have cost much time. However, the elements of delay may be an asset rather than a liability, as this tends to temper the passions of nations and provide opportunities for just settlements. An interesting outcome in the development of institutions reveals the tendency for the better policies and practices to survive, and the unworkable ones to become discarded. The most important thing about the League is to keep it alive, and in time the more effective phases of its usefulness will grow to meet the highest expectations of its present-day supporters.

CHAPTER IV

The Force of Moral Sanctions

Many opinions have been voiced as to how peaceful relations among nations are disturbed. One group will blame the munitions-makers as the instigators of war, because large profits are derived from the sale of munitions. Others hold that wars are caused by international trade rivalries, with profit as the underlying motive and it is said that if economic imperialism is stopped, wars will not be fought. Still others believe that people must be educated in the ways of peace; that if they thoroughly understand the horrors of war, they will turn against it. A strong sentiment prevails in this country that neutrality is the proper course to pursue and that we should bend every effort to keep out of war. Some believe that statesmen and diplomats are responsible for wars, and that they should be restrained. It is urged that before war is declared, the people should decide the matter by their vote. Indeed, some would go so far as to refuse to support the Government in time of war.

The framers of the Covenant of the League sought to devise means to avoid future wars and thus envisaged a world society in which secret diplomacy would have no place. The general opinion prevailed during and immediately after the World War that a handful of statesmen brought about catastrophes with no consideration for the wishes of the people. While this view deserves attention it must not be forgotten that the outbreak was also due to some inevitable tendencies among the peoples, as all important historical events are the products of inevitable trends. Popular conception during and after the war was that the chief functions of nineteenth century diplomacy was the formation of military alliances and the laying of plans to improve the military positions against potential enemies. Due to the terrible losses of the World War, some governments changed their practices in the conduct of foreign affairs to provide for more democratic control and new constitutions were drawn up embodying this principle. Thus for the first time in history public opinion exercised a voice in the control of foreign policies on a large scale.

The assumption of this responsibility by the electorate of Europe and America, placed a tremendous responsibility upon the people. The wise conduct of foreign affairs presupposes a knowledge of international relations and genuine understanding of the means for preserving peace. Herein lies also the danger of democratic control of foreign affairs, for in international economics, and other involved subjects, people often fail to formulate opinions that are for the best interests of their respective nations. Experience has revealed mistaken public policies in such matters as tariffs, international exchange, intergovernmental debts, and other financial and economic problems, due to the public attitude toward these questions. The popular mind is often poisoned with bias, prejudice, and antagonism toward foreign nations. History records not a few wars fought as the result of popular clamor. Thus popular conduct of foreign affairs may not be a sure guarantee of peace. Relations among nations may be improved through popular interference, only if a high degree of intelligence and fair-mindedness is to be found among the people.

Democratic influence on the conduct of international relations has been abandoned in some European countries, such as Germany and Italy. Nevertheless, it is precisely in these two countries that we find the greatest uncertainty as to future peace. The dictator has absolute authority in determining foreign policies, as freedom of discussion through the press and on the platform is prohibited. A healthy formulation of public opinion is not possible under such circumscribed conditions. Moreover, there is the likelihood of a dictator arousing the public to a high pitch of frenzy, which may lead to armed conflict in the face of well-reasoned judgment. Neither is it possible under dictatorial rule to develop a healthy opinion in favor of peaceful international relations.

The contrary condition exists in democratic countries where a wide-spread movement has developed in opposition to war. Besides, the deadliness of modern warfare holds no glamor for sensible youth. Numerous organizations have sprung up in this and other countries, with the aim of preventing wars, and they have made a tremendous appeal. These efforts are vital in paving the way for that intelligent public opinion which exerts great influence on governments in their conduct of foreign affairs. At this time, when international questions are so much in the forefront, these private international organizations merit popular encouragement and support. Many school textbooks are designed to foster a wholesome spirit of international cooperation and friendship. Active interest in international relations is to be found in churches, clubs, and other bodies. In most countries there are student movements that develop cosmopolitan interests in international studies, and this active interest is most significant. Although the decisions reached by these groups may not carry great weight at the moment, many of these students may later actively help determine the foreign policies of their governments. In the democratic countries, numerous voluntary bodies seek solutions to international questions prior to action by governments. This may be termed "constructive international lobbying" as the theory underlying their effort is the belief that public discussions will lead to equitable solutions. But here again the formulation of international policies by private organizations presupposes a high degree of intelligence, otherwise, misguided viewpoints may lead to disaster.

Much encouragement may be found in the fact that peoples everywhere ardently desire the governments to join in a march away from the dangers of war. This almost universal desire is new and has not been accurately understood, nor adequately expressed. It is a happy discovery for peoples in all lands to learn of this mutual desire for peace. In a book by William H. Chamberlain, entitled "Soviet Russia," the author states: "Nothing the Soviet Government has ever done has probably excited such general approval as its efforts in the direction of peace and disarmament." The popular desire for peace is a world-wide desire which has merely been expressed more definitely in some countries than in others. As these latent desires among peoples become crystallized, we may expect governments to pursue policies in keeping with them.

Many of the private international organizations are local or national in scope, while others maintain central offices to coordinate the work carried forward in various countries. Between sixty and seventy of these organizations maintain international headquarters at Geneva. Being thus situated, they are able to keep in constant touch with the various aspects of the League's work and officials of the Secretariat assist these private organizations by participating in discussions and in other ways. Representatives of international private organizations are called before League meetings as experts and their assistance is of great value in promoting its work. The purpose in establishing the headquarters at Geneva is, first, to obtain information at the center where many of the international developments occur, and second, to act as a liaison between the national countries and the League. This form of cooperation tends to crystallize public opinion on League matters, and guides these private agencies in formulating world policies. Governments are forced to take cognizance of popular movements and to a large extent to conduct foreign policies to conform with their aims and purposes. This is a splendid example of organized popular pressure upon governmental action. If public interest can be developed in this work, the governments may be led to pursue policies in keeping with their aims.

One of the surest ways of making the League effective as an organization of peace, is through wide-awake public opinion. The Covenant contains many provisions as to the procedure to be followed in checking an aggressor power. They may be of little consequence, however, if there is not strong insistence among the people to insure peace. This public pressure against an aggressor state has well been termed, "moral sanctions." Modern means of communication bring recent developments to public attention, thus creating an informed opinion. Former President Wilson envisaged the part people would have in the determination of foreign policies when he announced his Fourteen Points, one of which read: "Open covenants of peace, openly arrived at, after which there shall be no private international understanding of any kind, but diplomacy shall proceed always frankly and in the public view." The war-time President forsaw the day when governments would not make secret agreements as was done before the War, and when the people would have a voice in the formulation of treaties. This pronouncement by former President Wilson was quite logical, for secret alliances had, prior to the World War, wrought havoc in international relations, as they committed governments to military action. Article 18 of the Covenant was intended to change this. It states: "Every treaty or international agreement entered into hereafter by any Member of the League shall be forthwith registered with the Secretariat and shall as soon as possible be published by it. No such treaty or international engagement shall be binding until so registered." Full publicity is here given to every treaty, and public opinion may express itself as to the worthwhileness of international agreements. Governments which are responsible to the electorate must thus take into account the force of public opinion when treaties are negotiated. This is a marked advance over pre-War practices in the conduct of foreign relations.

Prior to 1914 it was not generally the practice to require parliamentary ratification of treaties. Indeed, treaties were often made without the knowledge of the parliaments concerned, and much less of the people. The governmental practices in the democratic countries of Europe have since then required parliamentary consent to treaties to make them valid. In the United States, the legislative branch of government has exercised a voice in the making of treaties from the beginning of our history. A two-thirds majority vote of the Senate in favor of proposed treaties is necessary before they may be ratified. The position of the Senate places greater control in the people than would be possible, should the executive head of the Government alone exercise this power. Popular control over foreign affairs by the American people is the result of the constitutional framework of our government.

During the earlier history of this country, the conduct

of foreign affairs was of minor concern to the citizens. The framers of the Constitution hoped to keep this function from popular interference. This was done by placing responsibility for consent to the ratification of treaties in the hands of the Senate, which was not responsible to the people during the greater part of our history. With the growth of democracy the citizens assumed increased responsibility for the conduct of government, but it was not until the World War that a marked interest was manifested in foreign affairs. Popular election of Senators, as the result of a Constitutional Amendment in 1913, gave impetus to this.

The machinery of the League is admirably constituted to respond to the free expression among the people of the countries constituting its membership. Unrestricted discussion takes place in League gatherings on all questions that may arise. Governmental representatives participating in the discussions must ever keep in mind the possible effects of their deliberations on the peoples in their countries. Public opinion is nowadays quite as ready to approve or disapprove of what takes place at Geneva as in the home parliaments, for the delegates to League meetings represent peoples and speak for them.

In this connection it should be made clear that the League is not a separate and distinct organization, dissociated from the governments which constitute its membership. The League is often referred to as having achieved this or that or as having failed to do so, when as a matter of fact the members are the real actors in the international drama, and the League merely serves as a meeting place for the nations to conduct negotiations.

The press of the world is amply represented at Geneva, as well over one hundred journalists from most of the countries of the world are permanently accredited to the League Secretariat. This number is augmented to three or four hundred during meetings of the Assembly and conferences meeting under League auspices. The Secretariat issued some six hundred press cards for the Disarmament Conference in 1932 and the same number at the London Economic Conference of 1933. With the Press of the World thus adequately represented at League meetings; it is possible for the peoples of various countries, not only to keep informed as to what transpires, but more important still, to have the opportunity of approving or disapproving of the measures passed.

Continued world interest is centered in the developments at Geneva as newspapers in this and other countries continually print articles on the activities of the League. This interest is general as people everywhere look with keen expectancy to what might take place at League meetings. This international institution holds a certain glamor which arouses the keenest imaginations both in those who may be bitterly opposed to its efforts, and those who hope for its success. Geneva is referred to by some journalists stationed there as the "capital of the world," and the small city on the banks of Lake Leman has indeed become a veritable news center of the world. The importance of the League, from the standpoint of general interest, makes it inevitable that the governments represented there should be keenly aware of the effect of their decisions on public opinion.

The public in various countries is also informed of the work of the League through the Information Section of the Secretariat, as this Section issues periodic communiqués, a Monthly Summary, as well as numerous articles and pamphlets on the various aspects of the League's work. It is occupied with the task of studying the attitude of the press throughout the world. The

Keystone View Company

LAKE GENEVA SWITZERLAND

Information Section is not carrying on its work so much in an effort to create a favorable League opinion in various countries, as to tabulate public reaction toward the League, and thus assist national representatives in carrying out the wishes of the people. The world press is extremely free in passing judgment upon the League's work and the Information Section must, of course, diligently seek to gauge this.

In 1932 a wireless station was erected near Geneva to provide more intimate contact with the people of various countries. This station serves a two-fold purpose. It may be used in times of emergency to provide the League with independent means of communication with all the governments. It is also available for official broadcasts of important messages, thus enabling the various officials at Geneva to maintain direct contact with governments. Short and long wave transmitters are used and it is possible to receive messages from Geneva by almost all stations in the world. The total cost of the installation was about four million Swiss francs, or well over a million dollars. There are regular broadcasts over this station, and special broadcasts as occasions may arise. The increasing use of the radio as a means of transmitting knowledge serves to emphasize the importance of this undertaking and it is to be expected that the League will, in the future, seek closer contacts with the public in an attempt to focus attention on its work.

Information relating to the League is also carried forward through publications by the various Sections of the Secretariat, dealing with disarmament, health, economic and financial, and other technical matters. The purpose of these publications is to facilitate international action in the numerous fields in which the League is engaged and through them favorable opinion is created as a result of these constructive efforts.

Experts and government officials make use of these publications, for they are not only extremely useful, but are in some instances indispensable as sources of information. The League's printing bill amounts to almost one million Swiss francs annually. The publications appear in English and French and are made available to the public at large through agencies in various countries.

The practice prevails of making meetings of the Council, Assembly, Conferences, and Committees public. Occasionally meetings are held in secret, but the decisions reached are made public. Secrecy was contrary to former President Wilson's pronouncement of "open covenants openly arrived at," but experience has shown that some discussions, such as those involving personalities, are not of primary public concern. What the public desires to know is not how, but what decisions are reached, and full publicity of discussion may tend to prevent freedom of decision. A very interesting prodecure is to find a League body meeting for a short session in secret and later admitting the public. The League bodies cannot justly be accused of conducting their work in secrecy.

In 1932 the Assembly deliberated on the problem of the dissemination of news of League meetings, as this affected its relation to the world at large, and the following resolution was adopted: "The Assembly, advocates the fullest possible publicity for League meetings; commends to the sympathetic consideration of the Chairmen of all Committees of the League of Nations the earlier and more complete distribution of documents; desires that the Secretariat should continue to devote its attention to the development, by all the means at its disposal, of the swift supply to the Press of the fullest possible information concerning the work of the League of Nations." It is clear that a large measure of the success of the League depends upon favorable reaction toward its work by the public in each member country. Thus the bar of public opinion is the court of last appeal in the success or failure of the League.

The framers of the Covenant realized the force of popular reaction to a world institution by embodying this idea in the preamble of the Covenant which states: "The High Contracting Parties, in order to promote international co-operation and to achieve international peace and security . . . by the prescription of open, just and honorable relations between nations, agree to this Covenant of the League of Nations." Open, just and honorable relations presuppose the free exercise of public discussion on all League matters. The controlling force of publicity has on numerous occasions been expressed on League matters. Perhaps the most conspicuous example of this is to be found in the influence of public pressure in the Italo-Ethiopian war, when a veritable outburst of public sentiment was directed toward a just settlement of this controversy. In England where public opinion exercises control over governmental affairs, there was especially a strong stand taken against Italian aggression in Ethiopia. The Government was at first slow to act and this hesitancy continued until there were strong manifestations of popular opposition to Italy. British opinion became alarmed in May 1935 when Anthony Eden, Minister for League of Nations Affairs, visited Rome and discovered that Mussolini was planning the complete subjugation of Ethiopia, thus threatening British interests in the Near East, and more particularly her route to India. This tended to turn the British people against Italy in such a manner as to make possible a strong anti-Italian stand by their Government. The British Government was likewise influenced in opposing Mussolini by a "peace ballot" which was conducted by the League of Nations' Union. Almost twelve million signatures were collected in England expressing the willingness by the signers to uphold the principles of the League Covenant, and over ten million of these voters favored economic sanctions. This large registration represented more than forty per cent of the total electorate and was the largest ever taken in England. On the basis of this, the British delegates to the League meetings could act boldly in supporting its measures.

British opinion was greatly aroused by a speech delivered by Mussolini on August 29, 1935 in which he declared: "Italian policy does not threaten, directly or indirectly, British interests, and the artificial scare raised in some quarters to this effect is simply absurd." To the average Englishman this declaration appeared to come from one who felt his power superior to that of England. Mussolini's assurance was regarded as an outburst of aggressiveness. The English Government was also prompted to adopt strong measures as a result of a resolution passed by the Trade Union Congress on September 5, 1935 when the Congress voted 2,962,000 against 157,000 to urge upon the Government to take a strong stand against Italy even though it might involve the risk of war. This move by British labor seems to have had far-reaching effects upon the British statesmen in the determined position which they took later. It is significant that the Labor Party in Great Britain, which has been strongly in favor of world peace, was in this instance ready to risk war in order to check an aggressor power. The development of the controversy between Italy and Ethiopia had continued over a period sufficiently long to give the people of Great Britain, as well as the peoples of other countries, an opportunity to fully express their sentiments. This is quite different from the events which led to the outbreak of the World War in 1914, for at that time diplomatic negotiations were held in secret, and the people knew little of the developments. Today the reading public is thoroughly informed on international developments and will not be blindly led into a struggle. Should a major war occur, it will be with the full knowledge and consent of the public. Exception to this must be made in countries where dictators rule. During the discussions of the Italo-Ethiopian controversy by the League Council and Assembly, full publicity was given to these deliberations. Public opinion, in countries whose representatives met at Geneva, was crystallized in opposition to Italian aggression and in favor of collective intervention. There was a noticeable trend toward international cooperation during the first months of this struggle.

Governments were willing to cooperate to check Italian aggression in East Africa when it became known that a preponderant majority of the people lent their support to this move and if the governments were later hesitant to restrain Italy, it was because of public caution. Certainly the British Intelligence Service, which knows so many things, was aware of Mussolini's plans from the very outset. British statesmen understood the significance of the agreement between Premier Laval of France and Premier Mussolini of Italy in January of 1935 when the latter seems to have obtained a free hand in Ethiopia. At that early date, however, public opinion in Great Britain was not aware of the dangers of the situation. If the nations had united to stop Mussolini at the very outset, the later impasse may not have developed.

Many believe that the League should have taken a definite stand against Italy in the early stages of the controversy. But public opinion was not ready then and no effective stand seems to have been possible until war actually broke out. It is the business of the League to explore all possible means of settlement before taking definite stand against a country. The members could not, under the Covenant, declare Italy an aggressor until she actually violated her treaty obligations. It was only after the Italian armies had crossed the boundary of Ethiopia, that the Covenant was openly violated and the machinery of the League could be set in motion to restrain her. This was done with the support of the people in practically every country.

Perhaps no single event in the history of this imperialistic adventure was more marked than the part played by organized opinion against an Anglo-French agreement, officially published on December 13, 1935, which aimed at giving Italy more Ethiopian territory than that occupied by her armies on that date. Premier Laval of France and Sir Samuel Hoare, Secretary of Foreign Affairs of Great Britain, agreed to a "peace plan" which it was thought would satisfy Mussolini's ambitions in East Africa. Upon the publication of this agreement there was an immediate outcry throughout the world. News of the "peace terms" was flashed to the newspapers, with the result that immediate denunciations were expressed in the press of every democratic country. Outspoken opposition against depriving Ethiopia of the exercise of sovereignty over more than half of her territory was voiced in the parliaments of Great Britain and France as well as in all other member countries except Italy. Mussolini received the Hoare-Laval proposal but sent no reply when it became known to what extent world opinion reacted against this land grab. The two statesmen were supposedly undertaking to find a solution to the Italo-Ethiopian controversy which would be satisfactory to Italy and Ethiopia, as well as to all other members of the League.

The member states refused to discuss this unjust plan, as it was contrary to the ideals expressed in the Covenant.

The impelling force which thus brought an end to the Hoare-Laval scheme was world opinion. Its inglorious end came in the meeting of Council on December 19 when the plan was presented but not discussed. This quick burial put an end to peace negotiations with Italy in so far as separate action by one or two countries acting independently of the League was concerned. The peace settlement between Italy and Ethiopia was a matter for the Council which, under the Covenant, assumes responsibility for such negotiations. Two statesmen could not enter into such discussions without the knowledge that other League members were looking over their shoulders as they negotiated. The rejection of agreements concluded behind closed doors is the most effective weapon to combat secret diplomacy.

After the Hoare-Laval peace terms were published, news was received from Geneva that the Secretariat was flooded with telegrams from the leading cities throughout the world, including the United States, in protest against the violation of League principles. The general belief prevailed that an imperialistic deal had been made with Italy by two major powers in which a weak country had been divided to satisfy nationalistic ambitions. Before the advent of the League such a deal by the powers may have been consummated with scarcely a ripple. In fact, many similar agreements were made before the War where territories of backward peoples were taken without their consent, and secret bargains were made by diplomats without the knowledge of their own people.

Before the League's existence, Italian aggression in Ethiopia would in no way have been regarded as unusual or strange, and no concerted protest would have been raised against the partitioning of territories belonging to backward peoples. World public opinion did not, at that time, regard such aggression as reprehensible. But the post-war period has witnessed a change in international morality which no longer approves these practices. On many occasions Mussolini referred to past imperialistic policies of other countries in an attempt to justify his war against Ethiopia. His contention was that other nations had exploited backward peoples and therefore he should be free to do the same. This method of reasoning, however, failed to take into account the changed conditions governing the conduct of nations. The newer concepts of international relations are not built upon the superior force of a single state, but upon the common consent of mankind expressed through organized institutions. Mussolini was very much opposed to outside interference in the Italo-Ethiopian dispute and he set forth the claim that this was a local matter over which the League lacked jurisdiction. He knew very well that for the League to intervene would mean an attempted settlement based upon just consideration.

Definite political action took place in England and France as a result of the Hoare-Laval proposal to partition Ethiopia. There were angry public protests against the British Government, which compelled the Cabinet to turn against the proposed treaty, and readopt economic sanctions against Italy. In order to avert a downfall of the Cabinet, Sir Samuel Hoare resigned his post as Foreign Secretary. A new Government had, shortly before this, been voted into office by an overwhelming majority of the electorate largely on the issue of effective cooperation with the League in stopping aggressor nations. The strength of Great Britain placed her in a favorable position to assume a leading rôle in collective security but this position had for the time being been given up. For the moment Great Britain yielded to the old art of secret connivance by disregarding the world forces opposed to imperialistic exploitation. She was destined to regain this leadership among the nations by the appointment of Captain Anthony Eden to the post of Secretary of Foreign Affairs. Mr. Eden had been outspoken in opposition to Italian aggression while he was Minister for League of Nations Affairs, prior to this crisis in the British Cabinet. A very brilliant man, young in years, and of great promise as a statesman, he enjoyed the confidence of the people in his efforts to vitalize collective action. Mr. Eden had to make amends, as far as possible, for the blunders of his predecessor and this was not easy. That the duties confronting the new Foreign Minister were arduous cannot be denied, yet he was destined to play a prominent rôle in leading England back to the League.

While Mr. Eden had played a conspicuous rôle in formulating policies to check Italy, it cannot be said that England was the leader in imposing sanctions in an effort to serve her own interests. The League members did not permit Great Britain to "use" the League as a catspaw to pull her imperial chestnuts out of the fire. The enemies of the League consistently accused England of supporting the League merely because her interest to check Italy was greater than that of any other country. The readiness on the part of the British Cabinet to "sell out" to Italy disproved the notion that Great Britain had greater interests in the success of the League than any other nation.

The same pressure which compelled reorganization in the British Cabinet was manifested in the French Parliament on December 28, 1935, during Premier Laval's defense of the rejected Anglo-French "peace plan." The Premier was able to remain in office only after a long speech in which he attempted to impress the members of Parliament with his wholehearted support of the League. Even so, a large minority in the Chamber of Deputies voted against him, because of his failure to take a strong stand with other League members against Italy. The majority of the members upheld the Premier after he promised faithfully to cooperate with the League powers in the future. Premier Laval attempted to impress Parliament with the active part which France had played in fulfilling her obligations under the Covenant. The parliamentary discussion led to the conclusion that no Government in France is secure which fails to fully collaborate with League members in important matters.

The high hopes of more than four-fifths of the peoples of the world, whose governments constitute membership in the League, were exalted during the September, 1935 sessions of the League Council and Assembly, when the leading delegates of England and France expressed the true feelings of their countrymen. In a memorable address before the Assembly, on September 11, Sir Samuel Hoare, then Foreign Minister of Great Britain, declared: "In conformity with its precise and explicit obligations, the League stands and my country stand with it, for the maintenance of the Covenant in its entirety and particularly for steady and collective resistance to all acts of unprovoked aggression." Premier Laval declared two days later that: "France is faithful to the Covenant; she cannot fail in her obligations. With undiminished fervor, the representatives of France have maintained and supported the doctrine of collective security. This doctrine remains and will remain the doctrine of France. The Covenant remains our international law." A few days later, delegates from twenty-six nations had spoken and pledged their Governments to fulfill their obligations under the

Covenant. Not a voice was raised against the policies that were being formulated in opposition to Italian aggression and one delegate after another arose to pledge the assistance of their peoples to the League. These were not empty words but the expression of deep conviction by the representatives of independent democratic countries. A certain tenseness and a feeling of uncertainty prevailed, and yet a real determination was noticeable in the efforts of the delegates to combine against an aggressor state. The dispute between Italy and Ethiopia had reached a stage where a strong stand was necessary. Either the League members would have to forego any effort to prevent Italian aggression in Africa, which might mean the breakdown of the League, or they would be required to take a strong stand against the aggressor involving the possibility of military intervention. The delegates at Geneva chose the latter course.

The September, 1935 discussions at Geneva revealed a new diplomacy of international solidarity as against the old idea of "balance of power." The result of united action by fifty-seven countries working together was definitely taking form. Throughout the world, people began to realize that if the member states of the League were successful in checking a major power in aggression, the League would be immeasurably strengthened. Many cynics pointed to this international institution as an ineffective organization for the maintenance of peace, but the united effort of League members to restrain Italy suddenly brought life to that body. League supporters grew very optimistic until the sudden military successes of Italy, and military occupation of the Rhineland by Germany, brought the greatest setback in prestige which it had thus far experienced.

Most governments in Europe have built up their foreign policies around the League Covenant, for they realize the necessity of support from a preponderant majority of nations to maintain international order. They cannot afford to let the League fail, for if the collective system breaks down, every nation will be still more endangered than at present. It is this cooperative effort that is especially needed in Europe. Some will point out that the Covenant has no teeth, and that the League is unable to enforce its decisions. In fact, some have advocated a League military force to give effect to its decisions. This proposal has never gained much headway because of the desire by each member state to retain independence of action. The governments which compose its membership are desirous of clothing the League with power if, and when, they agree this is needed. This freedom of action by each sovereign member makes possible the freer play of public opinion in the enforcement of decisions. With this thought in mind it is clear that the League is not something apart from, nor foreign to the governments which compose it. The League's strength will depend upon the attitudes of its members as particular questions arise calling for solution. If it succeeds or fails, it is not the League which is to be praised or denounced, but rather the governments that compose its membership. All wars have not been stopped by the member states of the League. Public opinion has been indifferent toward some of the wars in remote parts of the world and due to public lethargy, the peace machinery failed to function. Other wars have been stopped and, the members of the League have combined to prevent more wars than occurred without effective intervention. If this record continues, the existence of the League will justify the efforts in the field of international collaboration. The Covenant does not preclude all wars, as the framers well knew that unforeseen outbreaks might occur. Public opinion in the countries constituting League membership may not become sufficiently aroused to make it possible for it to take effective measures against all states disturbing world peace. The League, as an institution, is not stronger nor weaker to maintain order, than are the governments making up its membership. Herein is a weakness in the usefulness of this international organization as a means of preventing all wars.

It is not at all certain that public opinion in various countries will be greatly aroused, except when their immediate interests are affected. National interests are too often placed above those of world peace. However, in this modern world of ours, the interests of one nation are closely linked up with the interests of every other nation, so that no threatened outbreak can fail to react on the public mind throughout the world. It is to the benefit of all peoples that the nations combine to stop an aggressor power wherever it may be.

If public interest is sufficiently aroused to restrain an aggressor, there need be no difficulty in the procedure of the Council or Assembly, for various stipulations in the Covenant may be interpreted in such a manner as to make it possible for the League to take no action whatever. The loopholes in the Covenant have made it possible for the League powers to remain inactive in times when a nation has violated Covenant obligations. Such difficulties will not occur if there is the willpower to make the Covenant operate effectively. What is really needed is for public opinion to become so passionately zealous for peace that the League will become an effective institution for the prevention of wars in any part of the world. The masses of people do not understand, and care less, about the technicalities of the Covenant, and it is understood only by a few specialists. But the people do desire to see an international organization built up, through which their governments may effectively cooperate in times of crises.

Various Articles in the Covenant provide the procedure which the League bodies are to follow when the peace of the world is threatened, as well as the possible course of action in stopping war after it has broken out. Articles 10 and 16 are often referred to as the vital sections which give validity to League deliberation. Article 15 is seldom referred to, but it may contain the essence of a more effective course of procedure than embodied in the other Articles. This Article states in part that: "When a dispute arises between members of the League which is not subject to arbitration, the matter will be submitted to the Council and the Council shall endeavor to effect a settlement thereof, and if the dispute is not thus settled, the Council shall make a public report containing a statement of the facts of the dispute and the recommendations which are deemed just and proper in regard thereto." By making a report of the Council public, which contains the facts of the dispute, world opinion is given the opportunity to become mobilized against the aggressor. Such action by the Council will not be an empty gesture, or a mark of failure, if world opinion exists to make League members coerce a belligerent through concerted action. Mobilization against an aggressor must under all circumstances await the will of the people. This, after all, is essential, regardless of what procedure the League Council or Assembly may adopt.

The League is thus seen to be a body where public discussions take place, affording an opportunity to the peoples of various countries to formulate opinions on international questions. The World Press greatly facilitates this. Disputes automatically come before the Council, or the Assembly, where they are discussed in open forum, and an opportunity is given for both sides to present their cases. This procedure is new in international diplomacy. Sir Edward Grey of Great Britain stated in effect that if the nations of Western Europe had been able to meet around a Council table to discuss freely their problems in the Summer of 1914, the World War would in all probability have been averted. Since the establishment of the League this procedure is commonplace. The future of peaceful relations among nations rests above all else, upon the willingness of the nations to assemble at a common meeting place, backed up by a wholesome public opinion desirous of maintaining a stable world order.

CHAPTER V

Reduction and Limitation of Armaments

The primary task of the League of Nations is the preservation of peace, and although its activities are numerous and varied all are directed toward this end. The machinery for settling international disputes, important as it is, was regarded by the framers of the League Covenant as inadequate in preserving peace, therefore the issues which degenerate into conflicts must also be solved and not least among these is competition in armaments. Article 8 of the Covenant recognizes "that the maintainance of peace requires the reduction of national armaments to the lowest point consistent with national safety and the enforcement, by common action, of international obligations." One of the primary functions of the League is arms reduction, as it was recognized that no peace organization would prove effective in the midst of arms rivalry.

The League members have thus far not fulfilled their obligation under the Covenant to reduce armaments and as a consequence have not achieved international peace and security. It must be understood that both war and arms rivalry are deeply rooted in history and to end them suddenly was too far removed from the experiences of the nations and more so immediately at the close of the World War. Much criticism has been directed against the League for its failure to achieve this main objective but no institution created by the nations can operate contrary to their own experiences. The declaration of war and competitive armaments were legally recognized in international society until the establishment of the League, when they were formally renounced. The institution of war was officially outlawed in the Kellogg Pact of 1928. By this agreement sixty-three states solemnly declared "that they condemn recourse to war for the solution of international controversies . . ." and that the "solution of all disputes or conflicts . . . which may arise among them shall never be sought except by pacific means." The Covenant does not admit the right of member states to make war, as an obligation is accepted not to "resort to war." Commitments under the League, unlike the Kellogg Pact, are numerous and specific thereby making their enforcement difficult. Although the commitments set forth in the Covenant are far reaching, they could hardly have been less so and still meet the needs of international society. As the nations work together with the aims of the League as a goal, their achievements may in time measure up to the high standards set in the Covenant. A few failures along the way may hearten the League critics and discourage its friends, but fundamental conceptions of a better world society have been deeply implanted in the post-war era and will no doubt continue to claim the best interests of the nations until they are fully realized.

Reduction and limitation of armaments was attempted in a few instances before the founding of the League. The Rush-Bagot Agreement of 1817 limited the number and size of war vessels of the Great Lakes, and this Treaty was the beginning of continued friendly relations between Canada and the United States which led to the demilitarization of their entire three thousand mile frontier. In 1865 Russia and Turkey agreed to limit the number of warships in the Black Sea to ten each, but this failed. In 1905 Sweden and Norway agreed to establish a neutral zone along their common frontier where "no fortifications, naval ports or depots of stores for the army or navy may be retained in the neutral zone or may be established therein in the future." This agreement has met with admirable success. Similar efforts have been made between countries in South America but with mediocre results.

The First Hague Conference (1899) was called for the purpose of limiting arms competition but succeeded in this only to the extent of adopting a resolution stating that the "restrictions of military charges, which are at present a heavy burden on the world, are extremely desirable for the increase of the material and moral welfare of society." The Conference expressed the hope that the governments might in the future examine the possibilities of an agreement. This was done at the Second Hague Conference (1907) which, although it did not include arms reduction on the agenda, did consider the seriousness of the problem and sought to reach an agreement. Delegates from various countries including France, England, and the United States, were especially outspoken in denouncing the dangers of competitive armaments. The moves to achieve definite results were promptly checked by the German delegation, a member of which declared that "the German does not regard it [militarism] as a heavy burden, but as a sacred and patriotic duty to which he owes his country's existence, its prosperity, and its future." This is not the cry of a nation held in subjection by her neighbors and thus forced to arm as a measure of protection. Germany was responsible for the failure to advance the cause of disarmament at this International Conference where the question of armaments was carefully considered for the first time. In 1911 Great Britain sought to obtain Germany's consent to a naval holiday but was unsucessful. Thus rivalry in arms continued, accompanied by a feeling of tense anxiety which culminated in the World War.

During the War, German militarism was widely denounced, hence it is not strange that she was forcibly disarmed by the Allied Powers. The Treaty of Versailles abolished the German General Staff, limited her army to one hundred thousand officers and voluntary enlisted soldiers who were required to remain in service for twelve consecutive years to prevent large trained reserves, forbade her tanks, heavy artillery, and aircraft. The German navy was limited to six small battleships, six light cruisers, twelve destroyers, and no submarines. The Rhineland was demilitarized and was to be occupied by Allied troops for fifteen years, but the last contingents were withdrawn in 1930. Germany failed to comply with the terms of the Treaty, and pressure to enforce disarmament only brought ill-will. Thus the forcible disarmament of a great nation proved disastrous, as it could not be permanently maintained. The rapid building up of the German military system has again put her at the head of the armaments race in Europe and this race is spreading more rapidly than before the War.

As the one-sided disarmament of Germany failed, so also did the far reaching efforts to achieve general arms reduction. Political and economic rivalries the world over, augmented by the universal depression and the popular desire in some countries to glorify military systems checked these moves. Partial and temporary success was achieved in the reduction of naval armaments by the Washington Naval Conference (1922), called by the American Government and attended by five naval powers—United States, Great Britain, France, Japan, and Italy—and other powers interested in the Far East—China, Belgium, Holland, and Portugal. In the opening session Charles Evans Hughes, then American Secretary of State, startled the Conference by offering concrete plans of naval arms reduction. Secretary Hughes offered to abandon the American naval program, which at that time was very ambitious, in exchange for similar concessions from Great Britain and Japan. On the basis of this proposal, the participants agreed to scrap old ships numbering seventy-nine and to abandon the future building of capital ships. The agreement reached placed the United States and Great Britain on a parity of 5 to 5 ratio and Japan at 3, while France and Italy accepted a ratio of 1.67 each. Agreement was only reached on capital ships and the way was prepared for continued arms competition in all other types of vessels. The life of the Treaty was to continue until December 1936, and in case no signatory gave notice of termination two years before the Treaty expired, it was to remain in force indefinitely or until such two year's notice was given. Agreements were reached at the Washington Naval Conference concerning the defences in the Pacific Ocean where the status quo in the building of fortifications and naval bases was maintained. The sovereign rights of each country in the Far East were recognized. The nine Pacific Powers reaffirmed the principle of the "open door" in China which bound them to respect her sovereignty, independence, and integrity. This Nine Power Treaty was violated by Japan in 1931 when she invaded Manchuria, and again in July, 1937.

Due to the continued race in naval construction in all but capital ships, President Calvin Coolidge sought to gain the consent of the leading powers to extend the Washington Treaty so as to include other categories. Great Britain and Japan accepted the President's invitation while France and Italy refused to do so on the ground that this effort would hinder a similar undertaking by the League of Nations. The three Powers met in conference in Geneva on June 20, 1927 but accomplished nothing, since, unfortunately, the participants were composed largely of admirals and naval experts whose interests were bound up with large navies. Until this time the United States has been backward in the building of cruisers, hence the failure of this Conference led to an extensive building program of smaller ships.

An additional effort was made to extend the terms of the Washington Treaty when the leading naval Powers met in London for a Conference early in 1930. Cooperation between Great Britain and the United States was facilitated previous to this time by a goodwill visit of Prime Minister Ramsey MacDonald to the United States. He and President Herbert Hoover agreed on parity between the two countries relating to cruisers and smaller craft categories. On April 22, 1930, a Treaty was signed by Great Britain, Japan, and the United States to end the building of such combatant vessels until December 1936 and then to consider the question of continuing the Treaty. Limitation was placed at a high level which afforded each signatory the opportunity of carrying forward extensive building programs without violating the pact. Since Italy and France were unable to agree on any definite ratio, they did not sign the Treaty.

Japan served notice of her dissatisfaction with the existing treaty ratios, which resulted in unsuccessful naval conversations in London at the close of 1934. An attempt was also made by the three naval Powers to reach an agreement in 1935 but this likewise failed. The Japanese Government insisted on changing the old ratios to authorize a navy as large as that of Great Britain or the United States. The two latter countries were content with the ratios as previously fixed but Japan, as a growing nation possessed with an unusual amount of national pride, insisted that her position in the Far East required that she obtain parity with the two foremost naval Powers. As a result of the failure of these Conferences no treaty is in existence to prevent the nations from engaging in unlimited arms construction.

During the years when efforts were made by the leading Powers to limit naval competition, parallel attempts were made by the League to bring about general reduction of armaments. In May 1920, the Council appointed a Permanent Advisory Commission on armaments, as provided for in Article 9 of the Covenant, composed of military and naval representatives from each state represented on the Council. This Commission was instructed to furnish the Council with advice on the execution of Articles 1 and 8 of the Covenant, and on arms questions in general. This was a technical Commission, hardly fitted for the task, so the first Assembly (1920) decided that arms reduction was not merely technical in nature but involved political, social, and economic questions which could only be solved by persons competent to deal with them. A Temporary Mixed Commission was therefore created to study the armament problem and continued its work until 1924. In 1925 the Assembly requested the Council to undertake a preparatory study with a view to the calling of a general conference on arms reduction. The Council complied by appointing a Preparatory Commission consisting of representatives from other countries including the United States. This invitation to participate in the work of the League was accepted by us. The Preparatory Commission encountered many obstacles but continued its work until the end of 1930, when a suggested treaty was submitted as a model to be followed at the general conference on arms reduction.

The existence of the Preparatory Commission from 1925 to 1930 may be regarded as the second phase of the League's effort to achieve arms reduction. The numerous problems confronting the members of the Commission led them into divergent fields. The most important step not directly related to arms was the problem of security. A group of nations headed by France held that security by mutual assistance against attack was a necessary first step. On this point the position of France was particularly clear. The people of that country recalled that within a century the Prussian and German armies had invaded their country four times and on three occasions had entered their Capital. France, therefore, urged that the machinery of the League be strengthened, as there was no definite guarantee that the existing obligations of the member states to unite against an aggressor would be fulfilled. Article 10 and 16 of the Covenant permits each member state independence of action in fulfilling its treaty obligations, hence definite commitments were sought to obtain assurance before an attack that assistance would be forthcoming. If such assurance were given, France would gladly reduce her arms. Great Britain and the United States represented the second group of states which were reluctant to tie their hands in advance of any emergency preferring to exercise this freedom when the occasion arose. They contended that arms reduction would be the best guarantee of security. These divergencies of opinion continued to limit the concerted effort of the Preparatory Commission at its meetings from 1925 to 1930.

Official efforts were made to bring about closer binding relations among the League members to insure mutual assistance against an aggressor. The first attempt was undertaken in the drawing up of a Draft Treaty of Mutual Assistance (1923) which was designed to bind the signatories to guarantee assistance to a state which was attacked when the Council designated the aggressor. This Treaty was to become valid in case there was a general reduction of arms, but it failed of ratification. A new attempt was made in the framing of the Geneva Protocol of 1924 which provided for compulsory arbitration of disputes and any state refusing to arbitrate a dispute would thereby place itself in the position of an aggressor, and the League members would thus be definitely bound to unite against it. This Treaty was likewise closely linked up with arms reduction, as it was felt that the nations could safely reduce arms if they were guaranteed assistance against attack. This Treaty also failed to go into force, thus checking the movement for arms reduction.

An additional effort was made to achieve security through a proposal by Great Britain in 1925 to apply the principles of the Geneva Protocol to Western Europe, where the greatest anxiety was felt. Representatives of Great Britain, France, Germany, Italy, Belgium, Poland, and Portugal met at Locarno and agreed on a series of Treaties which obligated each signatory to renounce war against the other parties except in self-defense, and to settle all controversies among them by pacific means. The existing frontiers were to be maintained as fixed by the Treaty of Versailles, and any power disturbing the peace would meet the combined resistance of the other members of the Alliance. A provision was made that the Treaties would become binding when Germany became a member of the League. Germany was admitted into League membership in 1926 and the Locarno Treaties thus went into force. With the strengthening of military security in Western Europe and with Germany a member of the League the way was prepared for renewed activity in an effort to achieve arms reduction.

The Locarno Treaties left many political problems in Europe unsolved. While Germany was given certain assurances of assistance in case of attack, yet the powers were not willing to grant her equality in arms strength. Another weakness was the limited area to which the Locarno system applied, as provision was only made for the guarantee of peace in western Europe. Germany was unwilling to agree to her existing eastern frontier as a permanent boundary settlement, hence territorial disputes existed between herself and Poland which she hoped would be settled to her advantage at some future date. Great Britain and Italy were also unwilling to guarantee the status quo in eastern Europe which tended to make any agreement extending to this part of Europe non-enforceable. With unsettled conditions in Eastern Europe and the possibility of using military force in affecting boundary changes, the danger of arms reduction was real. As these conditions confronted the governments of Europe, no genuine desire was manifested to reduce their arms strength. It is not strange that there should have been little or no headway in the preliminary preparation for a general arms conference, as a wise divergence of viewpoints existed in regard to the military needs which each nation advanced as a minimum requirement for national safety.

Although there was a wide divergence of opinion among the nations as to the best means for reducing armaments, the League members nevertheless agreed to call a general Conference for the Reduction and Limitation of Armaments. This Conference met at Geneva in February 1932 with fifty-seven states represented, constituting the largest international assembly since the Peace Conference following the War. The Conference could not have met at a more inopportune time, as the Japanese were marching into Shanghai while the delegates were assembling at Geneva. The nations were likewise faced with world-wide depression, international economic rivalry, and rising tariff walls which did not augur well for a conference of this nature. Public opinion throughout the world was nevertheless strongly in favor of this Conference, and petitions bearing 10,000,000 signatures demanding real arms reduction were presented at the opening session.

The Conference got under way by setting up two principal organizations: the General Commission and the Bureau. The General Commission was the Conference proper, presided over by Mr. Arthur Henderson of Great Britain, while the Bureau, at times called the Steering Committee, directed the procedure. Five committees were appointed to deal with political problems, budgetary limitation, land, air and naval armaments. A draft treaty prepared by the Preparatory Commission during its sessions from 1926 to 1930, was presented to the Conference but was not seriously considered. Numerous plans were proposed by delegations which indicated a wide divergence of opinions and as the deliberations progressed it became increasingly clear that the demands of various nations could not be harmonized. Discussion on these proposals continued almost uninterrupted until July 1932, when the Conference adjourned, subject to a later call. The Conference was again under the control of military and naval experts who showed little disposition to yield on technical points, hence the desire to cooperate in reaching concrete results was not manifested. Prolonged discussion took place which at times resulted in deadlocks over irrelevant details, and thus from day to day problems presented themselves with increasing complexity with less and less hope for their ultimate solution. A sympathetic approach to the problems before the Conference proved beyond the ability of the delegates to solve them. A mistake was perhaps made in the attempt to deal with this difficult problem in all its phases instead of undertaking the task piecemeal as was done at the Washington and London Naval Conferences, both of which were partially successful. At the adjournment of the Conference in July a resolution was adopted which expressed little more than vague ideas. Diplomatic conversations were expected to continue at the various capitals preparatory to a second meeting of the Conference in the early months of 1933.

The Conference deliberations were further complicated by Germany's demand for equality in arms with the leading powers, as she maintained that the disarmament clauses in the Treaty of Versailles were conditional, and that the more important obligation of the Powers was expressed in Article 8 of the Covenant which is based upon the principle of equality in arms. The Germans argued these points with great force and threatened to withdraw from the Conference if their demands were not met, but conciliatory conversations on the part of representatives of the powers prevented their early withdrawal. Adolph Hitler's rise to power in Germany terrified her neighbors and made the nations unwilling to agree to the German demands of arms equality. France, in particular, proposed a period of arms supervision before any real reduction should begin. When it became clear that Germany would not obtain arms equality she withdrew from the Conference (October 14, 1933) and shortly thereafter from the League of Nations, the World Court, and the International Labor Organization. The Conference was further hindered in its work by the Far Eastern crisis which led to the withdrawal of Japan from the League in March 1933.

No progress was made in the discussion on arms reduction during 1934 although the Conference convened in the summer for a fortnight and was marked by heated clashes of interests with obstacles to arms reduction becoming increasingly difficult. All hope for a treaty had by that time disappeared. The Conference, while not technically ended, had failed to resume its deliberations while conditions developed to make discussion of arms reduction futile. The military operations of Italy in Ethiopia during the winter of 1935–1936, as well as the political interference by the powers in the Spanish revolution during the summer of 1936, made political conditions in Europe extremely unstable with the result that instead of arms reduction they were engaged in an armament race. In March 1935 Germany unilaterally renounced the military clauses of the Treaty of Versailles and introduced military conscription. On March 7, 1936, she violated both the Treaty of Versailles and the Locarno Pacts by announcing her intention to re-garrison the Rhineland. With these moves in defiance of existing treaties the hope for arms reduction came to a definite end. The long period of the League's effort to reduce arms must be therefore regarded as a failure. Yet this is not an indictment against the League but rather against the powers which refused to cooperate with it. This is a vivid example of the inability of the League to function where nationalistic policies are contrary to its aims and it is only if these policies give way to those of the League that progress may be made in arms reduction.

International arms rivalry has aroused great popular attention. This condition tends to make war inevitable although no one knows when or from what quarter it may come. Every nation is determined to be prepared for such an eventuality. Fear grips the nations, traditional jealousies cause international suspicions, boundary disputes intensify national hatred and lead to the desire to have larger armed forces. Alliances and counter-alliances are formed. The powers of the world watch one another uneasily and live in anxiety lest hostile neighbors steal a march on them. Hence competition in arms is larger today than ever before in history. Upward of $11,000,000,000 is spent yearly in this business. One of the foremost reasons for desiring arms reduction is the terrific cost of maintaining large bodies of men, supplies, and other equipment. The larger powers spend a preponderant share of their public incomes in paying the cost of past wars and preparing for future ones. Crushing financial burdens are imposed upon the taxpayers and the expenditures result in ill-feeling, budgetary deficits, and financial havoc. But far greater than this is the ultimate cost in the death and destruction of the people affected by war. Farsighted observers realize that the time to put an end to this military anarchy is before a cataclysm breaks loose.

Although nations are now spending more money for military and naval purposes than ever before, it is true that popular interest in arms reduction is also greater. The demand for relief from the crushing burden of huge armaments is told by the voice of the press and the people. Armaments are not generally spoken of in a laudatory spirit nor looked upon with a sense of national pride but are regarded as dangerous weapons of grim necessity.

The real issue is to eliminate war altogether but the practice of nations shows that this is not possible at present. A practical step would be for nations to agree to limitation upon all armaments which together with the control of arms would prepare the way for the second step: progressive decrease in arms. This can be done only by international agreements. Arms reduction by example—where one nation takes the lead with the expectation that others will follow—is not practicable since a nation is not willing to accept voluntarily an inferior position while others are left heavily armed. They all strive for equality of strength. A reduction of armaments of one nation is not dangerous if all are engaged in the progressive decrease at the same time. Security is a collective interest and must be sought collectively but no nation is secure today so long as the powers feel that they are exposed to serious dangers. Joint efforts by all powers are required to adjust controversies before they feel their positions secure, no matter how far they may be removed from the immediate scene of danger.

Armaments are used by nations to carry out their international policies. When these are aggressive other nations are endangered, hence adequate arms protection is necessary to meet these threats. The shaping of international policies is beyond the control of international action except insofar as nations are willing to unite in working out their common problems. In its ultimate form the achievement of permanent disarmament depends upon the establishment of law and perfected institutions capable of maintaining peaceful relations among the nations. While international disputes are inevitable in a changing world-society, it is not necessary to resort to war as the means of settling disputes. The swing from armed forces to conferences, treaties and courts as a means of adjusting differences represents a definite trend and not a sudden move by nations. History presents this important fact in an ever widening field of social and national relations. The reduction of the military forces of the original thirteen states in the United States was accompanied by the elevation of the United States Supreme Court to a commanding position in the peaceful settlement of numerous disputes among the states. The elimination of naval forces and armed troops along the border of the United States and Canada was followed by arrangements for arbitration in case of disputes. Efforts to limit or reduce world armaments in the post-war period has been accompanied by the constructive work resulting in the establishment of the League of Nations, the World Court and the peaceful procedure of conferences as substitutes for war. The transition from armed might to legal right and judicial procedure is a slow process requiring time as well as able leadership. Clemenceau, the "old tiger" of France, admitted that "the work of peace is more difficult and requires much more patience than the work of war."

We should refrain from denouncing any power for increasing arms as security against attack unless we are willing to help create a condition which will make wars less likely. Our Government led in a movement to renounce war as an instrument of national policy, which was readily accepted by all the other nations. The splendid position of the United States favors such leadership in international movements, but our Government will move only insofar as public opinion permits. We have reached the time when public opinion exerts itself so forcefully as to influence every great official act, and the pressure of popular opinion in international affairs has been increasing—particularly since the War. The growing importance of the arms problem requires that some methods be indicated for focussing attention on, and stimulating popular pressure, for, reduction of armaments.

A few general observations are here noted which may prepare the way for definite governmental action in achieving effective limitation of armaments. Progress may be made by a far-reaching program of education for peace. This must be continuous and untiring and must in time be undertaken by all nations. Today we have democratic, dictatorial, and autocratic forms of government. Because of these distinct systems, popular peace discussions have become extremely difficult. Is it possible to unite in a common task members of different nations, speaking different languages, having diverse class feelings? This is a herculean task but it is worthy of the world's best endeavor. Progress may be made by arousing a wider interest in the possibility of living in a world free from arms competition. One of the most serious obstacles to disarmament is the tacit acceptance of international anarchy. The idea of the possibility of living in a warless world is still outside the realm of popular imagination. Legal recognition of the outlawry of aggressive war has been achieved in the Kellogg Pact, but the full import of this worldwide agreement is rightly regarded as a dream yet to be realized, and particularly does this popular attitude tend to make the outlawry of war non-effective in times of stress. Again an intelligent electorate is necessary in democratic countries, for, as former Secretary of State Elihu Root has said: "A democracy which undertakes to control its foreign relations ought to know something about the subject." The expression of popular will by an illiterate and uninformed electorate will result in little more than a registration of multiplied ignorance. It is under conditions of illiteracy that the way is prepared for the acceptance of propagandist programs of all kinds.

Much can be done by improving the existing public international organizations whose purpose is to further the cause of world peace through cooperation. When representatives of governments meet for a conference to discuss their common problems, there is less likelihood of misunderstanding among them. It is not enough for us to insist upon general arms reduction while neglecting to bolster up the world peace machinery, nor can we afford to adopt a "do nothing" policy. We have too long prided ourselves on a neutral attitude toward many of the world's ills, and we boast that we have no enemies and give no offense to any country, but this negative policy will not insure world peace nor destroy arms competition. The policy of aloofness has too long been the American attitude and has led to the building up of armaments on a scale unprecedented in this country. It is easy to blame others for failure to cooperate in achieving disarmament, but our Government has in this respect been one of the chief offenders.

We do cooperate with other nations in numerous ways not directly associated with peace and war. We have shared in the enormous increase in active relations among nations in non-political fields of endeavor. Some of the newer international activities which claim our attention are to be found in the sciences, arts, intellectual cooperation, labor problems, suppression of opium traffic, and communication and transportation, etc. Elaborate conference machinery has been set up since the War for the purpose of promoting numerous forms of international cooperation in times of peace and the conference method which is an innovation, with new techniques, should tend to lessen international friction and ultimately lead to reduction of armaments. As interest centers upon these broad relationships the likelihood of wars may in time diminish. The prospects for future peaceful relations among nations are in some respects encouraging. Armaments and war need not be thought of as belonging to the natural order of society, but the social order of the future should be a truly cosmopolitan one in which popular interest will be centered upon those forces which enrich life instead of those that destroy it. May the time soon come when we can turn our thoughts away from armaments to the finer and richer fields of human endeavor.

CHAPTER VI

Technique of International Administration

WHILE a major part of the League's endeavors relates to international political and legislative undertakings through the formulation of policies to insure peace and better the conditions of the nations, these are not the only important phases of its work. Important as the settlement of disputes and the formulation of international policies may be, there are likewise instances where the nations find it advantageous to cooperate through the League in the continuous task of carrying out administrative functions in governing backward regions of the world, protecting minority groups in certain European countries, and in the governing of territories in Europe. International administrative control had its inception long ago through unified efforts in the internationalization of certain rivers and harbors with commissions appointed to exercise administrative control over them. These isolated instances of international administration were not sufficiently far-reaching to prove the effectiveness of unified control, nor did they result in developing international consciousness in continuous administration on a large scale. It remained for the nations to unite under the aegis of the League in an effort to extend this principle in new and untried fields and thus prove the feasibility of performing governmental functions on an international basis.

1. The Mandates System

The opportunity for administration was offered to the nations by the taking of the former colonies of Germany, as well as possessions of Turkey, and placing them under a system of mandates to be controlled by the League. In depriving these defeated countries of their possessions, the victorious powers in the War might have followed the traditional practice of carving up the territories and annexing them as legitimate booty by "right of conquest." This principle of imperialism was largely discarded by the Allies during the War when British and American statesmen announced their opposition to the old form of military conquest as a war objective. The victors might have returned these possessions to Germany and Turkey, but this was hardly to be expected and would not have been in keeping with the traditional policies of victors. Another alternative was the granting of freedom to the peoples who were under the former rule of these two governments, but this was deemed inadvisable as the inhabitants of those regions were not sufficiently advanced to govern themselves. The other and more feasible alternative was to place these territories under the trusteeship or mandate of various powers who in turn would be responsible to the League for their administration. This idea seems to have been first formulated by General Smuts, a British official of South Africa, who proposed the extending of the mandate principle over territories formerly belonging to Russia, Hungary, and Turkey. President Wilson, who was the prime mover in framing the Covenant, readily agreed in principle to this unique innovation and succeeded in applying it to the former colonies of Germany and parts of Turkey. The application of the principle of trusteeship was in keeping with President Wilson's humanitarian ideals of establishing a system of international administration that would operate for the benefit of the native populations. These aims here involved are in contradistinction to the older concept of colonial aggression for purposes of economic exploitation. With this higher goal as an end in the government of backward peoples, the framers of the Covenant drew up Article 22—one of the longest Articles in that document. In the reading of this elaborate Article, it may be clearly seen that the Mandate system places upon the Mandatories a trust or stewardship to be discharged in the interests of all nations and not alone for that of the trustee. Coupled with this is the obligation of "tutelage" to govern in behalf of the backward peoples with the aim of ultimately making it possible for them to become autonomous. Article 22 sets forth the objectives of the Mandates System as extending to those colonies and territories "which are inhabited by peoples not yet able to stand by themselves under the strenuous conditions of the modern world." As a consequence, "there should be applied the principle that the well-being and development of such peoples form a sacred trust of civilization and that securities for the performance of this trust should be embodied in this Covenant." This Article further states that this "sacred trust" shall be delegated to the more "advanced nations who by reason of their resources, their experience or their geographical position can best undertake this responsibility" . . . and that "this tutelage shall be exercised by them as Mandatories on behalf of the League." The above declarations make clear that the Mandates System places colonial government on a very high plane to operate to the advantage of their peoples and also to the benefit of all nations.

The Covenant does not deal with the distribution of the mandated territories nor indicate the mandatory powers. These matters were settled by the Allied

Supreme Council at two meetings in 1919 and 1920. Fifteen different mandated territories were established and divided into three groups as follows:—

Class A Mandates—in the Near East
1. Syria....................France
2. Palestine...............Great Britain
3. Iraq (until 1932)........Great Britain

Class B Mandates—Africa
4. Togoland................France
5. Togoland................Great Britain
6. Cameroons...............Great Britain
7. Cameroons...............France
8. Tanganyika..............Great Britain
9. Ruanda-Urundi...........Belgium

Class C Mandates—the Pacific and Africa
10. South-West Africa.......Union of South Africa
11. Western Samoa...........New Zealand
12. German islands south of the equator............Australia
13. German islands north of the equator............Japan
14. Nauru Island............British Empire
15. Territory of New Guinea Australia

The three groups of mandates were established on the basis of degrees of "backwardness" or as indicated in Article 22 according to the stage of development, beginning with Class A Mandates that would shortly be able to govern themselves, to Class C Mandates that would for a long period be incapable of self-government. The Mandated territories occupy an area of one million and a quarter square miles, supporting a population of upward of twenty millions. The magnitude of the task involved in administering these large and diverse areas places a major responsibility upon the above mentioned mandatory powers and the League to whom they are responsible.

This unique arrangement in international administration places full powers of legislation and administration in the Mandatory to be exercised "on behalf of the League" and subject to full inquiry by the Council. The Council receives annual reports from the Mandatory Powers and approves or disapproves of the way in which the territories are governed. Any change in the territorial status of these territories must also be approved by the Council. This latter provision has become important of late in view of Germany's demands for ownership of her former African possessions. While these requests have been made to Great Britain as the Mandatory Power, the reply to Germany has in each case been that such compliance can only be made by action of the Council, a condition that permits of little likelihood of the fulfillment of her ambitions.

The Permanent Mandates Commission acts as a liaison body between the Mandatory Power and the Council. It usually meets semi-annually to examine reports which each Mandatory Power is obliged to submit to it, and on the basis of full discussions of these reports the Council is, as indicated above, informed of the execution of the trust placed upon each Mandatory. Thus it is seen that the Council is, under existing international law, the body of last resort in which the sovereign power of these territories rests. While the Council ultimately determines policies relating to Mandates, these are of necessity based upon the findings of the Commission, composed of persons selected for their qualifications and competent to deal effectively with problems as they arise. The eleven members of the Mandates Commission do not represent governments, but are chosen by the Council to act impartially as an administrative body in obtaining the needed information relating to the inhabitants of these territories, and on the basis of the findings to make recommendations. The Mandates Commission obtains information from various sources outside these territories, from journals, from data gathered by the Secretariat on conditions relating to the well-being of the inhabitants, and as stated above, from the annual reports of the Mandatory Powers. From these sources the Mandates Commission keeps fully abreast of conditions, and is able to lay plans for the effective administration of these territories. Having indicated the responsibility of the Mandates Commission, it must nevertheless be stated that the active execution of administrative policies rests upon the Mandatory Powers who may, or may not, be zealous in fulfilling their obligations.

Numerous problems of major importance have arisen in connection with the Mandated Territories which have tested the League's ability to supervise effectively their administration. Serious political disturbances occurred in the former Turkish possessions of Syria and Lebanon, in 1925, due to racial, religious, and economic differences, culminating in the bombardment of Damascus by France, the Mandatory Power. This led to an inquiry by the Mandates Commission, and resulted in the replacement of a cruel military administration by a representative form of government with policies designed to effect closer cooperation with the natives to insure their social and political development. Peace was not permanently restored when disorders again occurred in 1936 and led to prolonged discussions with native representatives with the view to protecting the rights of minorities and to the conclusion of a working agreement that would operate to the benefit of the racial groups in Syria and Lebanon. In that same year France granted Syrian demands for the creation of an independent republic in 1939 under French protection. Turkey demanded that the district of Alexandretta in the northwest of the Syrian mandate be at once made independent, as eighty per cent of the inhabitants are Turks and their lives were in danger with French troops in the area. Tenseness prevailed until the Council peacefully settled the dispute on Jan. 27, 1937. Full independence in internal affairs was given to Alexandretta with Syria and the Council to control its foreign affairs. Thus terminated a serious crisis between France and Turkey.

This thorny problem has its parallel in Palestine troubles beginning in 1925, between Jews and Moslems, and continuing periodically to the present time. The basis of these disturbances is largely economic, and political, growing out of land ownership and questions of immigration. The British Government, as Mandatory, has found it exceedingly difficult to appease the two but has done much to develop a systematic plan of land distribution by providing homes in agricultural areas. At the present time it is trying to carry out a plan to partition Palestine, in accordance with the recommendations of a royal commission. The responsibility of the Mandatory over Palestine is singular in that the Government of Great Britain made a declaration in 1917 in favor of its establishment as a national home for the Jews. Certain privileges have been extended to the Jewish populations relating to nationality, land settlement, development of natural resources, and guarantees respecting their language and religion.

The purposes of the Mandates System were fulfilled in the case of Iraq when in 1932 its Mandatory regime was brought to an end. Iraq, formerly in the A group Mandates, developed rapidly from the position of tutelage to that of self-sufficiency. The Mandate came to an end at the request of the British Government, and Iraq was admitted to full membership in the League of Nations as an independent state. The inducement to complete independence, as provided under the Mandates System, supplied added incentive to the people of Iraq to develop along the lines of self-government. In accepting independence, Iraq agreed to protect the rights of minorities under League control.

The Commission was confronted with the problem of formulating guiding principles in determining satisfactory conditions to be met in changing the status of a mandate to that of an independent state. For that purpose the following observations were suggested by it. In order that a Mandate may become a state it must; "a.) have a settled government and an administration capable of maintaining the regular operation of essential governmental services; b.) be capable of maintaining its territorial integrity and political independence; c.) be able to maintain internal peace and order; d.) have at its disposal adequate financial resources to provide regularly for normal governmental requirements; e.) possess laws and a judicial organization which will afford equal and regular justice to all."

While Iraq had a settled government and maintained internal order, the Commission found that no military establishment existed sufficiently large to maintain political independence if encroached upon by the outside,—a condition that was hardly to be anticipated,—but the view was expressed that, if emancipated, Iraq would have the protection of the League and of the Anglo-Iraq Alliance. The Commission observed that the country's financial condition was sound, and with the possession of natural resources sufficient income might well be obtained to meet governmental needs. The judicial system was well organized and, subject to certain readjustments, would afford uniform justice to all.

The Mandates System offers a splendid example of an ideal to be attained by the powers in governing their colonies. Too often in the past, the rule over backward peoples has been established for the sole benefit of those that govern, with little or no regard for the well-being of the native inhabitants. The extension of the Mandates principles to all colonial territories would do much to raise the standards of colonial administration and the welfare of backward peoples. With the growth of international morality, the colonial powers must, of necessity, give greater consideration to their obligations in seeking the betterment of native populations. The standards set by the League may well form the basis of this aim.

2. Protection of Minorities

A task of first magnitude was thrust upon the League by provisions in several treaties placing upon the Council the responsibility of protecting minority groups in various countries of Central and Eastern Europe. This obligation was not embodied in the Covenant, and in this respect it differs from most other undertakings in which the League is engaged, although extensive discussions took place at the time of framing the Covenant as to the advisability of incorporating an article on this subject. The League was regarded as the logical institution to supervise the interests and rights of minorities as the problem is international in scope and import, and all such questions were in the future to be entrusted to this world agency.

The protection of the interests of minority groups did not emerge as a post-war problem, but has existed throughout modern history. Since the growth of nationalism there have been European minority groups incapable of assimilation, which have persisted in retaining their customs, languages, religions, and racial identities, too often at the annoyance of the majorities. There seems to be a natural inclination for people in Europe to cling to their former ways of living, and pass these traits on to succeeding generations. Efforts by ruling majorities to change these conditions have met with little success. These conflicting interests have often led to suspicions, and at times to open hostilities. Conflicts of this nature are regarded as patriotism by the minorities and as disloyalty by the authorities. Governments have often viewed the attitudes of minority groups within their boundaries in this light, and have undertaken to nationalize them forcibly. Striking examples are recorded in history, especially during the nineteenth century, of efforts at Germanization and Russification.

The boundaries of many pre-war European countries had been drawn in such a way as to include many millions of foreigners. This was in some cases inevitable, as drawing boundary lines could in no way eliminate all aliens. To change boundaries may merely substitute one minority group for another, and make the problem equally acute in that the dominant majority would, by rearranging borders, become in turn a minority, subject to the same oppression formerly exercised by it. Before the War the German Empire included Poles, Lithuanians, Danes, French, Dutch, Italians, Moravians, Czechs, and Masurians. The Russian Empire was disconcertingly faced with the problem of minorities, as millions of her population included Poles, White Russians, Jews, Tartars, Finns, Germans, Lithuanians, Kirghizes, Bashkirs, Letts, Armenians, Georgians, Rumanians, Estonians, and other smaller groups. The old Austro-Hungarian Empire counted among her minority groups Czechs, Slovaks,

Serbs, Croats, Poles, Ruthenians, Rumanians, Slovenes, and Italians. These conglomerate groups of Central and Eastern Europe frequently revolted. Such revolts were followed by repression, to say nothing of the continued unrest that prevailed in these countries. Extreme forms of persecution and massacres were committed in the old Turkish Empire against Armenians, Arabs, Bulgars, Greeks, Kurds, Syrians, and others, to such an extent as to arouse the hostility of the major powers of Europe. Turkey was obliged more than once to sign treaties guaranteeing equal treatment of various national groups within her domain, but frequently disregarded these committments.

Although various international treaties were signed during the period before the War obligating the signatories to protect minority groups, and although the nature of the problem was regarded as international, nevertheless, the efforts to thus solve the problem by international legislation did not meet with success. The chief reasons for these failures were due to inadequate national legislation to give the treaties force. Moreover, no international institution, such as the League, existed as a clearing house to supervise the execution of these agreements.

As if by coincidence, the very countries that contained the larger minority groups were the defeated powers in the War. Whether the minorities were a large contributing factor in bringing about this defeat may not be known, nevertheless they did receive encouragement from President Wilson's famous Fourteen Points, which contained a startling pronouncement guaranteeing self-determination of nationalities as an objective of this country in the War. Upon learning of the declaration of the American President, various oppressed groups took heart in the ultimate outcome of the War, for they saw in this the opportunity to be released from alien rule and were active in the latter phases of the War in counter-movements to overthrow the existing governments. This was especially true in Austria-Hungary, where President Wilson's Fourteen Points electrified many peoples and caused them to organize in opposition to the government and thus hasten the termination of the War. The principle announced by President Wilson was carried by him to the Peace Conference where he stood ready to champion its fulfillment. A Boundary Commission was appointed for the purpose of redrawing the frontiers on the basis of providing the greatest amount of autonomy for the largest groups possible. While this work could not be done with complete impartiality, and while the selfish interests of the victorious powers did have some part in the realignment of frontiers, nevertheless the new map of Europe did take into account the interests of many minority groups that had been ignored prior to the War. Thus the minorities of Europe were reduced from fifty-four million to about seventeen million as a result of redrawing frontiers based upon the principle announced by President Wilson.

With the creation of the new, but less acute minorities problem than that which existed before the War, the statesmen of Europe were confronted with the task of providing means of satisfactorily meeting future minorities problems. They well understood the nature of the previous crises and were aware of the disturbances created by minority groups, especially in Austria-Hungary where they led to the assassination of Archduke Franz Ferdinand. The prevention of such reoccurrences was uppermost in the minds of statesmen when the Treaties of Peace were signed.

To protect minority rights adequately, a series of treaties were drawn from 1919 to 1923, which included the following countries: Poland, Czechoslovakia,

Jugoslovia, Rumania, Bulgaria, Austria, Hungary, Greece, and Turkey. In time other small States were induced to sign treaties that obligated them to protect the minorities rights within those countries. The Treaty signed by Poland on June 28, 1919, serves as a model for other treaties of like nature that were to follow. In this Treaty certain obligations are set forth such as the protection of all peoples within her frontier "without distinction of birth, nationality, language, race, or religion," and the free exercise of "any creed, religion, or belief whose practices are not inconsistent with public order or public morals," a clause dealing with the right to become citizens, equality before the law for all nationals including civilian and political rights and the exercise of professions. The minorities are granted the right to instruction in their own language and maintain their own schools where the population is sufficiently large to warrant it. In substance, the Treaty provides for the retention of the rights of the individual which we find embodied in the Bill of Rights of our own national Constitution.

The means of enforcing minorities treaties is provided, first, in the laws of the countries where the obligations are accepted to execute scrupulously such treaties, and, second, in placing the jurisdiction of enforcement under the League as provided for in the treaties. A typical example of the League's jurisdiction is found in Article 12 of the Polish Treaty which, in part, states that "so far as they [the clauses of the Treaty] affect persons belonging to racial, religious, or linguistic minorities they constitute obligations of international concern and shall be placed under the guarantee of the League of Nations. They shall not be modified without the assent of the majority of the Council of the League of Nations ... Any member of the Council of the League of Nations shall have the right to bring to the attention of the Council of the League of Nations any infraction or danger of infraction, of any of these obligations. The Council may thereupon take such action and give such direction as it may deem proper and effective in the circumstances." The significant points in the above obligations are that the minorities problems are of international concern and are under the jurisdiction of the League and cannot be modified without a vote of the majority of the Council.

The procedure for supervising the fulfillment of these obligations has been worked out by the Council which organized a special section of the League Secretariat to act as a continuing agency to collect information relating to the problem together with a Sub-Committee of the Council consisting of the President, and two other members (or sometimes four) whom he may name to receive communications and hear complaints on behalf of minority groups in countries where such treaties are in force. The Council also receives petitions of persons or organizations, belonging to the minorities of the country concerned. These petitions must originate from authorized sources and may not be worded in violent language and must contain factual material that is not designed to arouse hostility or affect the existing political systems. The Committee of Three carefully sifts these petitions and decides what action is to be taken, if any, and may unofficially negotiate with the government concerned to settle a complaint or may refer the matter to the Council for discussion and recommendation. Matters settled by the Committee are communicated to the Council for its information and the findings may at times be published with the consent of the government concerned. The Official Journal, a monthly League Publication, lists these petitions and the decisions based on them, as well as other information which brings to light the work of the League in this field. Of course many petitions are sent to the Council by dissatisfied minorities that do not justly warrant consideration and are thus not received, for to do so would lead to friction and ill-will. The Council attempts to retain the goodwill of the governments concerned in these petitions, and often communicates directly with the officials concerned without giving publicity to a grievance or causing offense to them. To air all grievances might increase rather than allay bitterness between majority and minority groups in a country. Of the hundreds of petitions that have come before the Minorities Committees, only a few have been brought before the Council for settlement, while the remainder have been disposed of in one way or another by the Committee itself. In several instances the Council has referred petitions to the Permanent Court of International Justice for decision or advisory opinions on points of law, relating to the treaties, and most of these came about as a result of minority grievances by Germans living in Polish Upper Silesia. The cases involving appeals by Germany for unfair treatment of her nationals in Poland occupy a large section in the decisions of the Permanent Court of International Justice and are discussed in the chapter dealing with the Court.

The Assembly has played an important rôle in formulating plans for the more efficient operation of the minorities system, and among the numerous discussions of these questions, passed on September 21, 1922, a significant resolution designed to place a share of the burden upon the minorities for the successful operation of the treaties. This resolution states that "While the Assembly recognizes the primary right of the minorities to be protected by the League from oppression, it also emphasizes the duty incumbent upon persons belonging to racial, religious, or linguistic minorities to cooperate as loyal fellow citizens with the nation to which they now belong." The Assembly also urged the adoption of the principles embodied in the Minorities Treaties by other States not bound by these commitments as a goal to be attained in the just treatment of such groups in all countries faced with this problem. Certain countries, more especially those bordering on the Baltic Sea, were required as a condition of membership in the League to accept in principle the obligations imposed upon the States that signed minorities treaties. The principle has also been extended through the signing of certain bi-lateral treaties, as for example an agreement between Poland and Germany in 1922, which contain provisions for the mutual protection of minorities within their respective countries. Other countries where the minorities problem exists have escaped these obligations, although the need for international responsibility is perhaps as great as in the countries that submit to international control. Belgium, Denmark, France, Italy, and other countries, include minority groups within their territories, but have been able to resist all attempts to accept similar obligations.

Countries that signed Minorities Treaties have at times challenged the justice of these obligations as one-sided arrangements, and these indictments are not without ground. No particular reason exists as to why some countries should assume these obligations and others not. For example, Italy with large minority groups within her borders is not obliged to adjust their grievances, due to the absence of treaty commitments. The Polish representatives insisted before the Assembly in 1934 upon extending the provisions of Minorities Treaties to all members of the League, and as a condition of acceptance, announced the unwillingness of Poland to fulfill her obligations under the Treaty until this should be accomplished. Although at that time Poland withdrew her threatening proposal, as this was beyond her legal right of fulfillment, yet the efforts made to extend the system did not succeed and in fact Poland has since rendered her Minorities Treaty void. On April 22, 1937 an official communiqué was issued announcing that Jews would be barred from membership in the Polish "Camp of National Unity" which is the party of the new totalitarian state. This isolates Jews from public life in Poland. There have been recurring instances of oppression in Poland to the detriment of the whole system. The neglect of treaty enforcement by one country operates to encourage similar action in other countries and minorities rights are increasingly disregarded. Greater international tension and nationalism, coupled with economic stress, have resulted in more discrimination against these groups. The beneficial results are clearly seen in the principles involved, but practical fulfillment of these ideals do not measure up to established standards. Reason would dictate that the adjustment of minorities disputes can better be settled by an international body such as the League than by a single nation acting alone. Yet in dealing with a recalcitrant state the practical fulfillment of this method is likely to aggravate rather than settle disputes. National pride makes a government hesitant to have an international body question its acts and more especially so if this be a major power.

Justification for international interference in the internal affairs of a country becomes vital where conditions threaten "to disturb international peace or the good understanding between nations upon which peace depends." Such conditions have obtained at various times in post-War Europe. The machinery of Article 11 of the Covenant has more than once been invoked as a result of internal conditions considered to be of international import. While a nation jealously guards its sovereign rights, yet conditions may obtain within a country that have far-reaching repercussions.

The League's achievements in dealing with minorities have by no means met with the full approval of its supporters, yet a splendid beginning has been made and numerous acute grievances have been ironed out. Typical examples of these successes are in the tackling of the Albanian, Bulgarian, and Turkish minority problems in Greece, the Ruthenian minority in Czechoslovakia, Jewish minorities in Hungary, Polish and Russian minorities in Lithuania, and Lithuanian minorities in Poland. Where the governments concerned are willing to cooperate with the League in an effort to solve the internal problems of a country, fairness will in most instances prevail. Under such conditions the League will be able to serve a useful purpose in promoting international good-will. The importance of tackling the minorities problem in the right spirit can not be over-emphasized as a condition necessary to the maintenance of peace.

Other proposals have been made, and some tried, as to possible means of solving this thorny problem. Some would ignore minorities completely, by placing them at the mercy of the State, and thus compel them to accept their fate without hope of redress. While this method is harsh in the extreme, it is nevertheless maintained that if a group can expect nothing through protest, they will not be made. The weakness of this view was clearly manifested in the nineteenth century when no outside body existed to which appeals could be made and yet this did not silence dissatisfied groups. Another and more drastic solution of the problem was tried on a limited scale in the transfer of minorities in the Balkans and the Near East. Greece and Bulgaria signed a Treaty in 1919 for the exchange of minorities under the supervision of a Commission appointed by the Council. In 1923 a Turko-Greek Treaty was signed, providing among other things for the exchange of the minorities of these two countries under the supervision of a Commission chosen by the Council. This Treaty led to the transfer of hundreds of thousands of persons from one country to the other causing untold hardships through economic and social dislocation. The Greek Government was required to care for almost a million refugees as a result of these exchanges, thus placing a burden of the first magnitude upon her in the resettlement of the new inhabitants. This, to be sure, is a drastic step to solve the problem. Its advantage is in the permanency of solution, as all people of the same race occupy the same region. A move to meet the situation by the rearrangement of boundaries does not hold great promise, as minorities are not alone found on frontiers, but often inhabit interior regions. Even along frontiers we find two or more national groups, and to change boundaries may merely result in making the majority group a minority one.

To approach the problem of minorities effectively it is necessary to turn to the United States where this has been a foremost condition from the beginning of our history. Although instances have arisen where aliens within the country have been a source of annoyance, yet the problem has never been acute, and little effort has been made to carry forward a conscious program of Americanization. Foreigners in this country have almost unconsciously become assimilated, thus avoiding acute situations prevailing in many European countries. Although some alien groups have settled in compact areas in a few large American cities where conditions have favored the continuance of foreign modes of living, even there the desire of the second generation to sever all ties with foreign countries has resulted in Americanization. Racial differences offer a more trying problem. While assimilation is possible, the inability to progress toward a unified race is by the very nature of the problem impossible. Thus in the Southern States where some twelve million Negroes reside, the distinctiveness of racial differences has become a continuing condition in which there is no solution other than the willingness of all to abide by established social usages. Discriminations from one source or another, may be, and often are, practiced, but the acceptance of these by the Negroes in the South tend to alleviate rather than augment the racial problem. A splendid tradition has developed in this country, and is embodied in the Bill of Rights of the Federal Constitution, of assuring minority groups certain legal guarantees protecting them against majority tyranny.

The Asiatics in the United States have created a minorities problem of no small magnitude, as the settling of the Chinese and Japanese on the Pacific Coast during the nineteenth century made a tremendous impact on the living conditions of the inhabitants of that region. The diversity of economic, social, racial, and other interests of the two groups led to friction and, in some instances, to strife. Drastic steps were taken by our Government through the enactment of laws denying the right of these immigrants to become citizens and again in denying the Asiatics the right of admission to the United States. The Indian population has offered no serious problem as it has generally been segregated in reservations set aside by the Government. The Mexicans of the Southwest, while large in numbers, are profitably employed and do not manifest a clannish attitude or racial assertiveness. Although the Negroes, Asiatics, Indians and

Mexicans are distinct, unassimilable groups, and constitute a fair share of the total population of this country, they do not retain close ties with other countries that might otherwise continue to instill in them a spirit of alien loyalty. Much the same condition obtains in the case of Europeans who migrate here, as they almost always intend to make this their permanent home and are thus willing to sever their ties with the mother countries.

Many Europeans minorities, on the other hand, find themselves in countries against their choice, as this may have come about as a result of changes in frontiers. The smallness of many countries and intensive nationalism leads to more active nationalistic propaganda to retain the loyalty of these groups. These conditions make it far more difficult for the countries of Europe to solve their minorities problems than in the United States. The growth of good-will among the nations of Europe will do much to lessen the tension, but for the time being this hope falls far short of realization. National passions and prejudices can only have their repercussions in augmenting ill-will among the already dissatisfied minorities. These conditions exist in the face of League efforts to deal with these questions, and if success does not always accompany the League's endeavors, the short-comings cannot be attributed to it, but rather to national behavior that too often runs counter to international cooperation.

3. Territorial Administration

The administration of the Saar and Danzig was placed under the League of Nations when the Treaties of Peace were signed and when the League was not yet in existence. The active administration of territories by an international organization was new in the history of European diplomacy, and was also quite different from the administration of Mandates and minorities. This innovation meant actual international government of peoples rather than supervision over governments of peoples. The origin of League control over these two territories was based on much the same principle as that of the Mandates in that the choice was open to outright annexation by the victorious powers, their return to Germany or their internationalization. Some members of the Peace Conference desired to place the Saar under French rule and Danzig under Polish rule as a reparations move, but this was strenuously opposed by President Wilson. The inhabitants of these two areas are almost wholly German, and to transfer them to other countries was contrary to the President's principle of "self-determination" of peoples. A compromise was found by placing them under the jurisdiction of the League.

Provision was made for the administration of these territories in the Treaty of Versailles, and not in the League Covenant. The anticipation of organizing the League relieved the victorious powers from assuming independent responsibility for the enforcement of certain provisions of the Treaty. It was felt that this new Institution might well aid in imposing punitive measures upon the defeated countries—a plan that has operated to the detriment of the League. History has demonstrated the lack of wisdom of employing the League to enforce the Treaties of Peace for by so doing it incurred the enmity of Germany Austria, Hungary, Bulgaria, and Turkey. Had the League started out with no unsavory tasks to fulfill, these nations would have assumed a more wholesome attitude toward it. President Wilson well understood this handicap, but agreed to place these unpopular burdens upon the League in the hope that the harsh provisions contained in the Peace Treaties would be modified under its initiative.

The Treaty of Peace placed the administration of the Saar Basin under the League for a period of fifteen years. This small area in western Germany contains a population of almost eight hundred thousand, nearly all of whom are Germans. It is very rich in coal deposits. The inhabitants retained their German citizenship, and while the territory was placed under the administration of the League, yet the coal deposits were ceded to France "as compensation for the destruction of the coal mines in the north of France and as part payment toward the total reparation due from Germany for the damage resulting from the war." On February 13, 1920, the Council appointed a Commission of Five to govern this territory; these members to be composed of a citizen of France, a native of the Saar, who is not a French citizen, and three additional members of countries other than France and Germany. The members were appointed for one year and were eligible for reappointment. The Commission exercised sovereign power in the Territory and governed under instructions from the Council in addition to the authority contained in the Treaty of Versailles. Quarterly reports were submitted to the League members and printed in the Official Journal. In the first years of this international rule the influences of the French Foreign Office were sufficiently strong to dictate the policies of the Governing Commission in its own behalf, but after 1926 a more moderate stand was adopted and the best interests of the people were taken into consideration. An efficient administration began to be carried out throughout the period of the League's jurisdiction. Yet the very nature of alien rule tended to intensify the desire of the people to come again under German rule. As the termination of the fifteen year period drew closer, the nationalistic tension increased, and it was manifest that a preponderant majority were in favor of returning the Saar to Germany.

In the summer of 1934 the Council decided that a plebiscite should be held on January 13, 1935, and that all persons over twenty years of age, who had been residents of the Saar on June 28, 1919 were entitled to vote. The Council appointed a Plebiscite Commission to organize and supervise the election, in addition to a Supreme Plebiscite Tribunal to exercise jurisdiction over all offenses committed in connection with the plebiscite. To maintain order at the time of the plebiscite, the Council voted to place at the disposal of the Governing Commission an international force composed of troops from Great Britain, Italy, the Netherlands, and Sweden. Having made these elaborate preparations, the election was conducted without unusual incidents, and the result showed that of the 528,705 votes cast, there were 477,119 votes, or 90.2% in favor of return to Germany. The Council immediately took steps to complete the transfer of the Saar to Germany which took place on March 1, 1935. As France had acquired ownership of the coal mines in this region, it was necessary for Germany to repurchase them, in gold, and a payment of 900,000,000 French francs was made through the Bank for International Settlements. Thus the administration of the League over this thickly populated area came to an end and brought satisfaction to all parties concerned. This experiment in international government serves to show the inadvisability of detaching a large and compact national group from its country of origin and placing it under a rule contrary to the desires of the inhabitants. The Saarlanders spoke out against this in the plebiscite, and to continue League control indefinitely would have brought trouble to the inhabitants. The principle enunciated by President Wilson might better have been applied to these people from the very beginning, as the prestige of the League was enhanced only when the Council planned the plebiscite that led to the transfer of the Saar to Germany. In other words, the most notable effort of the League in connection with the Saar Basin was in relinquishing it.

The League fell heir to another task imposed upon it by the Treaty of Peace in assuming administrative control over Danzig. Like the Saar, this was to prove an onerous burden with no added prestige for the League in having thrust upon it the execution of a Treaty that proved difficult of enforcement. Unlike the Saar, the administration of Danzig did not provide a time limit when the inhabitants might themselves decide their future destinies. The Saar Territory was governed by a Commission directly responsible to the League whereas the inhabitants of Danzig were privileged to draw up a Constitution guaranteeing a large measure of self-government.

The territory of Danzig contains 754 square miles and has a population of 415,000, most of whom are Germans. This internationalized area is at the mouth of the Vistula, and has for centuries been a trading port on the Baltic Sea. Far back in history this was Polish Territory, but became Prussian in 1793. During the nineteenth century this region was Germanized in language, education, and economic interests; however, at the close of the War the opportunity of separating this territory from Germany was seized upon as a redress of injustices committed in 1793. The historic claim to this territory may be in doubt, but an important problem faced the framers of the Treaty of Versailles in finding an outlet to the sea for Poland. To adhere to the principle of self-determination of peoples by returning this territory to Germany would, it was argued, deny Poland this greatly needed concession for her economic life. As the inhabitants of this region are almost all Germans, the same principle of self-determination made it unfeasible to permit outright annexation by Poland. A strip of German territory to the west of Danzig and reaching to the Baltic was given to Poland, thus separating East Prussia from Germany proper. This region, known as the "Corridor," is now inhabited largely by Poles and does not give rise to the same intense national antagonisms as Danzig. To deprive Germany of Danzig was at first essential for the commercial interests of Poland as the ancient shipping center at the mouth of the Vistula was ideally situated for her commercial interests. Later Poland established the port of Gdynia on the "Corridor" harbor and this made her independent of the Free City as a shipping center.

The Treaty of Versailles provided that a Constitution should be drawn up for Danzig and that a High Commissioner should be appointed by the Council for a period of three years and be responsible to the League. The High Commissioner was to act as arbitrator between the Free City and Poland, since the latter government was given certain concessions as a result of which disputes were sure to arise. The conduct of foreign relations and defense were placed under the control of Poland with the provision that the Free City must consent to the treaties. The High Commissioner may disapprove of treaties but the Free City and Poland have the right to appeal to the Council against his decisions. The Constitution as approved by the Council in 1922, provided for an Assembly of 120 members as a legislative and administrative body. A President of the Senate is chosen by a majority vote of that body reflecting the political temper of the major party. This is significant in view of the coming into power of the National Socialist Party in Germany and Danzig in 1933, for there has since been constant friction between the President of the Senate and legislative leaders on the one hand, and the High Commissioner, Poland, and the League on the other. Provision is made in the Constitution for amendment by two-thirds majority of the Assembly, but this has not been guaranteed. The Nazi majority has on numerous occasions disregarded or openly violated the Constitution. Flagrant instances of such acts were presented to the Council in May, 1935, when a Committee of Jurists was appointed to probe the matter. Other protests were referred to the Permanent Court and the political leaders of Danzig were in both instances charged with illegal acts. The Nazi leaders justify these acts as expressions of majority rule. By expelling many public officials the Nazis obtained the qualified two-thirds majority to amend the Constitution in defiance of the Council. This in sum amounts to a coup-d'état. The time is ripe for reannexation by Germany but the danger involved may prevent this move and especially so if the union is complete except in name.

Growing disregard of the League's administrative control over Danzig has brought mild protest, insufficient to deter the Nazi agitators. The early history of this rule was marked by numerous disputes between Poland and the Free City, but in more recent years the League has been singled out as a more vulnerable center of attack by the Nazis. This departure from early quarrels with Poland to a denunciation of international administration proved effective in weakening the League's jurisdiction, as no forceful resistance was offered. In the summer of 1936 the Council placed upon Poland the responsibility of enforcing the Constitution of Danzig, an obligation that was not effectively fulfilled. Thus with the lack of outside pressure it may be safely stated that the government of Danzig will in the future be administered from Berlin.

The failure of this experiment in international administration is rooted in the desires of a people to determine their own destiny, and a governmental regime, set up in opposition to such desires, is bound to fail. The League may well be partly absolved of the blame for the failure of this system in intensely nationalistic Danzig as it was the victorious powers that thrust this burden upon it, although it should never have been done. In justification of this move on the part of President Wilson, the idea was advanced that injustices and mistakes, where such existed, could be rectified under the machinery provided in the Covenant. The concept of orderly process of adjustment was not, however, realized, whereupon the changes demanded by the people of Danzig were brought about in defiance of authority. The unwillingness of European powers to effect peaceful change, where such was needed, has operated to the detriment of the League which acts as a barometer in measuring pathological conditions. The League will succeed only insofar as the powers are willing to place upon it the responsibility of fulfilling tasks that are sincerely just and honorable.

The administrative jurisdiction of the League has extended in other directions than those previously mentioned, but these have been temporary or emergency undertakings such as the control over the financial stabilization of Austria, Hungary, and other small countries, the vast undertaking of settling refugees, and supervision over certain areas whose status was undetermined. Almost by accident, the League was given a measure of responsibility for the administration of

Memel, a city at the mouth of the Niemen, which was ceded by Germany to the Allies after the War. This trading center of 145,000 population on the Baltic offered shipping advantages similar to those of Danzig and is also almost wholly German. Yet the principle of self-determination of national groups, as advocated by President Wilson, was disregarded by compelling Germany to surrender this city to the Allies. Justification of this move was partly found in the excuse of giving Lithuania access to the sea.

An Allied High Commissioner, aided by French troops, administered Memel immediately after the War, until such a time as its status should be determined. It was thought that Memel would eventually be ceded to Lithuania, but this was delayed and the city prospered under Allied control which caused the Lithuanians to fear lest another "Free City" be set up, similar to that of Danzig. In view of these developments, Lithuanian "irregulars" entered the city in January, 1923, disarmed the French troops, and set up a provisional government. The Conference of Ambassadors requested the Council of the League to make final disposition of the city, whereupon a Commission was appointed, headed by Norman H. Davis, former Under-Secretary of State of the United States, which drew up a treaty, later accepted by the Council and Lithuania, providing for the transfer of Memel to Lithuania. Although the "Statute of the Memel Territory" gave Lithuania full sovereignty over the city, a degree of local autonomy was provided in the popular election of a Chamber of Representatives and the choosing of a Directorate of five Memel citizens to exercise executive power and to be responsible to the Chamber. Thus legislative, judicial, administrative, and financial autonomy was made local by the Statute. The Governor was to be appointed by the President of Lithuania with power to veto acts of the Chamber where they might be contrary to international commitments.

Memel was made an international port to be controlled by a Harbor Board of three members, one appointed by the Lithuanian Government, another by the Directorate of the Memel Territory, and the third by the Chairman of the Advisory and Technical Committee for Communications and Transit of the League. Periodic reports were to be submitted by the Harbor Board to the Lithuanian Government, to the Directorate and to the League. Inasmuch as a member of the Harbor Board was appointed by the League and reports are received by it, a large measure of supervision in the control of a foremost economic interest of the city falls under League supervision. The jurisdiction of the League was also extended to include responsibility for disputes between Lithuania and the Powers concerning Memel, and any infraction of the Treaty creating Memel an independent territory was also regarded as of concern to the Council.

The dual nature of partial control over Memel by Lithuania and the League operated satisfactorily until the coming into power of the Nazis, when, as in Danzig, the local National Socialists adopted an attitude of hostility to outside interference. The preponderant German population strongly desired to have their city annexed by Germany. Antagonism between Lithuanian officials and the Memel Nazis became extremely acute and necessitated interference by the Powers to prevent outright seizure of the city. Happily for the League, the control over Memel by it was indirect and failure of administration did not seriously detract from its prestige. Compliance with the wishes of an overwhelming majority of the inhabitants of Memel will no doubt in time lead to the complete return of this Baltic port to Germany.

The League has also exercised supervision over the administration of Upper Silesia, a territory rich in coal and iron deposits, and valuable as an industrial area. This region was given to Poland in the original draft of the Treaty of Versailles, but upon protest by the Germans that this did not accord with President Wilson's Fourteen Points, a concession was made by the Allies in providing that a plebiscite should be held. Article 88 of the Treaty stipulated that the boundary between Germany and Poland in this region should be determined in accordance with the wishes of the people concerned, and "with consideration for the geographical and economic conditions of the locality." This latter clause gave rise to a serious dispute following the plebiscite, for in March, 1921, the inhabitants voted overwhelmingly in favor of Germany. They carried thirteen of the seventeen administrative districts, but Poland claimed the districts having a Polish majority, while Germany contended that the region was an economic entity and should not be divided.

While this controversy raged, a force of irregular Polish troops overran a large part of the province. As French troops of occupation favored the Poles, six British battalions were dispatched to restore order. In the meantime an Inter-Allied Commission, failing to reach an agreement in fixing the boundary, referred the matter to the Council of Ambassadors who were also unable to solve the problem, and referred the dispute to the Council with full power to recommend a settlement. The task of the Council was to decide, in the light of the results of the plebiscite, where the boundary between Poland and Germany in Upper Silesia should run. This was a difficult task as the economic interests of the people were closely united, and the population was so mixed that any line would leave many Poles and Germans under alien sovereignty. At an extraordinary session of the Council, a Committee of four members was appointed with the aid of experts to study the problem. On the basis of its report the Council was able to recommend a division of territory in conformity with the plebiscite, and it was accepted at once by the Allies and later by Poland and Germany. The Council did not leave the matter there but recommended that a treaty be concluded between Poland and Germany whereby a special régime of fifteen years would be set up under League supervision to prevent economic disruption in the region due to the new frontier. The railway system would continue to operate as a unit, German currency remain a legal tender, water and electric units be maintained, and the crossing of frontiers by Poles and Germans be facilitated by the removal of the usual frontier restrictions.

The Committee of Four also recommended the creation of a Mixed Commission and an Arbitral Tribunal, each to remain in Upper Silesia during the transition period of fifteen years. Each was to be composed of two Germans and two Poles and an additional member of another nationality was to act as president, to be appointed by the Council. The Commission was to be given the task of enforcing the proposed German-Polish Treaty, while the Arbitral Tribunal was to be created to settle disputes growing out of it. The above recommendations were adopted by the Council of Ambassadors and were included in a general Treaty between Germany and Poland, signed on May 15, 1922. The Treaty was voluminous, containing 606 Articles, and was on the whole the most satisfactory settlement that could then be attained. The task before the Council was completed in a remarkably short time, and the precaution taken to maintain League jurisdiction over the joint interests of Poland and Germany in this region for fifteen years was also an achievement in League methods of settling disputes by orderly processes.

The territorial settlement of Upper Silesia operated to allay strife and discontent in a similar manner as did the plebiscite in the Saar. In Danzig and Memel, on the other hand, continual disturbances have served as indictments against the subjection of minorities contrary to their wishes. The democratic methods employed by the League in sponsoring plebiscites, where this was possible, has been far more successful than the harsher dicta of compulsion embodied in the Treaty of Versailles.

PART TWO

INTERNATIONAL LEGISLATION

CHAPTER VII

Non-Political Activities of the League

International political relations occupy the center of the stage in so far as public interest is focussed on the shifting scenes that threaten world peace. Spectacular happenings always claim concentrated attention, as may be noted in the newspapers. Interest in world affairs is centered on those conditions that may spell disaster, whereas little attention is given to the constructive processes of world planning that may lead to reasonable relations among nations. Interest in the League's work may be approached from either or both of these points of view. The side concerning political relations of nations, and peace has aroused popular imagination, whereas the other side dealing with what has been termed the second League, has hardly been touched upon and much less understood. The political work has been accompanied by successes and failures with undue emphasis on the latter, while the non-political or legislative work has gone steadily forward at an accelerating pace.

This world of ours happens to be divided into sixty or more separate political units, called states, each of which may be regarded as sovereign in so far as it exercises jurisdiction over a given territory. Yet self-interest does not end there, for each is closely linked up with the other. Ever since the Industrial Revolution, the relationship of nations has become more complex. Technical advances in communications and transportation of the nineteenth century have made the world exceedingly small. In fact, the magnitude and intricacy of the means by which people carry on transactions across continents, regardless of national boundaries, has grown so that we hardly appreciate the present extent of world solidarity. National boundaries no longer serve to isolate a nation, as was the case a century ago, when through force of circumstances it was necessary for each to resort to independent self-development. Science and technology have changed this, so that the growth of commerce, travel, communications, and other world-wide interests have created intricate international relationships and new methods to regulate them. If permitted to do so, trade is carried on between one country and another with the same freedom as within one country. The mechanism of finance is most certainly of international concern, as witnessed by the world-wide effects of fluctuation or breakdown of currencies. Formulation of policies relating to such questions as tariffs and monetary standards are thus of international concern and serve to illustrate their far-reaching ramifications.

Some form of international control of overlapping interests was obviously necessary for the orderly functioning of world society. International institutions and agreements in the nature of legislation developed in order to coordinate these multifarious problems. While the creation of the League was the boldest step in this direction, much conscious cooperation developed even before the War. Its pattern resembles in some respects the national legislative bodies but is greatly restricted as regards the fields that are covered. It is difficult to conceive of international legislation apart from a legislature. A world parliament with full power to legislate seems in history to have been a popular prerequisite to a well-regulated international society. A "federation of the world" loomed large in the minds of many thinkers of the past, with emphasis on the maintenance of peace and little attention to peaceful cooperation. Legislation suggests the power of a superior command, of which the state is the highest unit. Yet it need not be a command at all, for it is more nearly to be regarded as the enactment of rules between equals respecting those principles and interests that are to govern their relationships. Domestic legislation concerns itself with agreements among individuals, while international legislation relates to agreements between states. To effect such agreements it is not necessary that there should be a superior power, a permanent legislative body, established procedure, or a central enforcement agency. The initiation and the giving of effect to legislation is a sufficient test of its validity. Where states unite on a given course of action they are automatically bound by an agreement and thus employ their own methods of enforcement. The League Covenant provides international methods for the enforcement of certain political obligations, but for other agreements no such central machinery exists. The members of the League obligate themselves to respect scrupulously "all treaty obligations" as a condition of membership. Mild pressure may sometimes be brought to bear for the non-fulfillment of agreements, especially in the field of labor, but this has been negligible, as the nations have shown a marked willingness to execute commitments relating to their peace-time activities.

The early growth of international legislation was marked by feeble beginnings, in the first half of the nineteenth century to the eve of the World War. At the opening of the twentieth century hardly a year passed without the meeting of an international conference where treaties were signed embodying legislative provisions. Authorities differ as to the number of such agreements in force at the outbreak of the War but they were numerous, if we consider that no machinery existed such as the League to furnish a meeting-ground. The establishment of the League and the International Labor Organization hastened the pace to an extent never before witnessed. Marked improvement was noted in the development of international legislation since the War, not only in the extent of its growth but in the development of a technique.

The nineteenth century did not produce a definite international conference system, as there was no periodic time for meetings or organized membership of states. Conferences were more often held at the close of wars for the purpose of drawing up and enforcing peace treaties, the terms of which were of course not willingly accepted by the defeated powers. In calling a conference it was customary for a single nation to extend the invitation, but nations were often reluctant to attend as they had little voice in determining the subjects to be discussed and no voice in deciding what nations would be invited. As there were no established methods for planning the agenda of conferences, nor fixed places of meeting, responsible heads of governments often failed to attend. Experts who today perform invaluable services at such gatherings were conspicuous by their absence. In a few instances the technicians assisted in formulating agreements, as in the White Phosphorous Conferences of 1905 and 1906, and the Hague Peace Conferences of 1899 and 1907, but they were not regularly accredited delegates. Serious drawbacks resulted by the insistence upon the doctrine of equality of states and the requirement of unanimity in reaching decisions. Treaties did not in. many instances become operative except through unanimous ratifications. Secrecy often shrouded the conference deliberations and the language difficulties continually recurred.

An organized procedure in the appointment of committees and commissions to study technical matters before the opening of a conference, assistance during the sessions, as well as in the execution of the decisions, were not systematically developed. There was no follow-up machinery for obtaining ratifications and the initiative in this matter was left wholly to the signatory states with the result that some treaties were ratified while others were not. Neither was there a convenient center for depositing ratifications as the practice was ordinarily followed of depositing treaties in the archives of the country where the conference was held. This led to confusion in determining the volume of international legislation that was in force for it was hardly possible at a given time to list them. Varying methods were employed in promulgating treaties from that of publishing them in official Journals as in Germany, to the issuing of Presidential decrees as in France. These are a few of the difficulties that were encountered by the nations in the furtherance of international legislation. Hence a world institution such as the League was sorely needed. The world of 1914 had outgrown the haphazard conference machinery and the close of the War brought the realization of this condition to the fore. The pressure of forces that united the nations more intimately in an ever-widening field of action led to an increase in number of specialized conferences that replaced the full-dress diplomatic gatherings. We shall see how the methods for the progressive development of international agreements became thoroughly organized through the systematic work of the League, for it is to this new technique that we must turn in meeting the world's needs.

Little was accomplished during the War in the progress of legislation, while most of the previous agreements were suspended during that period. The practice of cooperation did however make great headway after the meeting of the heads of the Allied Governments at Calais on July 6, 1915. At this and subsequent meetings far more was accomplished than would have been possible by older methods of diplomatic intercommunication. Early in 1916 rules were agreed upon for the permanent organization of the Allied Prime Ministers' work. This marks the beginning of the Supreme War Council that continued until after the War. Cooperation among the Allies was greatly strengthened by coordinating governmental departments. Such international agencies were set up as the Allied Transport Council, Inter-Allied Council on War Purchases and Finance, Allied Blockade Committee, Allied Naval Conference, Board of Military Representatives and Food and Relief Commissions. Necessity forced the Allied Governments to pool their resources and cooperate in a wholehearted manner to attain their objectives.

While the Paris Peace Conference met for the primary purpose of framing a political treaty, it was nevertheless necessary to conclude a number of agreements that were distinctly legislative. In addition to this program, the Conference took the unprecedented step of establishing machinery for continuing the process of international legislation through the League. The formulation of its Constitution was the first systematic effort of its kind ever undertaken. To insure acceptance, the Covenant was literally smuggled into the five Treaties of Peace, so the Powers would be obliged to subscribe to it while agreeing to the Treaties. This was done because the feeling prevailed among the members of the Peace Conference that the League must be established then or never. Although the Covenant is a part of the Treaty, the League stands on a different footing by remaining in force after the other provisions had been fulfilled, and becoming an agency to function effectively in a changing world.

There are numerous stipulations of a legislative character embodied in the Treaties which lie outside the

Keystone View Company

THE "BIG FOUR" WHO CARRIED THE DESTINIES OF THEIR COUNTRIES THROUGH THE WAR: LLOYD GEORGE OF ENGLAND; ORLANDO OF ITALY; CLEMENCEAU OF FRANCE; WILSON OF AMERICA

Covenant having to do with the revival of previous agreements, the execution of which was entrusted to the League. Added legislation was agreed upon regarding labor, mandated territories, minorities, communication and transportation, and humanitarian efforts. Separate agreements were signed on aerial navigation, slavery, liquor traffic in parts of Africa, and the control of trade in arms and ammunitions of the defeated powers. These moves were independent of the League except for their enforcement. Legislative endeavors at the Peace Conference developed in part from the pre-War Congresses, the Inter-Allied organizations, and the formulation of original ideas by the delegates. The essential elements of periodic conferences developed from continued meetings of responsible ministers, coordinated action for the prosecution of the War, with special reliance upon experts, and the utilization of subordinate committees and councils at the Conference. After the termination of the work of the Paris Conference on June 28, 1919, the pattern there devised was in a large measure incorporated in the structure of the League. The vastness of the work undertaken at the Conference required effective organization. Such matters as foreign trade, labor, nationality, international control of ports, waterways and railways, were problems that would later come under League jurisdiction. While preliminary planning for peace-time cooperation was begun at a War Conference, the successful execution of the decisions awaited a more auspicious time. The international conference system of the post-War era gathered up the loose threads and salvaged much of the legislative initiative of the Conference.

When the Assembly was created, many believed it would replace the pre-War conference system, but this did not prove feasible, as its membership is composed of diplomatic representatives not conversant with technical problems and therefore not capable to deal with them. The Assembly also has a crowded agenda and cannot give the necessary time to the discussion of the numerous problems requiring international action.

Treaties have been concluded by this body, but this is not the accepted procedure, as special conferences are called to discuss and agree upon definite subjects. This practice operates to the advantage of non-member states of the League, invited to attend conferences although they do not attend the meetings of the Assembly. The United States has officially participated in League conferences and has signed and ratified treaties growing out of them.

The League has organized various departments to cover a wide range of specialized activities of a non-political nature. At the outset, a resolution was passed by the Assembly providing for the creation of the Communication and Transit Organization, the Economic and Financial Organization, and the Health Organization. These technical bodies, and others created later, were to assist the members of the League in coordinating mutual problems which had hitherto been unorganized. They form an organized part of the League and report regularly to the Assembly and Council and receive approval from them to deal with the member states. The Assembly agreed that the technical organizations "must keep enough independence and flexibility to make them effectively useful for the members of the League, and yet they must remain under the control of the responsible organizations which conduct the general business of the League." A few examples will suffice to illustrate the value of technical organization in assisting League conferences. The Advisory and Technical Committee on Communication and Transit meets frequently between sessions of the general conferences to discuss technical problems in preparation for intergovernmental action. The members of the Economic and Finance Committee are chosen by the Council as experts to deal with specialized questions under the jurisdiction of the League and to prepare the groundwork for international action. These experts engaged in prolonged preparation for the meeting of the London Economic Conference in 1933, which met under League auspices. The same technical preparation was made by these experts in drawing up draft treaties for conferences on customs formalities, abolition of import and export prohibitions and restrictions, in addition to related questions that have come before the conferences of the International Labor Organization. The health, opium, social and humanitarian, and other divisions of the League have experts to perform duties similar to those mentioned above.

The wide use of experts is a fortunate innovation, as they usually are free from national bias and are not held back by political considerations. They try to approach their tasks dispassionately, and rely upon sound perception and judgment. The experts are not subject to the same pressure of public opinion as are political officials, and can thus more readily reach scientific conclusions. They are highly trained and possess those qualities that make for success in international cooperation. As more reliance is placed upon them, the more certain will the nations be of arriving at equitable solutions of their common problems. Military and naval experts are exceptions to the above rule, as they are chiefly interested in devising means for building up armaments, and when called into conference are certain to seek advantages at the expense of other nations.

The conduct of the non-political work of the League is thus in a large measure undertaken by experts and their achievements usually culminate in the calling of international conferences. The preparatory work follows somewhat this procedure: A proposal for a conference may come from public or private initiative, or from officials of the Secretariat, and when put into proper form, is submitted to the Assembly or Council where it is debated, and if feasible, forms the basis of a resolution. The Council appoints a committee of experts to prepare a draft treaty, and if approved by it, the Secretary-General is directed to submit it to the governments for their observations and recommendations. On the basis of the replies, the Council may instruct the Secretary-General to invite the governments to send accredited representatives to a general conference for the purpose of formally agreeing to such proposals. This procedure is an improvement upon the pre-War conferences where the preparation, if any, was carried on by diplomatic correspondence before the opening of the conference. As a result of the thorough manner in which this work is now done, the conferences are ordinarily assured of a common basis of agreement.

A general conference may be regarded as a diplomatic assembly called by recognized authorities for the purpose of negotiating matters of specialized interest. The delegates express the wishes of the governments which they represent, and are given power to enter into agreements involving national obligations. Periodic conferences are conducted under established rules of procedure formulated to guide them. Uniformity does not prevail in all conference procedures. Some conferences require a simple majority, others a two-thirds majority, and still others a three-fourths majority vote to make treaties. Each delegation has one vote, and if a treaty is favorably acted upon, it is signed by the delegates and submitted to the governments for ratification.

Signatures may be affixed immediately, or at some future time, as provided for in the treaty. Privilege is usually accorded the states to become parties to treaties even though they were not represented at the conference. After they have been signed, most treaties are deposited in the archives of the Secretariat and are published as official documents. The conference can take no steps toward making treaties operative, for the decision to ratify is a matter for each state to determine. Even ratification does not create an international obligation under League practice, for notice of this must be registered with the Secretariat to consummate this official act. Governments are sometimes slow in ratifying treaties, due to pressing domestic questions, parliamentary opposition, or the wish to await ratification by other states. Hesitancy is also caused by the fact that when a government has once ratified a treaty, it may not repeal or amend it except by the unanimous consent of the other parties. Treaties are often operative for a term of years or for an indefinite time, if a sufficient number of signatories do not give advance notice of their desire to terminate them. This procedure is necessary, as the life of treaties is not without limit, regardless of the intentions of the parties. Outright denunciation without the consent of the other signatories is an exercise of bad faith and is seldom resorted to. Governments are committed to definite obligations only because of the advantages to be derived from them.

Of recent years there has been a material lessening in the number of general treaties concluded, largely due to excessive nationalism growing out of the economic depression. Although most governmental problems are national, an increasing number enter the international realm. The Assembly in 1926 agreed that housing, nutrition, cleanliness, education, recreation, and morals are national problems. Yet each of these questions has since come up for consideration by the League bodies or the International Labor Organization. The scope of international interest is ever widening, and as political tension lessens, the League may expect to register continued progress in non-political cooperation. The machinery has been set up to serve intergovernmental needs, so it is not a question of availability of a world conference center, as in the pre-War era, but of its utilization. Although not a member of the League, the United States is priviliged to unite with other states in sharing the benefits of the conference system. Sensing the importance of this form of international cooperation, a Division of International Conferences was created in the Department of State on July 22, 1937. There is thus a growing realization of the need for international collaboration through conferences. The extent to which this has already been done is discussed in another chapter.

CHAPTER VIII

The Economic and Financial Organization

From its inception, extended efforts were made through the League of Nations to promote close economic and financial cooperation among nations. While this important work may rightly be regarded as technical, yet numerous political factors contradict this classification. Perhaps this side of the League's work may more rightly be regarded as semi-political in that political authorities have often interfered with the work of experts in their attempts to solve international economic and financial problems. Hence it is at times difficult to distinguish between the political and non-political phases of the League's work, as the two may overlap. While the primary objective of the League is the maintenance of peace, thereby making it political in nature, the founders realized that a durable peace must be based upon a stable world order. They therefore wrote into the Covenant certain provisions which would permit the League to extend its activities outside of the main scope for which it was established.

Among the numerous activities in which the League is engaged, the economic and financial work is one of the most important. Article 23 of the Covenant contains a short statement to the effect that the League "will make provision to secure and maintain . . . equitable treatment for the commerce" of all member states. This phase of the League's work was undertaken very early when in 1920 the Council summoned the International Financial Conference to meet in Brussels to lay plans for the solution of many pressing problems resulting from the War. This Conference recommended the creation of an Economic and Financial Organization

Keystone View Company

KING GEORGE OPENS ECONOMIC CONFERENCE OF DELEGATES FROM 69 NATIONS

by the League. In creating this organization, the Council and Assembly appointed Committees to direct the work in various specialized fields, the most important of which are the Economic and Financial Committees. They are composed of experts who usually meet at Geneva three or four times a year to work out various economic and financial problems which might come before the League. The numerous economic and financial problems of international importance since the War have greatly increased the work of these bodies. While these Committees serve in the first instance to advise the Council on matters coming under the latter's jurisdiction, an additional duty has been that of working out intricate problems preparatory to the calling of international conferences. To rightly understand the two divisions of this organization it will be necessary to deal with each Committee separately.

The work of the Financial Committee is concerned with, first: general financial questions; second: advice to the Council in lending assistance to governments; and third: advice to the Council on financial questions capable of international solution. The Committee took the initiative in preparing for Conferences which have dealt with Suppression of Counterfeiting Currency (1925); Suppression of the Falsification of Documents of Value (1930); Convention on Financial Assistance (1930); and the problem of "double taxation" which was forwarded to governments for their approval (1933). The Financial Committee was requested by the Council (1928) "to examine into and report upon the causes of fluctuations in the purchasing power of gold and their effect on the economic life of the nations." A comprehensive study was made of the gold problem in relation to international exchanges and it was concluded that gold "remains the best available monetary mechanism."

Following the War some of the weaker governments of Europe faced financial bankruptcy and turned to the League for assistance. At the request of the Council the Financial Committee devised plans for meeting these requests. In general, the plans provided for the granting of loans to these governments under guarantees for repayment through close supervision over their finances by experts appointed by the League. In 1922 Austria was in a state of economic collapse and appealed to the League for financial assistance which was granted. Ten European Powers arranged a loan of 650,000,000 gold crowns ($130,000,000) for a period of twenty years. This plan guaranteed the complete independence and sovereignity of Austria, but with supervision of her public finances by a commissioner-general appointed by the League. The economic position of Austria greatly improved under this arrangement, so much so, that the Council in June, 1926, decided to terminate League control over her finances. In 1923 Hungary requested the Council to lend financial assistance, which was also granted on conditions similar to those of Austria. Greece experienced a financial strain, and in 1927 received a loan under League auspices. The same was true in the case of Bulgaria, Danzig, Estonia, and Rumania.

The work of the Economic Committee has been more varied and comprehensive than that of the Financial Committee. The extensive researches done by this body are contained in its publications which include the following: *Monthly Bulletin of Statistics* which contains tables and graphs on selected subjects of economic interest; the *International Trade Statistics*, an analysis of the foreign trade of sixty-five countries, including practically all world trade and the changes which this trade has undergone in recent years; *Balances of Payments* containing information concerning international accounts, such as outstanding foreign debts and assets of various governments as well as the receipts and expenditures, treasury position, and public debts. Other publications are: *Money and Banking, Statistical Year Book, Review of World Trade, World Production and Prices*, and the *World Economic Survey*.

The Economic Committee made preparations for

the International Conference for the Unification of Economic Statistics which met at Geneva in 1928 where methods were devised for unifying statistical material which had previously varied greatly in different countries. This unification has made it possible to collect economic data with some degree of uniformity. Again the Committee made needed preparations for the Conference on the Simplification of Customs Formalities (1923) which, as the name suggests, formulated plans to facilitate the movement of goods without being restricted by many customs regulations.

A practice which handicapped foreign trade was the variation in national laws and practices relating to bills of exchange, promissory notes, checks, and other commercial instruments. A conference convened in Geneva in 1930 and agreed to a system of unification of commercial practices which has since greatly aided in facilitating international commercial transactions. At the request of the Assembly (1925) the Economic Committee undertook a study of the treatment of nationals in foreign countries who were often discriminated against while engaged in various professions, industries, and occupations. This led to the calling of a Conference which met in Paris (1929) and while definite results were not achieved, certain principles were formulated which may in the future lead to a more equitable treatment of foreigners engaged in gaining a livelihood. The Economic Committee made the necessary preparations for a Conference on the Abolition of Import and Export Prohibitions and Restrictions (1927) which sought to abolish numerous barriers to trade. A treaty was signed and put into force by some countries, but not by the more important commercial ones. This was the first international treaty to regulate commerce among nations and to establish methods for settling disputes growing out of trade practices. In 1928 two Conferences met at Geneva and agreed to abolish restrictions relating to the export of bones, hides, skins, and similar animal products. An international Treaty was signed in 1935 which had for its purpose the regulation of the transportation of animals and animal products to prevent the spread of diseases.

In 1927 the Economic Committee undertook to devise a systematic method of listing the names of all classes of goods on which tariff duties were collected. Until then each country had its own classification of goods for purposes of customs duties, which led to confusion in determinating tariff rates. As the result of a systematic classification of almost one thousand items it may now be possible to apply duties more equitably and thus increase international trade. Governments have reacted favorably to the work of the Economic Committee and an international treaty embodying this classification may be agreed upon in the near future. In 1934 the Economic Committee engaged in a study of foreign tourist traffic in relation to the economic policies of certain countries. Countries visited by tourists have at times been obliged to negotiate trade agreements which provided for the importation of goods from countries unable to export the money spent by the tourists. These conditions often restrict tourist traffic and hinder the normal flow of goods, hence the Economic Committee has sought to find a solution for this annoying problem. The Economic Committee has also given much attention to plans for the arbitration of commercial disputes growing out of international trade. It drew up a model treaty on this subject and presented it to the Assembly in 1927, outlining the procedure to be followed in the settlement of economic disputes. The Committee has also dealt with "indirect protectionism" or the practice of customs officials to bar goods by administrative rulings for one reason or another which often resulted in great financial losses to shippers. Closer cooperation in this respect is now sought and is greatly needed. Due to the constant improvement in whale fishing there developed an irrational exploitation of this source of wealth. The Economic Committee devised means for regulating the whaling industry and submitted it to the Assembly, which, in turn, agreed to a Treaty (1931) which was submitted to the governments for ratification. This promises to be a constructive move through the efforts of the Economic Committee and the League.

Special attention has been given to the possibility of international agreements affecting agricultural products such as wheat, sugar, hops, tobacco, et cetera. Because of their importance, these products require international control of exports and imports. The lack of international cooperation in the production and marketing of farm products led to a serious drop in agricultural prices and resulting economic difficulties. With these conditions prevailing, the governments most affected were willing to place various commodities on a rational import and export basis. Several treaties were signed, establishing quotas among exporting countries with international supervision in their execution. The United States as a leading country in foreign trade agreed with other nations to regulate the price and shipments of various commodities.

In recent years the Economic Committee has been engaged in a study of the immediate economic conditions affecting the welfare of the nations. The reports of these experts show that the economic interests of each country are closely bound up with world economic interests and that no nation can prosper independently of conditions beyond its own frontiers nor can the shutting out of foreign goods by tariffs achieve lasting benefits to the country which adopts such measures. These conclusions were vividly portrayed in a report to the Council in 1935 and were discussed at length in the Assembly in the same year. The Assembly adopted a resolution urging the nations to return to a more liberal economic policy, and as an immediate step recommended commercial agreements between countries in order to encourage more trade. Secretary of State Cordell Hull sent a message to the Assembly commending it for this action. Unfortunately, many bilateral trade treaties have been made in recent years that have discriminated against all other countries. Our own Government entered into such agreements but adhered to the so-called most-favored-nation principle which is not discriminatory. The annual report of the Secretary-General of the League (1936) pointed out that the new commercial policy of the United States, as inaugurated in 1934, was in harmony with the Assembly's recommendations opposing discrimination in trade agreements. Liberal trade agreements are designed to increase foreign trade with all countries and may be the means of furthering economic progress.

The Economic Committee was for many years engaged in making careful preparation for a world economic conference which was to promote increased trade and financial relations among the nations. As a result of the preparatory work of this Committee, the Assembly in 1925 decided to call an international economic conference. Careful preparations continued, the most elaborate in history, and the World Economic Conference met in Geneva in May 1927 with unofficial representatives from fifty countries, including the United States and Russia as non-members of the League. The international aspects of numerous commercial, industrial, and agricultural problems were discussed and the Conference formulated policies which, if followed, would have done much to avert the crisis of 1929. A significant statement was made in the report of the Conference to the effect "that the time has come to put an end to the increase in tariffs and to move in the opposite direction." Unfortunately the governments represented at this Conference did not comply with this proposal but continued to place obstacles in the way of international trade. The develop-

THE ECONOMIC CONFERENCE OF 1927

ment of scientific methods of agricultural, and industrial production led to an expansion of output with the result that nations became increasingly anxious to shut out foreign goods. They therefore moved in the opposite direction from that recommended at the Economic Conference in 1927.

In the early phases of the depression, the Economic Committee paid special attention to the immediate problems confronting the nations and attempted to formulate plans for recovery. While this work was under way, the principal parties to the Treaty of Versailles met at Lausanne (1932) to consider the question of reducing German reparations. They adopted a resolution inviting the Council to summon a world economic and financial conference and outlined the subjects to be considered with the additional request that a committee of experts be appointed to undertake the necessary preliminary work. The Conference also requested the Council to invite the Government of the United States to be represented on the proposed committee which was in time duly accepted by us. The Council called the Monetary and Economic Conference to convene in London on June 12, 1933, where over sixty nations were officially represented. The subjects to be discussed and acted upon were contained in an agenda which included the following: monetary and credit policy, exchange difficulties, level of prices, movement of capital, tariff policies, prohibitions and restrictions of foreign trade quotas as well as other trade barriers, and producers' agreements.

The Conference met at a very inauspicious time as the world depression had resulted in an almost universal collapse of currencies and the drying-up of foreign trade to a small percentage of its former volume. The deplorable economic and financial conditions throughout the world made the nations willing to meet in such a gathering but made them unwilling to reach compromises in order to improve international economic conditions. The nations were pursuing independent economic policies in an effort to overcome the depression, hence it was hardly to be expected that they would alter these policies at this critical time. The United

States had a few months earlier depreciated the gold dollar. While our currency was unstable we were unwilling to enter into an agreement on stabilization with the result that no progress was made at the Conference in this direction. Failing to reach an agreement on stablization, the Conference hesitated to proceed with the solution of major economic questions. The sessions continued six weeks and resulted in little more than the focussing of attention on numerous economic problems. This was a most unfortunate result after long years of endeavor by the Economic and Financial Organization of the League which had labored to bring about better economic and financial relations among the nations. This failure in the realm of economics and finance cannot be charged against the League, as its work was carried forward along the right paths, but it is to be attributed to the mistaken policies of the nations which disregarded the interests of other nations in the hope of benefiting themselves.

The report of the Preparatory Commission of Experts for the Monetary and Economic Conference contained a diagnosis of world economic ills which authorities on international economic problems will agree was fundamentally sound. The report stressed the need of economic action in the following language: "Three years of world-wide dislocation have generated a vast net-work of restraints upon the normal conduct of business. In the field of international trade, prohibitions, quotas, clearing agreements, exchange restrictions —to mention only some of the most widely employed forms of regulation—throttle business enterprise and individual initiative. Defensively intended, and in many instances forced by unavoidable monetary and financial emergencies these measures have developed into a state of virtual economic warfare. It is not only in the field of trade that this tension exists. In the difficult sphere of international monetary and currency relations and in the world capital markets, free international cooperation has given place to complex and harassing regulations designed to safeguard national interests. If a full and durable recovery is to be effected, this prevailing conflict of national economies must be resolved." This analysis of world conditions was considered at the Monetary and Economic Conference but not acted upon nor has it received serious official consideration since that time.

An unofficial International Conference was held in London, March 1935, with leading Americans present to decide upon "steps to be taken to restore confidence by promotion of trade, reduction of unemployment, stabilization of national monetary systems, and better organization of the family of nations to give security and to strengthen the foundations on which international peace must rest." This Conference added to the Commission's report to the Monetary and Economic Conference by enumerating the world's economic and financial ills and recommended among other things that "the leading governments . . . should consult one another without delay for the purpose of coming to a provisional stabilization of exchange on the basis of gold . . . with a view to the establishment of a stable world gold standard" and that the basis for a stable world order must rest upon "the preservation of peace and the restoration of political confidence and security." To this end the Conference recommended the "strengthening of the League of Nations and increasing its influence and authority as an impartial instrument of all the nations."

While important conferences have been held in recent years where there was general unanimity of opinion in regard to the nature of the world's economic and financial difficulties and where there was general agreement as to their solution, the nations, nevertheless, are seemingly unable to unite in carrying them out. It is regrettable to find that never before in history has there been such a retreat from international economic and financial cooperation as in recent years. The roots of the evil are to be found in the slow but sure growth of nationalism which controls the internal economic forces of each country. The industrial depression of recent years has only served to intensify this condition. Each country has attempted to develop its own industries, thereby freeing it from the necessity of buying abroad. A nation steals a march on its neighbors by first making itself, insofar as possible, a self-sufficient economic unit; and second, by capturing foreign markets that would otherwise be claimed by others. These unequal conditions result in the placing of high tariff duties on goods entering a country, by setting quota restrictions which limit the quantity of goods admitted, and by various forms of exchange-control that hamper foreign trade. Typical examples of these restrictions may be found in the case of Switzerland which began to manufacture automobile tires to meet domestic needs. England finding her market for tires closed in Switzerland proceeded to stimulate the manufacture of watches by means of a high tariff on the Swiss product. France has been busily engaged in developing her motion picture industry, largely at the expense of the German producers. Germany, as an importer of French commodities, thereby finds it more difficult to meet her payments to France. The price of sugar doubled in England through the subsidizing of the British sugar beet industry which deprived the countries of eastern Europe from supplying this commodity while they were at the same time unable to purchase the equivalent in other goods from England. The internal price of wheat in Germany and France has been more than twice that of the world market, as a result of protective tariffs in these two countries. These attempts to become economically self-sufficient can only lead to all-around curtailment of production and resulting hardships.

Definite benefits accrue to a nation when extensive trade relations are carried on with the outside world, as each country enjoys special advantages in the production of certain commodities that should make it the logical production area for their output. These advantages may be due to skilled workmanship, proximity of raw materials, availability of capital, technical processes, and accessibility of markets. All countries do not enjoy these advantages alike and to attempt to carry on parallel activities in each country only results in high production costs and often in inferior quality of goods. The practice of restricting international trade among all countries becomes inevitable when once begun by a few countries, for if they decide to import as little as possible a situation is created of unequal trade balances if all other countries continue to buy from them. It is well established that an unfavorable trade balance cannot continue indefinitely in any country. In order to avoid trading with countries that restrict imports, those whose markets are shut off are forced to develop an economic self-sufficiency of their own and close their markets to goods from foreign countries. This vicious practice has continued to grow until the whole world has become enmeshed in trade practices that stifle world commerce.

A problem closely related to the artificial barriers to trade is the unequal value of world currencies. Some countries have remained on the gold standard while others have left it voluntarily or have been forced off. The currencies of gold standard countries are necessarily high in value, which makes the price of goods in those countries extremely expensive to foreign buyers in countries with depreciated currencies. With the wide discrepancy in the price levels as between countries, unequal trade advantages must follow. Currency fluctuations have persisted in various countries which have made the buyers and sellers of foreign goods hesitate to make commitments, as it has not been possible to know the amount of money that will be paid or received for goods. The political instability of governments as well as unbalanced budgets have tended to undermine their credit structure, which in turn cause currency fluctuations. Thus we see that stable political conditions are a prerequisite to a healthy economic society. While it cannot be denied that the numerous political upheavals since the War have brought economic chaos, nevertheless, only through orderly economic conditions can we hope to achieve political stability. The two go hand in hand.

The United States has fortunately enjoyed political stability, but economic chaos has reigned. We have been among the foremost offenders in choking the channels of international trade, due to our restrictive trade policies. Our tariffs were already too high in 1929 when the industrial depression began and should have been lowered, but instead we raised them. Other countries retaliated by raising tariffs with resulting tariff wars and the drying-up of world markets. After 1929 our foreign trade dropped at an alarming rate as the total exports fell from $5,157,000,000 in 1929 to $1,149,000,000 in 1933, while our imports sank from $4,339,000,000 in 1929 to $1,122,000,000 in 1933, which represents the lowest point in our foreign trade since the War. This sharp decline proved a severe blow not only to our merchant marine but to the railroads, seaport cities, banking institutions, and foreign investments. The drying-up of this trade also threw out of employment longshoremen, seamen, truckmen, stevedores, repairmen, and many other groups numbering tens of thousands. The capital invested in the United States foreign shipping and port facilities was tied up and thus affected the financial structure of the country.

The economic dependence on foreign trade of our seaport cities is strikingly illustrated in the economic decline of New York City. From 1929 to 1934 the value of goods entering and leaving the Port of New York decreased 62% while in actual volume there was a 50% drop in seaport activity. The economic effect of this decline upon the people of New York was such as to cause widespread unemployment and economic distress. Relief agencies attest the fact that a large percentage of the unemployed were formerly engaged in ocean-going commerce in one form or another. No degree of imagination is required to visualize the effect of this stagnation on every type of business and industry of this metropolis. These conditions were fairly representative of the other seaport cities of this country where the populations total sixteen to eighteen millions.

The economic welfare of our seaport cities is closely allied to that of the interior regions, as no part of the country can prosper alone. Few appreciate the vital importance of world commerce. While the total percent of our foreign trade in relation to that of domestic trade may appear to be relatively small, yet the economic importance of this difference in our volume of business becomes enormous. The foreign trade Bureau of the Merchants Association of New York estimates that employment growing out of world commerce during normal times is surprisingly large. This Bureau estimates that of the 42,829,920 gainfully employed in 1930 not less than 14,400,000 were dependent on foreign trade and of this number about 7,000,000 derived all or part of their income from business connected with imports. Excluding 3,000,000 farmers engaged in raising export crops such as cotton, tobacco, etc., the remaining 11,400,000 persons still constituted 22.5% of the total of those gainfully employed. While comparative figures may not be accurate, yet the fact remains that the people as a whole have not been conscious of the part which foreign trade plays in the economic life of the nation. A study made by the American Manufacturers Export Association shows that there was a total of 48,000,000 persons gainfully employed in this country in 1930 which is higher than that given above. However, this report indicates that of this number 14,300,000 or 29.4% were directly or indirectly dependent upon foreign trade. A Department of Commerce report reveals that in 1931 about 2,250,000 persons were directly engaged in the production of goods for export. From this same source comes this startling fact that imports affected the jobs of 7,200,000 people. The figures here obtained from various sources indicate the vital relation between foreign trade and gainful employment.

In the South alone some 20,000,000 people formerly relied directly or indirectly on the sale of cotton. During the years before the War about two-thirds of all American grown cotton was sold in foreign markets while in the years prior to the depression about one-half of our cotton was sold abroad. This decrease continued until 1934 when only one-third of the cotton grown in this country was exported and to this must be added the startling fact that the cotton acreage had been decreased by 15,000,000 acres as a result of the governmental policy of restricting agricultural output.

For some years Japan was this country's best customer but she turned to other countries for cotton in retaliation for the treatment accorded her manufactured exports, as she was able to exchange goods more freely in other markets. Cotton has for years constituted the largest single item of our export trade but there is danger that this trade may be permanently curtailed by our unwillingness to receive other goods in exchange for this commodity. Responsibility for the danger of permanently losing foreign markets for cotton places a great responsibility upon our Government in determining our foreign trade policies. More than fifty other countries are now growing cotton and we have been indifferent toward this expansion of acreage in other lands as "King Cotton" has ruled the South during the larger part of our national existance. American cotton growers enjoy natural advantages over other areas and the superior quality of the staple will make it possible for us to compete successfully in foreign markets provided no conscious restrictions by the Government prevents it. On the other hand, if we continue to stifle the flow of goods into the country the cotton producers may find foreign markets permanently cut off and the economic consequences of such a policy would be difficult to contemplate.

Secretary of Agriculture Henry A. Wallace urged the importance of expanding our trade with other countries in order that we may dispose of our surplus agricultural products. Many hold the disposal of the country's surplus farm commodities to be the key to complete economic adjustment. For years there has been a wide discrepancy between the prices of farm products and manufactured goods. As long as low farm prices prevail it is not possible to sell manufactured goods in large quantities to our largest group of consumers who are the farmers. A larger distribution of surplus foodstuffs to the people of this country will not solve the problem, for a large surplus would still remain. The policy of restricting agricultural output offers no permanent solution to the problem, as this would increase the already large unemployment in this country.

A far better way is to supply peoples of other lands with the farm products they need in exchange for goods which we may profitably receive. While imports will compete with certain interests and may cause some unemployment, the harm thus caused is in no way comparable to the hardship caused by our inability to export farm surpluses.

Our Government has in recent years pursued a policy of negotiating reciprocal trade treaties with other nations. Numerous agreements of this nature have been made. They offer an advance in the restoration of foreign trade as tariff bargaining will equalize imports and exports while the general raising or lowering of tariffs results in one-sided trade balances. Foreign trade restrictions, as practiced by practically all nations, make it impossible for any one country to act alone in the lowering of tariffs. Therefore we may expect to find an increasing number of trade agreements between countries if international trade is to be restored. The nations enjoyed prosperity at times when goods moved freely from one country to another but experienced economic distress during periods when international trade was restricted. It is not unreasonable to conclude that complete prosperity may only be attained as the nations develop close economic cooperation.

CHAPTER IX

The Communications and Transit Organization

The greatest single event in modern history was the emergence of new technical processes of production commonly referred to as the Industrial Revolution. The coming of the machine age produced many changes not only in the techniques of production, but greatly altered transportation and communications, which served to unite the nations into a single community. Numerous problems that before the Industrial Revolution were regarded as national began to transcend political frontiers and emerge as international questions requiring the united efforts of the nations in their solutions. The urgency of international action impelled these nations to meet in conferences for the purpose of enacting legislation governing their relationships.

International legislation was removed from the experiences of the nations prior to the nineteenth century and hence it was difficult to develop the international conference system and bring about agreements governing the larger peace-time contacts. Again nations were reluctant to meet and legislate in those fields affecting their common interests, as no world parliament existed for this purpose. Some sort of a world federation had been the dream of philosophers and theorists for centuries, manifesting interest in an orderly world society. However, these efforts were in the main directed toward various schemes for the maintenance of peace. For centuries statesmen had assembled in international conferences usually at the end of wars, to settle diplomatic questions, and when pressing peacetime problems presented themselves the nations almost unconsciously entered into agreements to solve them.

While modern means of travel was instrumental in bringing the peoples of the world closer together, it likewise brought many inconveniences, as delays were occasioned at various points of transit from one country to another due to complicated frontier restrictions. In the shipment of goods from one country to another separate bills of lading were required for each country through which goods were sent. Later, complications arose in the rightful use of automobile licenses when crossing a national frontier. The telegraph, telephone, wireless telegraphy, and postal systems transcended national boundaries, and hence required some form of international control to make them effective agencies of communication. In the absence of international legislation regulating these technical innovations chaotic conditions were bound to prevail. The absolute necessity of international regulation in these fields served to bring the governments together in an effort to achieve a common good. International cooperation in non-political fields did not occasion strife, nor arouse the fears of nations, but tended instead to allay them. Political interests remained nationalistic and did not keep pace with the unifying forces of technology.

There is general agreement among writers that the first notable example of a deliberate attempt to enact such international legislation was in the Congress of Vienna in 1815. The Treaty then signed contained certain principles governing the navigation of the more important rivers in Europe, but it did not contain adequate provision for the carrying out of its administrative features and as a result, was only partially fulfilled. A long period elapsed after the Congress of

Vienna before new efforts were undertaken to regulate international communication or transportation. In 1856 a Conference of European governments created the European Commission of the Danube to regulate the navigable waterways of south-eastern Europe. The administrative duties of this Commission extended to the maintenance and improvement of waterway traffic, collection and apportionment of tolls, and the enforcement of various navigation rules.

The invention of the telegraph created the problem of utilizing this method of communication on an international scale. This was made possible by a meeting of the continental states of Europe in 1852 when steps were taken to unite in the control of this invention. At a Conference in Paris in 1856 the International Telegraphic Union was established as an administrative body to replace the former control by separate governments. A Bureau was established at Berne, Switzerland, to administer the agreements entered into. This combined effort by the nations has brought far-reaching benefits and is a splendid example of the advantages of international cooperation.

The international legislative Act "which stands out most prominently because it touches every man's daily life" was the formation by the Powers in 1874 of the General Postal Union which later became the Universal Postal Union. The postmen of all the nations serve as international agents in delivering mail from various parts of the world. A permanent administrative Bureau was set up at Berne to fix rules for the execution of this agreement. This Bureau has succeeded in uniting all member states of the Union into a single postal territory with fixed uniform rates for foreign mail matter. The money collected from the sales of postage is retained by the state of origin. Numerous regulations are in force relating to all phases of the international postal system. Periodic congresses meet to formulate the general policies of the Postal Union and by majority vote, decisions are reached, sometimes over the protest of one or more of the powers. The essential need of uniform control in the world postal system makes it necessary to adhere to a majority rule. The International Postal Union has reduced postal rates to a minimum, in addition to providing rapid communications to all parts of the world.

National frontiers do not act as barriers in the control of radio waves, hence a method of regulation requires international cooperation for the proper utilization of this technical innovation. Sensing the need of this, twenty-nine governments sent delegates to Berlin in 1906 where a multi-lateral Treaty was signed which established the International Radiotelegraphic Union to fix rules relating to this mode of communication. A second Conference met in London, 1912, and gave special attention to wireless communication on ships. The sinking of the liner Titanic had revealed the special need for this service. Again a Radiotelegraphic Congress met in Washington, 1927, and drew up regulations allocating radio wave lengths to the countries represented and fixed rules for the effective transmission of wireless messages.

While the nations showed a greater willingness to unite in solving technical problems than political ones, their united efforts did not keep pace with the need for international legislative control. With the exception of some conspicuous successes, as in the examples mentioned above, the period before the War must be regarded as lacking in notable progress in the control of numerous problems pressing for action. It was not until after the War that far-reaching progress was made under the impetus given by the League of Nations to advance various forms of international cooperation.

While several international organizations were established during the Nineteenth Century with permanent administrative offices to carry forward activities in specialized fields, they were without any centralized institution such as the League to serve as a coordinating agency. The growth of these organizations in a society of nations presented a condition somewhat analogous to the growth of numerous semi-governmental agencies in a given territory without a central government through which they might function. It was the aim of the founders of the League to bring these administrative organizations within the purview of the League. Various international organizations were firmly established, such as the International Telegraphic Union and the Universal Postal Union, and would not be materially benefited by giving up their independent existence and becoming organs of the League. Article 24 of the League Covenant states in part that, "there shall be placed under the direction of the League all international bureaus already established by general treaties if the parties to such treaties consent. All such international bureaus and all commissions for the regulation of matters of international interest hereafter constituted shall be placed under the direction of the League." Invitation was extended to all international bureaus or organizations to unite with and operate under the League with the additional statement that future international unions shall automatically come under the League's jurisdiction. When organized in this manner, the permanent agencies tend to strengthen the League and give it a degree of continuity which would not be possible if its work was confined solely to the settlement of international disputes. The administrative bureaus on the other hand benefit by the League as the foremost recognized institution in world cooperation. The work of coordinating various administrative agencies of the world was undertaken by the League at the time of the establishment of League organizations so that the nations now have one recognized clearing-house where most of the business of world-wide interest is conducted.

While Article 24 of the Covenant envisages the incorporation of the numerous independent unions and bureaus within the orbit of the League, opposition to this inclusion has been expressed by some governments who participate in their work but are not League members. In some instances, however, these organizations have cooperated with the League although they have not become part of it. These include the International Educational Cinematographic Institute, the International Institute of Intellectual Cooperation, the International Institute for the Unification of Private Law, the International Institute of Agriculture, the International Hydrographic Bureau, and the International Commission for Air Navigation. The League acts as a clearing house for these organizations, thus utilizing the services of technicians already engaged in related undertakings. The League does not seek to direct the work of these independent associations, but attempts to coordinate their activities in a way to achieve the maximum results.

Article 23 of the Covenant sets forth various undertakings of world-wide import to come within the province of the League. Among these it was decided that "subject to and in accordance with the provisions of international conventions existing or hereafter to be agreed upon, the members of the League . . . . will make provision to secure and maintain freedom of communications and of transit and equitable treatment for the commerce of all members of the League." In a meeting of the Assembly in 1920 the Communications and Transit Organization of the League was created, while the Barcelona Conference in the same year drew up a Statute or Constitution, later revised, under which it was to operate. The Constitution provides for an autonomous body of experts who carry forward their work without interference from the League. Members of other Organizations are appointed by the Council while those of the Communications and Transit Committee are chosen directly by the governments represented. Each member of the Council and other states which enjoy "technical interests and geographic representation" appoint members to this Organization. Aside from the continuous work of the technical committees, provision is made for calling of general conferences of delegates chosen by the governments and responsible only to them. This high degree of autonomy makes possible the conduct of work without interference by political authorities.

An Advisory and Technical Committee was set up to act as a consultative and technical body with permanent headquarters at Geneva, meeting twice a year, to discuss technical questions which call for solutions by inter-governmental action. Subjects of mutual interest are presented in the form of draft treaties and submitted to the governments for consideration and comment, after which they may be taken up in the General Conference and formulated as general treaties. The General Conference meets every four years, and draws up treaties in various technical fields and submits them to the governments for ratification and enforcement. This method of international action leads to uniformity in the control of transportation and communication to the benefit of all nations.

The work of the Advisory and Technical Committee is enlarged through six permanent sub-committees made up of technical experts in their respective fields. These committees are: Permanent Committee for Ports and

Maritime Navigation; Permanent Committee for Inland Navigation; Permanent Committee for Transport by Rail; Permanent Committee on Electric Questions; Permanent Legal Committee; and Permanent Committee on Road Traffic. Additional committees are organized to carry forward work in specialized fields of a temporary nature and they include the following: Air Transport Cooperation Committee; Committee of Enquiry on Questions Relating to Public Works and National Technical Equipment; Preparatory Committee for the Unification of Buoyage Rules; Technical Committee on the Tonnage Measurement of Ships; and Committee for the Unification of River Law. The members of these committees are also experts, able to work out plans for the solution of the intricate problems that unite the world into an integral unit. The growing importance of engineering problems transcend national frontiers and require international action if full utilization of technical advancement is to be obtained. The efforts of the Communications and Transit Organization are confined to those subjects of international concern which are most likely to achieve results. Some technical fields are excluded by this Organization because other independent bodies adequately deal with them, but as technical changes continue to present themselves this phase of the League's work will grow in importance. The specialized branches in which accomplishments have been attained will be briefly discussed.

Passport Facilities

Immediately after the war governments made it difficult for travelers to pass freely from one country to another. Passports were required to cross national frontiers and these tended to discourage international travel. An effort was made to alleviate these conditions by the convening of a Conference in Paris, 1920, on Passports, Custom Formalities, and Through Tickets. A second Conference met in Geneva in 1926 and adopted resolutions of uniform passport practices to be enforced by various states. The Conference recommended the reduction of passport and visa fees, and their abolition by certain countries, as well as the unification and simplification of frontier customs formalities. An agreement was reached in a Conference in Geneva in 1929 whereby transit cards for emigrants were to be given by the shipping companies without charge when they passed through countries other than those of destination. This agreement was readily accepted by the governments and has since been in force. In 1927 other agreements were reached, and put into force by various governments, dealing with identification certificates for Russian, Armenian, and other refugees, as well as certificates of identity for those without nationality or of doubtful nationality. Problems of this nature come properly within the scope of international action, and are grappled with by the branch of the League concerned with transit problems.

A Treaty concluded at the Barcelona Conference in 1921, provides for complete freedom of transit of persons and freight where the transport originates in one state and crosses a second into a third. Practices had grown up which subjected those crossing a country to various frontier restrictions, and tariffs were exacted in the shipment of goods through a country, to the detriment of the shippers. Such measures lead to retaliation and reprisal on the part of the countries thus injured. By the Barcelona Treaty which went into force in 1922 these handicaps to travel and trade were removed and the movement of persons and goods across a country without special customs duties and vexatious fees were made possible.

Transport by Rail

The early development of railway transportation was primarily planned with a view to meeting the needs of specific countries rather than the larger benefits of many countries. These practices led to numerous technical difficulties at frontiers by preventing traffic from moving freely. Sensing these practical obstacles, the nations of Europe met at Berne in 1890 and agreed to create the International Union of Railway Freight Transportation. The Organization was given extensive jurisdiction over international transport of merchandise, settling accounts among various railway administrations, collecting debts and deciding numerous disputes arising in the course of routine business transactions. This beginning in the regulation of transport by rail led to the calling of other conferences and the establishing of specialized organizations to facilitate international commerce. Although much was accomplished pertaining to the technical standardization of railway transport prior to the founding of the League, there nevertheless remained much to be accomplished to still further disencumber railway transit. This was undertaken by the Transit and Communication Organization of the League.

A general Treaty on the International Régime of Railways was concluded at Geneva in 1923 which is a comprehensive code drawn up to facilitate greater service to international traffic by close international supervision of railways. The agreement is of a technical nature and is divided into six parts as follows:—"interchange of international traffic by rail; reciprocity in the use of rolling stock and its technical uniformity; relations between the railway and its users; tariffs; financial arrangements between railway administrations in the interest of international traffic; and general regulations." By this general agreement through-railway service is made possible without interference by a single country; discrimination by one country against other countries in international traffic is prohibited; time-table connections are provided on an international scale, through trains to pass from one country to another with the least possible delay due to customs and passport formalities; working agreements regarding the exchange and mutual use of rolling stock, through-ticket contracts and as far as possible the adoption of uniform rates; reasonable traffic tariffs; and the avoidance of discriminatory practices against any of the contracting nations. Numerous problems grew out of the transfer of railway properties in the change of boundary frontiers by the peace treaties after the War. Disputes resulting from the ownership of such properties were to be settled by the Transit and Communication Organization. Many disputes of this nature have actually been settled, more particularly in areas which formerly comprised the Austro-Hungarian Empire. The settlement of disputes of this nature requires technical knowledge.

Highway Traffic Control

The growing importance of automobile traffic has necessitated the adoption of certain uniform measures relating to the regulation of this mode of transportation. An international Treaty was signed in 1909 and revised in 1926, providing for certain uniform practices in the regulation of motor vehicle traffic. These agreements inaugurated a system of uniform traffic control which was later to become a part of the work of the Transit and Communication Organization. An European Conference on Road Traffic was called by the League and met at Geneva in 1931 at which time two Treaties were concluded relating to the unification of road signs and uniform taxation of foreign motor vehicles. By adopting uniform road signs, foreign motorists are able to interpret the highway markings in all European countries. This is a vast improvement over the older practice whereby each country maintained a distinct system of its own. Under the Treaty of 1931, motorists of the signatory countries are permitted to remain in a visiting country for ninety days without the payment of taxes or other charges incidental to the possession or circulation of motor cars. These agreements by the European countries under the initiative of the League will do much to encourage international automobile tourist traffic.

A Permanent Committee on Road Traffic has been created to cooperate with the Advisory and Technical Committee of the League in formulating international rules for street-light signaling. This effort is undertaken with the view of introducing a single design known as the three-color system of signals which is steadily growing in use. The Committee recommended to the governments the use of red, amber, and green lights with the expectation of obtaining general consent in the adoption of this system. The question of civil liability of motorists for damage due to traffic accidents has also been considered by the Committee, as greater uniformity is desirable in this matter among the various countries. This question is closely linked with that of compulsory insurance and gives rise to numerous complications where uniform laws do not prevail. The countries of Europe have responded favorably to these efforts by the League in adopting uniform practices in numerous fields relating to traffic problems.

Ports and Maritime Navigation

The Transit Organization has been actively engaged in working for more uniform practices in international maritime commerce. Through the preparatory efforts of the Organization several conferences have been called by the League that have tended to abolish discriminatory practices by a nation against other nations engaged in maritime shipping. The equality of opportunity as regards navigable waterways dates back to the Congress of Vienna when rules were formulated which defined international waterways and outlined the rights that nations were to enjoy in their use. A Treaty was signed at the Barcelona Conference in 1921 which specifically defined navigable waterways as "all parts, which are naturally navigable to and from the sea, of a waterway which in its course . . . . separates or traverses different states," and waterways placed under international control by treaties. Under the above Treaty the contracting powers "accord free exercise of navigation to the vessels flying the flag of any one of the other contracting states." The nationals flying such flags are in no way discriminated against by riparian states that are parties to the Treaty. Dues may be levied in the interest of navigation and for the upkeep and improvement of such waterways, but these expenses are equitably allocated.

Inland navigation presents many problems of international concern which have received the attention of the Permanent Committee on Inland Navigation, organized in 1924. The effort at tonnage measurement of vessels was undertaken prior to the organization of the League, but renewed attention was given to this subject in a Treaty signed at Paris in 1925 when uniform measurement for registration of vessels and certificates of issuance, validity, and duration were agreed upon. Three Treaties were signed in a special Conference on the Unification of River Law at Geneva, 1930, which established regulations in the field of mortgages of vessels and commercial rights of vessels, unification of rules pertaining to collisions including payment of damages and registration of vessels.

A Treaty on the International Régime of Maritime Ports was signed at Geneva, 1923, which forbade discrimination against foreign shipping in the ports of the parties to the Treaty. This equality of treatment extended to dues, customs, and other regulations where discriminations were formerly practiced. By this Treaty, which went into force in 1926, all vessels irrespective of flag are accorded equality of treatment in the ports of the countries, parties to this Treaty. With this assurance of fair treatment for shipping interests there is no longer the fear of unjust treatment in the ports of foreign countries.

A Conference for the Unification of Buoyage and Lighting of Coasts met in Lisbon, 1930, when agreements were reached concerning maritime signals, the fixing of standard storm warning devices, and problems bearing upon ocean and channel conditions. A series of recommendations were made bearing on lighthouse characteristics and radio-beacons, which were submitted to the maritime governments for adoption. The Conference also discussed the unification of buoyage characteristics but did not reach an agreement due to the expense involved in inaugurating a new system. Agreement as to the unification of buoyage rules was reached by a preparatory Committee in 1933 with the view of gaining the future acceptance of governments. Favorable replies were received from more than twenty maritime governments in which they expressed their desire to conclude an agreement embodying these recommendations. An expert committee met in London, 1936, at which time uniform buoyage rules were adopted and subsequently submitted to the Council. The Council forwarded these rules to the signatory governments of the Lisbon Conference for final acceptance.

The Transit Organization considered the question of sea pollution by oil because such pollution destroys sea birds, fishes, and maritime plants, and spoils the water at bathing resorts. A draft treaty was drawn up by a committee of experts and submitted to the governments for their observations and comments with the view of calling an international conference to legislate on this subject. The replies were received and recommendations based upon them were submitted to the 1936 Assembly of the League.

Aerial Transportation

An international agreement was reached at the Peace Conference, 1919, which had for its purpose the regulation of aerial navigation. This Treaty recognizes "that every Power has complete and exclusive sovereignty over the air space above its territory, and that the signatory Powers agree to permit freedom of innocent passage" to the aircraft of the contracting states. The Treaty provided for markings and signals, rules relating to air traffic, licenses and medical certificates for pilots, meteorological information, and customs regulations. An administrative body was created with headquarters at Paris to supervise the carrying out of these regulations. Other treaties have been signed, more especially in the Western hemisphere, with a view to greater uniformity of air transport. The Transit Organization of the League created the Air Transport Cooperation Committee to examine more especially the establishment of an international air network of important air connections throughout the European continent and the joining of important points of air traffic to avoid duplication of air lines and to regulate schedules. The economic position of air transportation in Europe was studied by the Committee in 1935, and preparation was made for an international agreement of European governments which would exempt air transport fuel from customs duties. The European governments were asked in 1934 to state whether they would agree to this customs exemption, and the replies received were most favorable to the proposal. With these replies in hand, the Council was in 1936 called upon to consider the conclusion of an agreement embodying the recommendations to grant exemptions to liquid fuel employed in air traffic. After favorable consideration by the Council, the governments of Europe were invited to sign an agreement embodying these recommendations.

Transmission of Power

With modern means of transmitting electric current over high-voltage lines for long distances, effective utilization of electric power is at times not limited to a single country. The transmission of electric current across national frontiers is only made possible by treaties. The advantages of full utilization of electric power led to the creation of the Permanent Committee on Electric Questions by the Communications and Transit Organization. This Committee seeks to further utilization of electric power on an international scale.

A Treaty on the Transmission in Transit of electric power signed at Geneva, 1923, and in force 1926, provides for the transmission of power produced in one country across the territory of a second country and used in a third. The contracting governments undertake to cooperate to the fullest extent in the construction and upkeep of transmission lines, and in general to place no obstacles in the way of the fullest utilization of electric power development. The Treaty further provides that if a dispute arises among the governments concerned, it shall be settled by the parties themselves, or by the Communications and Transit Organization, if they so desire. A second Treaty was signed at the Geneva Conference of 1923, and entered into force in 1925, on the Development of Hydraulic Power Affecting More Than One State. The two Treaties are in most respects similar in that they make possible greater utilization of power in two or more countries. One nation agrees to negotiate with another in the development of hydraulic power where the interests of the second are affected. Where two or more signatories agree to the development of hydraulic power, such agreements are based upon this Treaty. This includes the establishment, upkeep, and operation of the works; equitable apportionment of expenses toward construction, operation and upkeep, technical control, public safety, regulation of the flow of water, and protection of the interests of third parties. This Treaty is designed to facilitate agreements that may be entered into for the development of hydraulic power, as a uniform plan of procedure in this respect is here contemplated.

Miscellaneous

In 1931 a Committee of Inquiry undertook a study of public works with the view of expanding numerous works projects on an international scale in order to alleviate unemployment. The study revealed that numerous large-scale public works projects could be profitably undertaken but only if several countries united in these undertakings. A country engaged in construction projects on a large scale is ordinarily required to import materials which it could not readily do if other countries were not engaged in undertakings that would make it possible for such a country to sell goods in exchange for those purchased. In other words if one country acted alone in this matter large imports would result without corresponding exports. Hence, international cooperation was necessary to carry forward large public works projects. At the request of the Assembly, the Organization sent enquiries to all governments to obtain information regarding the wisdom of this proposal, and the replies indicated widespread favorable reaction. As a result of the endorsement of this program by the Assembly in 1933, some twenty-nine governments undertook building programs in thirteen categories of works, largely in the field of communications. This was a splendid example of coordinated effort by the nations to relieve unemployment and hasten economic recovery.

The International Chamber of Commerce and the International Astronomical Union brought the question of calendar reform before the League and a special Committee of Inquiry into Reform of the Calendar was appointed which studied the question from 1923 to 1926. The drawbacks in the use of the Gregorian Calendar are numerous and give rise to inaccuracies or difficulties in statistics, accounts, transport, and commerical transactions, determinations of salaries, interest, insurance, pensions, leases, etc, when measured in terms of periods of less than one year. On the basis of studies made up largely of replies to questionnaires sent to governments, religious, and other organizations, the Committee of Inquiry into Reform of the Calendar was able to draw up three workable plans, any one of which would be preferable to the calendar now in use. A similar effort was undertaken in an attempt to fix the date of Easter, which recieved wide acceptance by numerous governments and private organizations. However, calendar reform and stabilization of Easter have received temporary setbacks as a result of strong opposition by certain religious bodies.

While the League has been markedly successful in furthering international cooperation in numerous technical fields, there have nevertheless been strong retarding influences at work during recent years due to the excessive growth of nationalism. Many of the salutary reforms that were accomplished during the earlier years of the League's existence have, for the time being, become of doubtful value due to national jealousy and frontier rivalry. It is to be hoped that with the re-establishment of closer political cooperation the nations may again more closely unite in developing their common technical and scientific interests.

CHAPTER X

SOCIAL AND HEALTH QUESTIONS

THE historic conception of the function of government was to maintain internal order and insure independence from external interference. The political stability of all countries has been maintained by adequate police systems and armed forces. With the passing of time, the scope of governmental functions went beyond this concept and included numerous services designed to improve the living conditions of the people. The newer responsibilities embodied measures to protect health, morals, economic, social, humanitarian and other general welfare interests of the people. These activities, numerous and comprehensive in scope, were undertaken by governments acting independently of one another. These efforts often proved ineffective in a world of growing solidarity. Numerous problems which at one time were quite adequately solved by each nation acting alone could no longer be thus approached in a world closely knit together by kindred interests. Rapid means of modern transportation brought into being new and involved problems heretofore unknown.

A striking example of the insufficiency of national endeavor was the inability of nations acting independently to prevent the spread of disease. Increased movements of people from one country to another caused contagious diseases to spread until international cooperation was shown to be absolutely essential in the control of this problem. As in the case of the control of contagious diseases by intergovernmental action, so also was this method of approach necessary in the solving of numerous social and humanitarian problems confronting the nations. The advantages of coordinated action in the solution of welfare problems tended to make the nations willing to forsake national interests in the interest of world cooperation.

Prior to the War, the nations acted more or less spasmodically in seeking solutions by collective action for numerous social and humanitarian problems. International conferences assembled and agreements were reached affecting specialized fields of human welfare to the distinct benefits of the participating nations. The isolated efforts of international cooperation to better the conditions of the people, although beneficial, proved insufficient by virtue of the limited scope and number of undertakings which the nations had been willing to attempt. Prior to the War the significance of world cooperation in numerous fields of human betterment was not fully realized by the nations, and only a few far-sighted statesmen foresaw the increased benefits that would accrue from collective action.

The founders of the League recognized the need for greater international control over numerous matters of general welfare confronting the nations, and therefore the future task of meeting many of these needs was entrusted to the League. The framers of the Covenant especially envisaged the League as a medium through which nations would work to enlarge their scope of interest in numerous fields yet unentered. With this in mind, Article 23 was embodied in the Covenant as an enabling clause to extend the authority of the League into fields yet untried. Provisions are contained in the Article regarding the activities which may properly come within the scope of the League, but the Covenant contains no statement that would prevent the nations working through the League from extending their activities. While the League bodies have, in fact, united in numerous undertakings not specifically mentioned in the Covenant there are, however, definite functions, as for example Article 23, which place obligations upon the member states to "entrust the League with the general supervision over the execution of agreements with regard to the traffic in women and children, and the traffic in opium and other dangerous drugs."

1. Traffic in Opium and Other Dangerous Drugs

A Treaty for the international control of opium and other dangerous drugs was signed at the Hague, 1912, but was not brought into force, with the result that a second conference met at the Hague in 1913, and a third conference in 1914, for the purpose of hastening ratification. The Hague Treaty came into force as a result of action taken by the signatory powers of the Peace Treaties after the War when it was agreed that ratification of the Treaties of Peace would also make the aforesaid Treaty operative. With the coming into force of the Hague Treaty, the first Assembly proceeded to appoint an Advisory Committee on Traffic in Opium and Other Dangerous Drugs, "to secure the fullest possible cooperation between the various countries" in checking the traffic in dangerous drugs over and above the quantities needed for legitimate purposes. Various steps were taken by this Committee to make the international effort effective, but sufficient progress was not made to check the traffic. Difficulties were encountered in preventing the smuggling of opium due, first, to the concentrated form in which the commodity is sold, and second, to the unwillingness on the part of exporting countries to cooperate in curtailing illicit traffic.

Realizing the ineffectiveness of existing international control of the drug traffic, the fourth Assembly passed a resolution convoking two international Conferences, the first to be composed of delegates from governments having colonies in the Far East, and the second to include delegates from the governments concerned with the problem. These Conferences were held in Geneva in 1924–1925 when a comprehensive Treaty was drawn up which contained seven chapters, the titles of which are: 1. Definitions; 2. Internal Control of Raw Opium and Coca Leaves; 3. Internal Control of Manufactured Drugs; 4. Indian Hemp; 5. Control of International Trade; 6. Permanent Central Board; and 7. General Provisions. The stringent obligations imposed upon the signatory powers by this Treaty delayed its ratification until 1928, when the nations of the world for the first time began in a serious way to cooperate effectively in controlling this social evil.

To assist in the enforcement of the Treaty, a Permanent Central Opium Board was created consisting of eight experts who, by their technical competence, impartiality, and independence from influence by governments, would be able to supervise the enforcement of the Treaty. Quarterly reports are submitted to the Central Board by the opium exporting and importing countries for the purpose of determining possible excess quantities of narcotics over and above that required for medical and scientific purposes. Where such excess shipments occur the Board may request explanations from the country under suspicion. Under this Treaty the Central Board may even call the Council's attention to a breach of the Treaty, whereupon the Council may decide that no further trade in drugs shall be entered into with the offending country until such trade is confined to traffic in drugs for legitimate uses. A significant provision in the Treaty on Traffic in Opium and Other Dangerous Drugs is the requirement of import and export certificates from those engaged in this trade by obtaining authorization from their respective governments certifying to the licit nature of the transaction. The governments are also required under the Treaty to enact the necessary legislation to give full force to the carrying out of these international commitments.

On the recommendations of the League Advisory Committee a Conference convened at Geneva in 1931 for the purpose of limiting production by a system of quotas and thus instituting international control over the production of narcotics at its sources. A Treaty was signed and entered into force in 1933. It was a long step forward in the campaign against the illicit traffic in narcotics. Under this Treaty a Supervisory Body of four members was appointed to examine the estimated requirements submitted by governments, and to determine these requirements if the governments fail to do so. A significant phase of the Treaty of 1931 is the direct quantitative limitation of the export of narcotic drugs as determined by a system of estimated needs for medical and scientific requirements. When such requirements have been determined for the needs of a country, the Supervisory Body prevents the shipment of additional quantities of narcotics to that country. The decisions of the Supervisory Body are binding on the governments and this gives an international agency control over the internal affairs of a country. A new problem has arisen in that the illicit traffic in harmful drugs has changed from one of supply obtained from licensed factories, to the secret manufacture of such drugs in unpoliced areas. This unlawful peddling of narcotics is possible because of the ease with which the technical processes of production may take place. Such practices make supervision by the

SOCIAL AND HEALTH QUESTIONS

League and cooperating governments extremely difficult.

Certain shortcomings in the Treaty of 1931 led the Council to call a Conference on the Illicit Traffic in Dangerous Drugs to meet in Geneva in the summer of 1936 when a Treaty was concluded providing for more effective enforcement of the earlier accords. Severe penalties are provided for offenses against the laws relating to drug traffic with provisions for meting out punishment to persons engaged in such traffic, and mutual agreements for the extradition of those committing offenses in foreign countries. Severe penalties are here provided, when accepted by the governments, for the punishment of those engaged in any phase of the illicit drug operations. The governments have seriously turned their attentions to this problem, and wholehearted cooperation will do much to successfully cope with the evil.

2. Traffic in Women and Children

Progress has been made in international legislation in the suppression of the traffic in women and children by the framing of treaties requiring the signatories to give effect thereto in national laws. Due to modern means of transportation this traffic has become an international scourge against which national measures are wholly inadequate. The white slave traffic has for many years been operating upon an international scale, as white slave agencies have transported prostitutes from one country to another on a commercialized scale. Often the traffickers do not themselves leave the country in which they operate, but carry forward their nefarious practices through international rings, which makes it difficult to cope with these practices.

Through the efforts of private international organizations the French Government called a Conference in

1902 that led to the signing of a Treaty in 1904 to which the United States was a party. This Treaty provided for the establishment of centralized authorities to obtain "all information concerning the procuration of women and girls with a view to their debauchery in a foreign country" and to provide punishment for anyone engaged in this criminal practice. A second Conference was held at Paris, 1910, when a Treaty was signed which among other things was designed to strengthen the earlier one by providing swift punishment for those engaged in white slave activities. These two Treaties were not effectively enforced and did not include a large number of countries, with the result that the framers of the Covenant realized that a central body capable of stimulating the governments to take effective steps to suppress this evil was needed. With this in view, a legislative provision was incorporated in Article 23 of the Covenant which intrusts to the League "the general supervision over the execution of agreements with regard to the traffic in women and children." An official of the Secretariat was appointed in May, 1920, "to keep in touch with all matters relative to the white slave traffic," and at the request of the first Assembly in 1920, the Secretariat assumed the task of ascertaining what measures were being undertaken to combat the traffic. The Assembly at the same time invited the Council to convene an international conference, which the Council did, and consequently the International Conference on the Traffic in Women and Children was held at Geneva in 1921. The preparatory work for this Conference was not carried forward with the thoroughness that generally characterizes conferences meeting under League auspices. Hence the deliberations were only based on information obtained from questionnaires sent to the various governments by the Secretariat. It was agreed at this Conference to strengthen and extend the Treaties of 1904 and 1910 and to urge their immediate ratification. Other provisions were made to extend the scope of international control, but the real significance of this Treaty was its acceptance by forty-eight countries, and the setting up of a permanent Committee by the League to supervise enforcement. In 1921 the Council appointed the Advisory Committee on Traffic in Women and Children and reconstituted it in 1924 as the Advisory Commission for the Protection and Welfare of Children and Young People. This Commission was divided into two parts, one dealing with Traffic in Women and Children, and the other with Child Welfare. The members of the two Committees are appointed by the governments which they represent, and meet periodically to examine proposals for future action, and study annual reports from the governments relating to the enforcement of the Treaties. The efforts met with marked success, and much has been accomplished through the League to eradicate commercialized prostitution.

While the League made marked progress in this humanitarian effort, there nevertheless remained certain weaknesses in the enforcement machinery which led to the calling of a Conference in 1933 to extend the existing agreements to impose penalties for those engaged in the international traffic in women of full age, even with their consent, for immoral purposes in other countries. Consideration was also given to the protection of children and young people respecting the nature and extent to which they might be subjected to similar perils.

The League has also in recent years concerned itself with the problem of child welfare insofar as this relates to protection against economic misfortunes, public morals, criminal responsibilities, child imprisonment, age of marriage and consent, status of illegitimate children, blindness, and the problem of foreign minors. Not wishing to go too far, the Council suggested in a resolution that this form of social welfare work "is not primarily a matter for international action . . . the purposes which the League can serve in this direction are limited." These interests like many others have both national and international implications and the states that have developed beneficial experiments in child welfare work may likewise cooperate with the less progressive countries for the betterment of childhood. The legal systems and customs vary widely from one country to another, thus affording League authorities an opportunity to study the existing practices and to collect and coordinate information to be used by backward countries in enlarging public responsibility toward children.

In March, 1924, the Council, on the petition of the International Association for the Promotion of Child Welfare placed that body under the permanent direction of the League. The Assembly ratified this action, and also endorsed certain guiding principles known as the "Declaration of Geneva" which in substance provides that the nations "recognizing that mankind owes to the child the best that it has to give" will provide for the normal development of the child, and when hungry, sick, orphaned, and delinquent will give the necessary assistance. Relief in times of distress, protection against exploitation, in addition to assisting the child to earn a livelihood and devote his talents to the service of mankind, are the ideals included in this declaration. The Child Welfare Committee was especially successful in coordinating a study of laws relating to the age of marriage and consent, and succeeded in inducing several governments to amend their laws to raise the marriage age. A similar study has been made of the laws governing the admission of children to motion picture performances, insofar as the films might harmfully affect children; and constructive measures have been taken for the production and presentation of recreational films suitable for young audiences.

On the basis of comprehensive questionnaires and replies from thirty-seven governments, the Child Welfare Committee examined the legal status of illegitimacy in various countries, with reference to the obligations of parents toward illegitimate children, the legal rights, including inheritance, their position under social insurance laws, and in general their moral and physical well-being.

Varying practices were found in countries respecting the treatment of children and young people imprisoned for crime which led the Committee to recommend the abolition of detention of minors as punitive measures, and substitute character training and education as corrective measures, since these have proved more successful than repressive measures. The Child Welfare Committee's work has been extended to include problems relating to the protection of blind children, the boarding-out of children in families to provide for the normal experience of home and community, and the effects of the economic depression and unemployment on children and young people. Constructive steps have been taken to improve the position of young people through vocational and industrial training by extending the time required for school attendance, and also planning a wiser use of spare time. The work of the League in behalf of the welfare of children commends itself to every thinking person as a work of extreme importance within the scope of social work.

3. Obscene Publications

In close connection with the efforts of the League to deal with the moral protection of women and children was the international problem of traffic in obscene publications. As early as 1910 an attempt was made to suppress obscene literature when a Conference met for this purpose in Paris, but failed to achieve results. The seriousness of this growing menace led the Assembly to convene a Conference. It met in Geneva, 1923, when a Treaty was successfully concluded which has since been ratified by more than forty governments. This social endeavor was not specifically provided for in the Covenant, and yet it was a task to which the League readily turned. As previously noted, while the Covenant definitely grants to the League bodies jurisdiction in certain fields of international legislation, it does not exclude it from undertaking tasks not mentioned in the Covenant. Doubt as to jurisdiction was overcome by the Assembly when it was agreed that Article 24 of the Covenant was sufficiently broad to include work of this nature.

Following the action of the Assembly in 1922 to call a Conference, questions that were likely to come up for consideration were addressed to the governments, and on the basis of the replies received it was possible to meet in conference with a fair knowledge of the best course to pursue. The International Conference for the Suppression of, the Circulation of, and Traffic in, Obscene Publications, 1923, succeeded in drawing up a Treaty that obligated the signatories "to take all measures to discover, prosecute, and punish any person engaged in . . . trade, distribution, public exhibition, or possession of obscene writing, printed matter, and pictures of obscene objects." The Treaty also prohibited, under penalty, the import or export of all obscene matter, and provided obligations for the enactment of national legislation where it did not already exist. The supervision over the execution of the Treaty rests with the Committees concerned with the traffic of women and children, and they receive annual reports from governments in regard to law enforcement and new legislation on the subject. While obscene publications have not been wholly suppressed through international cooperation much has been achieved by obtaining consent of forty-five governments to make this circulation and traffic a legal offense—a condition that did not prevail before the League undertook to outlaw sordid literature.

4. Refugees and Relief of Distress

One of the outstanding achievements of the League in the realm of humanitarianism has been the repatriating of, the giving of financial assistance to, and the finding of homes for millions of refugees scattered throughout Eastern Europe and Asia Minor. The problem grew principally out of the World War as large numbers fled from their countries of origin due to pressure of one form or another, or were driven out because they held political views different from those in power and also because they were of a different race from the national majority. There was an exodus from Russia where a million and a half persons fled the country, a million and a half Greeks left Turkey, three hundred fifty thousand Armenians left Asia Minor, one hundred twenty thousand Bulgarians fled from Greece, one hundred fifteen thousand left Germany, twenty-five thousand Assyrians fled from Iraq, and eight thousand persons quit the Saar, not to mention the Italians who fled from their native land with the coming into power of Mussolini and the exodus from Spain with the setting up of dictatorial rule in that country. These expatriates not only severed their connections with their mother countries, thus no longer enjoying national protection, but found themselves in unfriendly lands where great reluctance was in most cases shown in accepting them as subjects or citizens.

This precarious situation led the Council in 1920 to appoint Dr. Fridtjof Nansen, High Commissioner, to undertake the task of rehabilitating the homeless multitudes. Dr. Nansen was the moving spirit in this work from 1921 until his death in 1930, and due to his great organizing ability and sympathetic attitude was able to carry forward this great work at very little cost. His prime achievement was in connection with an exchange of Greek and Turkish populations resulting from the bitter hostilities of the Balkan War, the World War, and the Greco-Turkish War in 1923. In the early years of this distress American charitable organizations greatly assisted in giving financial aid to the refugees. When this was discontinued, the Council undertook a program of permanent settlement of these people by advancing funds for the establishment of homes. The Greek Refugee Settlement Commission was set up to supervise the financing of the settlement work through loans from leading European banks which, over a period of years, led to the permanent settlement of almost one hundred fifty thousand families on farms in Greece, while many others were provided homes in urban centers. While the cost of rehabilitation was tremendous, yet the outlay per family was remarkably low due to the efficient manner in which the League agency performed its work. The League served the useful purpose of supervising the expenditures obtained from contributions, and funds advanced through the aid of governments, in the work of resettlement. A Greek Refugee Settlement Commission, headed for a time by Charles P. Howland of New York, was set up in 1923 to assist the High Commissioner in this task. The League did not at first attempt to tackle the problem at its source by attempting to obviate the causes of emigration, but sought only to aid the refugees after their departure. In more recent years attention has been directed toward the liberalization of the majorities toward the minorities and also to seek to repatriate many exiles.

The position of the Armenians has for many years been harsh due to massacres under the Ottoman rule, and this was intensified during the War when it appeared that a policy of extermination of these people would be carried out. Many escaped to Russia and fought in the Allied Armies and after the War universal sympathy was extended to these unfortunate people. The hope of return to Turkey, after the War, ended with the coming into power of a harsh government that showed no sympathy for the exiles. Many remained in Russia, many more settled in Syria, while large numbers went to France and other countries. These movements of peoples without legal status or identity papers led the League to issue the so-called "Nansen Passports" to protect them in their peregrinations. Since 1927 the governments have, on the recommendation of the League, issued "International Passports" or certificates similar to the "Nansen Passports." Arrangements were made under the Nansen Office for cheaper railway tickets, the advancing of money, and the finding of work for these unfortunates.

The Russian migrations between 1918 and 1924 were caused by the Revolution and Civil War. Most of these people had been sympathetic toward the Tsarist and Kerensky governments and their return was not welcomed by the Soviets. Indeed out of a million and a half who left, less than one per cent were given full amnesty. On the inability of the Russian refugees to return to their native land, they began to seek permanent homes in different parts of the World. Some four hundred thousand settled in France, one hundred thirty five thousand in China, seventy-five thousand in Germany, to mention only a few countries where they migrated.

With the coming into power of the National Socialist Party in Germany in 1933 policies were adopted which resulted in the exodus of large numbers of Jewish and other citizens from that country. Of these roughly one hundred thousand were Jews, and the other fifteen thousand were Communists, Socialists, pacifists and other groups who were hostile to the Nazi regime. Large numbers have settled in Palestine, the United States, Netherlands, and smaller numbers are scattered in other countries. The acuteness of the problem of the expatriated led the Assembly to pass a resolution in 1933 calling for the appointment of a High Commissioner to obtain assistance directly from the governments where these exiles had migrated. The Council appointed James G. McDonald, an American, as High Commissioner to undertake the raising of funds to alleviate the economic stress of these expatriated Germans. League efforts through the High Commissioner were more indirect than in the case of the "Nansen Office," as it was deemed advisable not to have the League interfere in the affairs of Germany due to her withdrawal of League membership and general hostile attitude toward its activities. Financial assistance for this work was not forthcoming from the League as in earlier years for similar work, but funds were sought from other sources. Large contributions were obtained in this, and other countries, to alleviate economic stress and to provide permanent settlements. The initiative taken by the League caused the drastic results of the policies of the Nazi régime to be mitigated. The High Commissioner continued his duties until the end of 1935, when active steps were taken by the Assembly to provide a permanent organization to deal with the future refugee problems as they might arise. This very necessary work is of international concern and properly comes within the scope of the League.

The one hundred twenty thousand Bulgarians that fled from Greece after the War were, unlike the Russians and Germans, welcomed in their homeland. However the burden of absorbing such large numbers proved too great for the government at Sofia, hence the League was called upon for financial aid in establishing homes for these people. After requesting financial assistance from the Council in 1926, an international loan was floated and funds thus obtained were used to provide homes for more than thirty thousand families.

The economic depression of the last few years has again intensified the refugee problem due to vast unemployment caused by it. These people needed employment, and in the face of loyalty to indigenous groups who were given preference over aliens in this matter, great hardships were encountered. The refugees also suffered far more than others from unemployment as governments at times withdrew the permits to work from those enjoying temporary visas to remain in the country. Precarious conditions prevailed when refugees were expelled from a country but were not admitted by other countries. Indeed many were imprisoned for violating government regulations relating to the nature of the hospitality enjoyed by them. It was a tragic occurrence to find a person imprisoned for working in violation of a government order denying him this right, but many abnormal situations existed during the depression years. The refugee problem is by no means of sole interest to the student of history, but will recur from time to time as a great humanitarian problem, thus calling for international intervention in behalf of subjugated groups.

In 1927 an international Conference met at Geneva

and drew up a Treaty which provided for the creation of an International Relief Union. The Union was organized and had as its object the extending of aid from League funds to member states overtaken in disaster. With funds thus available, the Union is in a position to act promptly in providing relief for losses due to earthquakes, floods, and other disasters. The continued building up of funds has made it possible for the League to come to the assistance of countries already visited by calamities. The International Relief Union operates in close conjunction with the International Red Cross Society which makes possible the pooling of League funds with those received from private contributions.

The League has concerned itself with penal and penitentiary questions by seeking to find certain standards or rules for the treatment of prisoners. This work is based upon a report submitted by the International Penal and Penitentiary Commission in 1929. Many conflicting practices in penal administration were observed which led the Assembly in 1934 to approve a uniform body of rules. It then submitted them to the member states for acceptance. Some twenty-nine countries agreed to this proposal as a move to introduce more scientific methods in the treatment of prisoners.

5. The Slave Trade

Few persons realize that in this enlightened age the institution of slavery still exists in certain countries. The problem is an old one and the more advanced nations long ago turned their attention to the suppression of slavery and slave traffic. This could not always effectively be done by each nation acting separately, as the lucrative practice gave the recalcitrant nations economic advantages over those that were willing to abolish slavery. Through coordinated effort a sufficient number of governments were able to formulate policies that were in time destined to lessen this evil.

The first international step of importance to abolish slave trade was taken at the Congress of Vienna, 1815, when the European powers agreed to condemn the traffic, but did not provide machinery for enforcement. Numerous treaties were signed between countries which provided for the right to search vessels suspected of engaging in this trade. An international Conference assembled in Berlin, 1885, when an attempt was made to suppress slave traffic at its source, and the powers here agreed "to secure the complete suppression of slavery in all its forms and of the slave trade by land and sea." Of greater importance was the attempt at the Brussels Conference of 1890 to abolish slavery in any form within the territories of the signatory powers, and also to police closely the routes used by slave traders. This Conference succeeded in obtaining the consent of countries that still recognized the institution of slavery as they agreed to abolish it.

Since efforts to abolish slavery and slave traffic prior to the War were not wholly effective, the earlier international Treaties were revised in 1919 when the Powers, meeting in Conference, renewed their efforts to suppress slavery in all its forms. The traffic nevertheless continued in some backward parts of the world, especially in regions bordering on the Red Sea. Abyssinia was one of the chief offenders, and when she applied for membership in the League in 1923, strong opposition to this request was expressed, especially by representatives of the British Empire, Holland, and Switzerland. Other nations, more particularly France and Italy, favored Abyssinian membership, and she was finally admitted upon agreement to fulfill the provisions of the anti-slavery Treaties. Singularly enough one of

Italy's foremost grievances against Abyssinia in 1935, when Italian armies occupied that country, was the existence of slavery. This appeared to be a mere alibi, as similar protests were not expressed by the Italian delegation when Abyssinia was admitted to League membership.

The framers of the League Covenant took cognizance of the evils of all forms of involuntary servitude by including in Article 23 of the Covenant the statement that the members "undertake to secure just treatment of the native inhabitants of territories under their control." The Assembly and Council undertook quite early the task of combating slavery by obtaining information from the governments as to the best means of dealing with this thorny problem. The preliminary work led to the creation in 1924 of a Temporary Committee on Slavery which drew up a report that formed the basis of subsequent action by the Assembly. The Assembly deviated from ordinary League practices by formulating a general Treaty on this subject instead of inviting the Council to call a special conference. This extraordinary procedure indicated the urgency of the situation as a Treaty of far-reaching import was signed in the fall of 1926 and entered into force the following spring. More than forty countries have bound themselves to suppress the slave trade and abolish slavery as soon as possible. The Treaty was ratified, or more correctly stated, adhered to by the United States Senate with reservations relating to the provisions regarding forced labor. The forced labor clauses apply to certain regions in Africa where natives are compelled to perform services by European overseers for public or private gain with little or no benefits accruing to the natives themselves. These practices were condemned in the slavery Treaty of 1926 and more fully elaborated in a Treaty drawn up by the International Labor Organization in 1930.

Slave traffic, as it was carried forward in a large organized manner, disappeared as a result of the coordinated efforts through the League, but isolated cases of buying and selling human beings still continued in certain remote regions. This led the Assembly in 1931 to reexamine the situation in an effort to give assistance in apprehending slave dealers in these outlying areas. The Assembly accordingly appointed an Advisory Committee of Experts on Slavery as a permanent body to study the matter and to cooperate with the governments, even to the extent of recommending financial aid by the League. The government of Liberia requested the Council "to ascertain on the spot whether slavery or forced slavery existed in Liberia as a normal social system," and a Commission was subsequently sent to that country to investigate conditions. The Committee's report indicated that a form of slavery did exist, but of real importance were the steps taken to change these conditions. Of equal importance was the acceptance in principle of these recommendations by Liberia, acting in cooperation with the League to abolish this ancient institution. We thus find the League's endeavors directed toward freeing men who have been held in bondage from time immemorial. While the task is not yet completed, great strides have been made, as permanent machinery operates to continually direct inter-governmental efforts toward this end.

6. The Health Organization

Modern means of transportation have brought the peoples of the world in close contact with one another, thus spreading contagious diseases. National frontiers do not serve as deterrents in the movements of germs, neither are epidemics peculiar to national groups. The spread of diseases from one part of the world to another and more particularly from the eastern countries to Europe has engaged the attentions of governments for a long time. Rigid measures were taken by nations acting single-handed to isolate themselves when the danger of epidemics was apparent, and strict quarantine regulations were set up. Contagion was not effectively controlled, however, through these isolated efforts, and hence the nations were drawn together in international conferences to deal collectively in promoting health measures. International Treaties were signed at Paris in 1903, and revised in 1912, obliging each signatory to notify immediately the other parties to the Treaties of outbreaks of plagues, cholera, or yellow fever within its territory. Delay prevented the operation of these agreements and thus little was achieved by way of concerted action in the control of epidemics prior to the establishment of the League. The International Office of Public Hygiene with headquarters at Paris was created by international agreement in 1907 to act as a center for the collecting of information regarding the spread of infectious diseases. In 1905 a Pan-American Sanitary Treaty was signed to check the spread of yellow fever, cholera, and plague, with a regional office at Washington to act as a clearing center in health measures under the aegis of the Pan-American Union. An endeavor was also made to check the spread of African sleeping sickness, caused by germs carried by the tsetse fly, but it met with little success before this work was undertaken by the League.

Since most epidemics in Europe have been caused by diseases carried from the Orient, special precautionary measures were taken in inspecting vessels passing through the Suez Canal, the Persian Gulf, and other routes from Asia. An International Sanitary and Quarantine Board was stationed at Alexandria to supervise the work of preventing the transmission of diseases into European countries. A similar center was established at Constantinople and other key cities. These organized undertakings on a regional basis did much to check the spread of infectious diseases, but did not meet the situation on an international scale. Hence it was logical that the framers of the League Covenant should write into that document provisions for the promotion of health on a world wide basis. Article 23 of the Covenant states that the members of the League "will endeavour to take steps in matters of international concern for the prevention and control of disease." In 1920 the Council summoned an International Conference of Health Experts to draw up a plan for the organization of the health activities of the League. The Conference agreed that the International Office of Public Hygiene at Paris should be continued and be officially represented on the Health Committee of the League. The Paris Office was unable to comply, due to the objections by one of its members, namely the United States. This was a logical move by the Paris office, as Article 24 of the Covenant provides for the incorporation under the League's jurisdiction of the existing organizations whose consent is obtained. The International Health Office at Paris had voted to do this, but inasmuch as the United States was not a member of the League, this decision was rescinded. However the Assembly and the Council continued to carry out the provisions of Article 23 of the Covenant, and in 1923 established the Permanent Health Organization. This consists of the Advisory Council, the Health Committee, and the Secretariat. The Advisory Council is appointed, despite earlier objections by the United States, by the Permanent Committee of the International Office of

Public Hygiene in Paris, to receive reports and to prepare international treaties to be submitted to the governments for criticism and adoption. The Health Committee, composed of medical experts, acts as the advisory body to the Council and Assembly on health questions, as this takes the form of enquiries and investigations of a preliminary nature "on which the final deliberations of the Advisory Council may subsequently be based." The Secretariat is the executive agency of the Organization with its duties directed by the Health Committee, and constitutes the Health Section of the League Secretariat. The nations of the World have thus been able to expand health work on a scale far greater than was possible before the Health Organization was established.

The International Health Organization serves as a clearing center for information in regard to the outbreak of epidemics and other health problems which might be solved by concerted action. Numerous publications are issued, based upon researches, which makes it possible for the medical profession to benefit by discoveries in all parts of the world. National health authorities of one country are brought into close contact with those of other countries, whereupon the latest medical knowledge tends to be more widely disseminated. Governments are increasingly turning to the Health Organization for information and expert advice in the control of diseases peculiar to certain regions, and the more backward countries have especially benefited by the services the Organization is able to offer.

A unique phase of this work was the establishment of the Eastern Bureau at Singapore, where since 1925, the Health Organization receives information regarding the outbreak of infectious diseases and plagues. This information is sent weekly to Geneva and the Central Quarantine Office in Paris. Almost all ships coming from the far-eastern countries touch at Singapore on their way to the western world. Thus valuable information is here obtained concerning the health of passengers through these routes, as well as the health conditions in the countries from which they come. Far-eastern countries receive radio broadcast information of such outbreaks and are enabled better to cope with the recurring scourges so often visited upon them.

The introduction of the airplane has greatly augmented the danger of disease, as persons travel rapidly from one country to another and may spread disease before diagnosis is possible. Ships plying the waters require a longer period of time, which makes possible the discovery of outbreaks before they dock. Air transportation has necessitated closer supervision over contagious diseases in the countries of origin by more careful analyses of symptoms in the early stages and through the requirement of certificates of health issued by public authorities. The Health Organization has succeeded in obtaining the cooperation of numerous governments more rigidly to enforce health measures designed to prevent the infected persons from traveling abroad. Although travel by air has thus made possible the spreading of communicable diseases, the efforts of the Health Organization to enforce treaties designed to localize such outbreaks have counteracted its ill effects.

The concrete types of international control of diseases are carried forward on two fronts through the development of techniques in combating diseases and again through assistance offered to countries in need of aid. The greatest headway has been made in combating malaria, a sickness more wide-spread than any other. Some two hundred and fifty million people are attacked by this disease in Russia, the Near East, the Far East, southern Europe, Central and South America, Africa, and parts of the United States. The harmful effects of this form of sickness is incalculable. The League's Commission has visited numerous countries stricken by malaria with the object of rendering assistance to the health authorities. Various conferences have met to plan large-scale treatment and to devise the best remedies based on experiments conducted in various countries. The older methods of treatment were costly and could not therefore be utilized by vast numbers who required treatment. The world's total production of quinine, a drug used to combat malaria, was inadequate, and after a careful study by the Commission, methods were devised to increase the yield and cheapen the cost by new methods of extraction. Synthetic drugs have also proved effective.

There are supposedly over three million lepers in the world, mostly in China, Japan, and India. For many centuries man had little knowledge of the causes and the remedies necessary to cope with this scourge. A Health Committee of the League undertook to investigate the prevalence of leprosy and methods of treatment are now practised. A research center was established at Rio de Janiero where the Health Committee has carried forward many useful experiments. Other centers have been organized by the Health Committee and are closely cooperating with the authorities of countries visited by the disease. The benefits of these isolated experiments are shared by all countries through this central clearing agency of the League. Marked headway has been made, to the point where the nature of this disease is better understood and remedies may therefore be applied.

In 1928 the Health Organization undertook a thorough study of the results obtained in the treatment of syphilis based on analyses of more than twenty-five thousand cases. Detailed case-record cards were kept on the basis of carefully noted results, which enabled the Health Organization to publish an ambitious plan for the successful treatment of this disease. The Health Organization has busied itself with ways of checking loathsome smallpox—a disease that has wrought great havoc in time past, but is now confined primarily to the more backward countries. A Commission of experts has studied with marked success various aspects of this problem with special reference to preventive vaccination and the value of primary vaccination in infancy. The treatment of cancer claimed the attention of the Health Committee in the early years of the League's existence, when a Cancer Committee was appointed to study the various methods of treatment of the disease, and to determine, if possible, the most successful methods of treatment. Through the collection of statistical data the best and most up to date information available has been made accessible to the health authorities of all countries.

The Health Organization has carried forward extensive investigations in the treatment of tuberculosis, sleeping sickness, rabies, trachoma, and sicknesses of infancy. In an effort to improve health conditions, active steps have been undertaken to improve rural hygiene, urban and rural housing, and dietary standards of workers. With reference to dietary standards, the Health Experts have actively cooperated with the International Labor Office, the Economic Section of the League, and the International Institute of Agriculture to determine the most wholesome diet for the workers, taking into account the incomes available for the purchase of foodstuffs. If the problem be rightly approached, the workers are able to consume wholesome food on relatively low family budgets. This is a new and interesting field which promises to bring far-reaching benefits to the working population of the world. A

Committee appointed by the Assembly in 1935 adopted a unanimous report which defined the nutrition problem in its international aspects, and made available information that will guide the governments in directing the attention of the people to the best solution of the problem of consumption.

By no means least in importance has been the work of the Health Organization to standardize sera, vaccines, and biological products. The establishment of international standards for the treatment of diseases will especially benefit those nations that have been backward in such medical experimentations. Coupled with this is the effort to disseminate medical knowledge in the hope that conditions of health throughout the world may thereby greatly improve.

The Health Organization has accepted invitations from various governments to assist in reorganizing and strengthening their health services and has done this with marked success. Bolivia appealed to the Health Organization in 1929 for assistance in reorganizing the Public Health Service, with a view to more effective public supervision over infectious diseases. Sanitary measures were undertaken in Greece in 1928 with the cooperation of the Health Organization, when measures were adopted which materially improved health conditions in that country. Chile likewise invited the League to assist in a study of nutrition problems of that country, which led a Committee of health experts to visit Santiago. The state of health of the people was improved due to the steps taken by the visiting Committee in 1934. China, a backward country in the treatment of diseases, received assistance from the Health Organization in 1929 to combat sickness, known to be rampant in that country. Steps were taken to provide more extensive medical education and train individuals to disseminate information relating to sanitation among the people, and to cope with smallpox and cholera in the populous centers. The Health Organization has received active support from the Rockefeller Foundation, and through this dual effort, far-reaching gains have been made in the development of a sound federal health administration in China.

Czechoslovakia in 1931 requested the Health Organization to assist the national health authorities to develop more effectively the rural public health services as well as other related organizations in various parts of that country. In 1933 Rumania likewise requested assistance to combat pellagra, whereupon an investigation was made by health experts to determine the causes of this malady and propose remedies to overcome it. Other and similar assistance has been extended to Liberia, Siam, South African Union, Bulgaria, as well as France and Japan. The health work of the League has assumed vast proportions and promises to continue as one of the foremost international enterprises.

CHAPTER XI

Intellectual Cooperation

A UNIQUE phase of the League's work may be found in its efforts to promote cooperation in various educational fields, where it is possible, on an international scale. Scholars throughout the world have many interests in common and through organized endeavor are able to share effectively one another's contributions. Impediments do not stand in the way of international intellectual cooperation such as exist in international political relations. Indeed there is not only willingness, but a keen desire on the part of scholars throughout the world to cooperate in making their contributions available to all. The English may find it difficult to see eye to eye with the Italians politically and the French and Germans may be antagonistic toward each other, but scientists, engineers, physicians, artists and other groups in the intellectual world cannot permit national frontiers to act as barriers in the advancement of their callings. Scholars are eager to keep abreast with the world literature in their respective fields, for advances in one country are anxiously awaited in all others. The history of scientific development has been the gradual building up of discoveries and improved processes based on earlier contributions until the work of many men, irrespective of nationality, has culminated in the intricate scientific and technological society of today. This form of international cooperation is genuine and lasting, meriting every encouragement. Thus distinct contributions may be made in stimulating international good will.

Prior to the War, few learned societies existed where scholars could pool their intellectual resources. Hence with the coming into being of the League, a most natural development took place in the formation of a branch of its work in intellectual rapprochement. While the Covenant makes no mention of international intellectual cooperation it comes within the spirit of the Preamble. The object of intellectual cooperation is set forth in a Committee's report of July, 1930, as "international collaboration with a view to promoting the progress of general civilization and human knowledge, and notably the development and diffusion of science, letters and arts." In the advancement of cooperation in the intellectual fields, closer union and better understanding between peoples should follow and thus the creation of a favorable international atmosphere will aid in the guarding of world peace.

In 1922 the Council set up the Committee on Intellectual Cooperation and work was at once begun to find remedies for the sufferings of intellectual workers in various callings as a result of the War. Numerous appeals for assistance had come to the League from Eastern and Southern Europe, and after facing this acute situation the Committee turned its attention to the development of permanent programs. The expansion of work led to the enlargement of the Committee so that it consists of nineteen members, all eminent scholars from various parts of the world including one member from the United States. They are appointed by the Council and meet annually at Geneva, where a full agenda is made up of a wide range of subjects calling for solutions. An Executive Committee was set up in 1930 to carry out the decisions. Seven permanent committees of experts have been chosen to carry forward specialized work. They are: 1. Permanent Committee for Arts and Letters; 2. Advisory Committee on League of Nations' Teaching; 3. Experts' Advisory Committee of the International Museums Office; 4. Directors' Committee of the Institutes of Archaeology and of the History of Art; 5. Committee of Directors of Higher Education; 6. Committee of Library Experts; 7. Committee of Expert Archivists. The Secretariat of the Organization is the Intellectual Cooperation Section of the League, and its duties are to organize meetings, contact the different governments, and maintain a center from which information relating to the work of the League is disseminated.

At the invitation of the French Government, the International Institute of Intellectual Cooperation was established in Paris in 1926. This is really an executive body of the Organization and undertakes to carry out numerous specialized tasks in close conjunction with decisions reached at Geneva. Some forty-five countries are connected with the Institute and its officials represent seventeen nationalities. This body is highly organized and its work covers a wide range of subjects, but more especially those dealing with literary, aesthetic and scientific questions, as well as intellectual rights and education. The Institute is financed by governmental grants, a large share of its funds being supplied by France, and also by donations from individuals and private institutions. The work of the Institute is reported each year to the French Government and to the Coucil, and these reports are in turn communicated to all members of the League. The Institute's program of work is drawn up by the International Committee on Intellectual Cooperation, and its Governing Body consists of all the sitting members of the Committee. As the programs are thus jointly planned, it is difficult to differentiate clearly between the work of the two bodies. The permanent staff of the Institute is able to accomplish much through continuing efforts, whereas the Committee meeting at Geneva assembles at periodic intervals and can only plan broader lines of work.

An International Motion Picture Conference met in Paris in the fall of 1926 with delegates from thirty-one countries present. The Conference voted that "a provisional international committee be appointed immediately with an office in the League of Nations" to work in conjunction with the Committee on Intellectual Cooperation. This plan was not immediately fulfilled, but in 1927 the Council accepted an offer by the Italian Government to found an International Educational Cinematographic Institute in Rome with initial funds to be provided by Italy. The aim was noteworthy, as "the object of the Institute is to encourage the production, distribution, and exchange between the various countries of educational films concerning instruction in art, industry, agriculture, commerce, health, social education, etc., by any means which the Governing Body may consider necessary." Like the Institute of Intellectual Cooperation at Paris, the Cinematographic Institute of Rome is closely aligned with the Committee of Intellectual Cooperation at Geneva. It is engaged in continuous efforts to promote the best forms of visual education. The motion picture industry has become tremendously important and logically lends itself to some form of international control. Films are sent from one country to another and if rightly directed may do much to promote international good will. Films that depict a strong nationalistic bias, or express contempt for other peoples will cause animosity between nations and thus do great harm. It is the purpose of the Institute at Rome to use this great instrument for peace. The Institute has especially directed its efforts toward the circulation of films of an educational nature with particular emphasis on the education of the youth. The showing of films that adversely affect the morals of youth is discouraged, while emphasis is placed upon the increased use of films that visualize moral and intellectual themes. The publications of the Institute lists the worthwhile films in catalogue form and they are distributed widely in all countries.

An international Treaty was concluded in Rome, October, 1933, and had as its object the facilitating of the circulation of films of an international character in all countries. The Institute has directed its efforts to the obtaining of ratifications of this Treaty so that there are now more than twenty countries that have obligated themselves to unite in this commendable work. In 1934 an International Congress on Instructional and Educational Films, attended by delegates from forty countries, met in Rome where broad plans were formulated for the more effective use of films in the schools, and with a view to the exchange of ideas relating to teaching methods in this field. It is planned to have a depository center for films that may be borrowed by educational institutions, and instruction is also given in the use of apparatus, lighting systems, and accessories. The Institute has undertaken to develop the field of television by establishing an information center with an experimental transmitting station, and a demonstration laboratory. The future possibilities in the use of television as an agency of education is yet unknown, but a wide avenue may possibly be opened up in the direction of better relations among nations.

The International Institute for the Unification of Private Law was founded by the Italian Government in 1926 after proposing to the Council that an annual grant would be made by Italy to its upkeep, and like the other Institutes mentioned, would operate under the direction of the Committee on Intellectual Cooperation at Geneva. The Italian proposal was made to the Council and accepted by it when the object was revealed to be a study of the "methods for the assimilation and coordination of private law as between states or groups of states and to prepare for a gradual adoption by the various states of uniform private law legislation." The purposes as here revealed clearly show the need for such a central agency to take the initiative. The Institute for the Unification of Private Law works also in close conjunction with the International Labor Office and the technical organizations of the League. In the first few years its work was largely advisory, but since 1930 it has worked to bring about international treaties on unification of river law, equal treatment of foreigners, uniform laws on bills of exchange and checks, laws relating to sales, arbitral procedure, closer international supervision over copyrights, the publishing contracts, and the legal position of international associations. The Institute has a wide scope in which to operate and if its work is carried forward with vigor, far-reaching achievements should result.

The Committee on Intellectual Cooperation has a comprehensive range of subjects to engage its attention, but they are all directed toward the fulfillment of the aims and purposes of the League. As an example of this, the Organization worked in close conjunction with the Conference for the Reduction and Limitation of Armaments in 1932 when a program of moral disarmament was initiated by the Arms Conference. To foster the aims of the League in various countries, the Committee has undertaken to fix its concept more firmly in the minds of people, and more especially to ensure that school children are instructed in the ideal of peace. As a result of these endeavors a number of governments have taken steps to include in the teaching of history, geography, languages and civics, the newer ideas regarding the inter-dependence of peoples, the settlement of disputes by peaceful methods, and higher regard for other nations. The Committee has induced government officials, responsible for the choice of textbooks, to forsake the use of those which have been incompatible with the theory of good relations among nations. Young men and women have been encouraged to travel and study in foreign countries, for it is felt that in so doing a wholesome appreciation of other peoples will be developed. Young people are urged to familiarize themselves with the songs and folk-lore of foreign countries and thus develop an appreciative attitude toward others.

The Committee, recognizing broadcasting as an agency of good or ill-will among nations, has striven to induce the governments to accept a general treaty obligating them to refrain from making use of the radio in such a way as to give offense to foreign countries. This movement dates from 1931 when the Assembly instructed the Institute of Intellectual Cooperation to undertake an inquiry into all questions raised by the use of broadcasting in regard to good international relations. The following year found experts active in examining conditions relating to the framing of a draft agreement on this subject. The proposed draft was twice submitted to the governments for observations, and inasmuch as a majority of the replies were favorable, the Assembly requested the Council to call a conference, inviting both League and non-League States, to meet in Geneva in September, 1936. Delegates from thirty-seven countries attended and agreed to a general Treaty embodying the purposes and ideals for promoting better mutual understanding between peoples. This Treaty was not signed by the United States as our government does not exercise the kind of control over broadcasts as contemplated in the Treaty. Through the efforts of the Committee a number of governments have already taken note of this work and have encouraged broadcasting for peaceful ends. If rightly employed, radio broadcasting may be utilized to promote international friendship and familiarize the people with the finer traits and gifts of peoples in other lands. This will enrich life as each nation has something constructive to be shared by others. The British Broadcasting Corporation exemplifies this practice to a marked degree by impartially informing the people of Great Britain of the cultural, political, and social life of others. Glaring instances of hostile broadcasts have occurred in central Europe resulting in a frenzy among the people and thus leading to official governmental protests against these practices. The seriousness of such broadcasts is especially marked on the continent of Europe where the ether waves readily carry messages of one country to many others.

A significant step was taken in an Agreement on Radio-Communications, signed at Buenos Aires, June, 1935, by the delegates of six South American countries, which provides concrete measures for the prevention of broadcasts that are likely to offend the feelings of other nations. This Treaty grew out of the preparatory work of the Intellectual Cooperation Organization and was a splendid beginning of what was again attempted in Geneva in 1936.

The growth of well-organized public libraries is comparatively recent in most countries. When wide interest began to be manifested in free libraries, the more advanced governments assumed direct control in devising techniques for the more effective use of their facilities. The organization of libraries proceeded along different lines in various countries so that complicated systems grew up, and little thought was given to superior techniques that may exist in other countries. Like so many other questions that were at one time considered national in scope the library experts realized that they too had problems in common with those of other countries, and thus began in an international way to bring together the best techniques existent in all countries. The benefits from the sharing of one another's experiences led the Committee on Intellectual Cooperation to take advantage of the detached national library systems by attempting to coordinate them into a unified system. A Committee of Library Experts, composed of directors of large central and national libraries, was appointed by the Organization to develop means of coordinating national systems. A similar committee of Archives Experts was set up to carry forward work in this sphere. Plans were formulated for the most desirable construction of buildings for libraries, and of equipment for most effective use. Published material to serve as a guide has been made available to countries wishing to make use of these ideas. This material contains recommendations relating to the cataloguing, the index system, and the training of librarians. A guide to the planning of archives and the effective use of documents have also been studied.

The kind of work undertaken in connection with the public libraries and archives has also been attempted in the organization of museums. An International Museums Office was created and has been particularly successful in devising plans for the protection of works of art and the preservation of historical monuments. Conferences were held in Rome for the preservation of paintings, in Athens for the preservation of artistic and historical monuments, and in Madrid for the study of general museography looking toward the general coordination of effective national administration and the preservation of works of art and historical monuments.

More than one hundred universities and other institutions including some in the United States are members of the Museums Office, and they collaborate in expanding its program of work.

In 1934 the Committee on Intellectual Cooperation recommended the setting up of a National Committee in each country, and this led to the formation of forty-two such organizations including one in the United States. The latter is composed of twenty-eight prominent scholars under the chairmanship of Professor James T. Shotwell. They serve as a link between the International Committee and leading intellectuals in all parts of the world. The National Committees conduct inquiries on the conditions of intellectual life and upon request transmit this information to other national Committees, to their respective governments, and to Geneva. This exchange of information is valuable in drawing attention to the differences in the cultural and scientific life of all countries. In some instances these Committees are official agencies of their governments, but usually their status is independent. International conferences are called at which representatives of these Committees assemble to discuss their mutual problems. A Conference was held at Paris in the summer of 1937 in connection with the Universal Exhibition of Modern Art and Techniques. So important has the work of the National Committees become that an "Intellectual Cooperation Month" was designated in their honor at the Exhibition in Paris for their meetings.

The National Committees collaborated with the Organization in the extension of activities to include social and political sciences affecting international relations. Professor James T. Shotwell took the initiative in proposing these studies as he felt that earlier collaborations during periods when national interests were paramount would serve to guide them in more effective present-day contributions. The first studies began in 1935 and dealt with: The Adaptation of Mechanization to the Conditions of Human Labor; or, Man and the Machine. The Organization is carrying forward this work in collaboration with the International Labor Office.

Since 1928 the Organization has sponsored a Permanent International Studies Conference with the aim of centralizing the work of the principal national institutions which are engaged in the scientific study of international relations. Numerous institutes of this character maintaining high standards have come into being in several countries since the War and their work is now being more closely coordinated for purposes of the scientific study of international relations. Representatives from these national institutes have met in conferences to formulate programs with common aims in view. A meeting in London, 1934, attended by some twenty different groups was typical of the work of the International Studies Conference. This Organization has collaborated with scientific circles in different countries studying many questions relating to foreign policies and mutual political and social relations of peoples, including monetary, agricultural, internal economic, unemployment, and other problems affecting, directly or indirectly, international cooperation. The governmental attitudes toward these matters have varied greatly, and a distinct need existed and still exists for the harmonizing of these views. The Rockefeller Institute made a generous grant for the expansion of the Internal Relations Service in addition to donating large sums for the development of national institutions specializing in the study of these current issues.

The Permanent International Studies Conference met at Madrid in 1936 and devoted itself to the discus-

INTELLECTUAL COOPERATION

sion of "methods of peaceful change" under the direction of Professor James T. Shotwell, and also to a discussion of "university teaching of international relations." The discussions included ethnological questions, raw materials and markets, colonial national and racial problems, and matters relating to the Danube region. These Conference discussions will be continued as it is believed that they are highly important as a means of bringing about better understanding among nations.

In 1930 the Permanent Committee of Arts and Letters was created to study on a high and disinterested plane problems relating to intellectual cooperation. This Committee met in Frankfort, 1932, in connection with the Goethe centenary and from it sprang a series of "conversations" on cultural relations. A session in Madrid, 1933, dealt with the "Future of Civilization," in 1934 the "conversations" at Venice related to "Art and the State" and "Contemporary Arts and Reality," and "conversations" at Nice, 1935, took up "The Intellectual Training of Modern Man and the Purpose of Education."

The recent "conversations" have perhaps been more vital than the earlier ones, in that they have dealt with the "effects of new theories and recent discoveries in physics on intellectual life," the current trends of thought among university students, "The Rôle of the Humanities in the Training of Modern Man," and the "Present Relations between European and American Cultures." These "conversations" bear upon basic matters that vitally affect the relationships of the peoples in each continent of the world. Comparisons were made on the state of intellectual relations between different peoples with the hope of uniting them in peaceful aims.

Another method adopted by the Committee has been

that of "open letters" organized in the form of correspondence between a few chosen scholars able to contribute to modern thought. The critical correspondence is published by the Organization and the first four volumes are: "A League of Minds" dealing with the attitude of intellectuals toward war; "Why War" by Einstein and Freud; "The Mind, Ethics and War"; and "Civilizations" which contains correspondence on "East and West" and "The Northern and Latin Mind." These studies are of particular interest in view of the conflict of different types of cultures. Emphasis is placed upon their possible synthesis rather than the working at cross purposes of differently cultured groups. The above are a few representative titles of numerous other publications by the Organization.

The Committee on Intellectual Cooperation began its work on entirely fresh ground in an experimental way, with no definite standards to gauge the results, such as has been possible in most other League enterprises. In becoming more fully established, the Organization experienced numerous definite achievements. In addition to those already enumerated, the reorganization of public education in China was undertaken by means of sending experts to that country and having Chinese educators visit Europe. By this exchange of personnel, professional and technical education in this backward country was greatly advanced. The Organization has undertaken more adequately to protect inventors, authors, and research scholars, and to ensure renumeration to those who, through creative thinking, benefit mankind. Emphasis has been placed upon the direction of higher education, and the encouraging of cooperation among international student organizations. Unemployment among intellectuals, and more particularly among university students, has, in conjunction with the International Labor Office, come within the jurisdiction of the Organization during recent years. The exact and natural science bodies have been encouraged to collaborate more freely in their respective fields to their mutual benefits. Published collections pertaining to Ibero-American relations, those of Japanese culture with the West, and a similar study on Russia have recently been made available. Closer supervision over international architectural competitions is now administered by the Organization. Control over excavations of international concern, especially in the near East, comes within the purview of this body. Work of this type should in time lead to better understanding among nations.

CHAPTER XII

The United States Cooperates with the League

AFTER refusing to become a member of the League of Nations at its inception, the American Government not only disregarded the League and its activities in its earlier years, but showed a distinctly hostile attitude toward it. Following the War a reactionary wave swept the country and strong isolationist propaganda readily appealed to the people. The ideal of cooperation experienced a sharp setback in the selfish manifestations of the Peace Conference, where the antithesis of internationalism was displayed. But the American delegates carried the high ideals of unselfish interest in international cooperation into that Conference by making no demands for war spoils. Upon the return of the American delegates, however, the fervor cooled and partisan politics resumed its place. The basic concept of the League being a willingness to unite with other nations in achieving useful results, the changed opinion in this country operated to the detriment of our membership in it.

Then came the national election of 1920, when the Republican party tried to make political capital out of any issue. As President Wilson and his party could claim the credit for inaugurating this new world Organization, the political opponents desired to deprive them of this achievement. Partisan politics was responsible for keeping this country out of the League.

Inconsistency dominated the oratory of Republican

campaign leaders in 1920 as some represented the League as a super-state and others compared it to a "rope of sand" with no authority to fulfill its obligations. Thirty of the most prominent members of the Republican party confused the voters still further by issuing a joint statement during the campaign in which they maintained that the election of Mr. Harding was the surest way of getting the United States into an "association of nations." The argument was advanced that the British Empire would have six votes to our one, a view that was without foundation. Much was made of the binding nature of Article 10 of the Covenant. Republican orators maintained that the armed forces of this country would be at the beck and call of the Council to insure the territorial integrity of all members of the League, and this would require the sending of our young men to remote parts of the world to engage in wars. Mr. Harding favored some form of association of nations in the hope of winning the support of many peace-loving citizens, and this too confused the voters. It must be stated that the Republican victory in 1920 did not hinge on League issue alone, and it is doubtful whether a true expression of the voters was obtained in this matter. It is not strange therefore that the early years of its existence should find the political partisans hostile toward the League and its work in the same manner as they had opposed American membership. After winning the election in 1920, largely on the ground of confusing the voters regarding our membership in an association of nations, President Harding stated in his first message to Congress that the United States would "have no part" in the League. America's abstention proved to be a blow to this new Organization as the nation most responsible for giving it birth had with-held its support. The expression was frequently heard in this country that "the League is dead." Confidence in other countries was undermined and especially so as they were in the beginning lukewarm toward the idea.

The opposition of the Harding Administration was expressed in its most extreme form by the failure of the Department of State to answer communications from the Secretariat. The American Consul at Geneva informed the Secretary-General that the United States had no relations with the League and therefore would not reply to his communications. But the work of the League grew wider in scope, including questions in which the United States had a vital interest, and thus our Government could not ignore it altogether. Our earlier contacts were indirect by having the French, Swiss, and Netherlands governments occasionally transmit information from the United States to the League. Numerous private individuals and organizations of this country actively participated in the League's work in one form or another. Elihu Root, a leading American statesman, was appointed by the Council to lay plans for the World Court. The Rockefeller Foundation aided the League in the development of the world health service, and other Americans accepted posts in directing varied League activities.

The growing emphasis upon the non-political phases of the League's work made a strong appeal to Americans as it was felt that this work was wholly detached from international politics. Our Government soon realized that America's vital interests dictated the necessity of our presence. It was not enough that Americans should participate in these deliberations on unofficial missions, but the State Department found it expedient to be present. This was at first rather embarrassing, as it was by no means certain that the member States would welcome us. We began in a halting manner to send "unofficial observers" to certain non-political meetings of the League even before the end of the Harding Administration. It was pointed out that this participation was not to be interpreted as a move toward American membership, but solely for the advancement of her interest. Our Government merely meant to keep up with the growing practice of nations to deliberate on questions of common interest to all.

Full-fledged American participation in the work of the League came late in 1924 when official delegates attended the Second Opium Conference at Geneva, and again in 1925, when a delegation participated in the Conference on Traffic in Arms. Having sensed the benefits of international collaboration, and experiencing no ill effect from it, the American Government grew bolder in accepting invitations to League gatherings. This momentum increased until the time came when the United States participated in practically every conference, and sent representatives to many commissions and committees meeting under the aegis of the League. Some of the Committees in which we have participated are: Health; Traffic in Women and Protection of Children; Double Taxation; Counterfeiting Currency; Maritime Tonnage Measurement; Opium; the Preparatory Commission for the Disarmament Conference; the Council's Committee to draft reforms for Liberia; technical aid to China; the Lytton Commission in Collaboration with the Department of State; and the Organizing Committee of the Council to prepare for the International Economic Conference of 1933. Our Government enjoys official representation on some important permanent committees such as: the Advisory Committee on Social Questions; the Bureau of the Disarmament Conference; and the Opium Advisory Committee. Even the Council meetings have been attended by an official American representative. At a session of the Council in 1932 the American Consul at Geneva met with it in an advisory capacity, and in the following year the American Minister to Switzerland participated in the election of members to the Permanent Central Opium Board.

The Republican party, which in the early years of the League would have no part in it, wrote a significant plank in the platform of 1928 which in part states that "we have most usefully assisted by cooperation in the humanitarian and technical work undertaken by the League, without involving ourselves in European politics by accepting membership." There seems to be no objection to our participation in League conferences where political discussions are omitted. This side of the League's work has, as is indicated elsewhere, developed rapidly and promises to continue to grow in importance as the world becomes more and more interdependent.

The Council, which is entrusted with the duty of calling conferences, has shown a generous attitude by inviting the United States to participate with League members on an equal footing. We have aided in the preparatory work and have sent delegates with full powers to negotiate and sign treaties, some of which have been ratified by the Senate. Insofar as the formulation of international legislation is concerned, the United States is to all intents and purposes a member of the League. But this relationship rests upon uncertain ground, since great doubt exists as to the continued willingness of the Council to invite our Government to participate in conferences. No agreement has been made between the United States and the League relating to a well-defined relationship between the two. Our financial assistance for the conduct of conferences is not definitely established although such contributions have been made. Our delegates attend as "guests." Our Government is disposed to collaborate with other nations in furthering our world-wide interests—and there are many of them—but does not feel obliged to share in the responsibility of creating a strong institution at Geneva. When American interests are discussed in a conference we are anxious to attend, but when they relate to matters affecting other nations we are disposed to remain aloof. A more vigorous participation in international planning, where it does not immediately affect us, would not only strengthen the conference machinery, but would gain the respect of other nations for America's willingness to cooperate. We have a contribution to make to world progress in view of our disinterested position and influence as a great nation. Nothing is to be feared in a more active rôle, and much may be gained for ourselves and others.

The method practiced by the League in formulating international legislation through conferences at which the United States takes part, is roughly as follows: a preparatory or advisory commission is created to explore a field in an effort to determine the need for international agreement. The commission studies the varying views of governments on the subject in order to effect a compromise. A summary of these observations in the form of a compromise is sent to each member state as a draft treaty with requests for comments. If there is some assurance of uniformity, the Council is free to invite the governments to send plenipotentiaries to negotiate and sign a general treaty. In the preparatory work as well as in the conference deliberations the officials of the Secretariat assist in guiding the deliberations along established lines of procedure. The Secretariat is conversant with the conference technique and can plan the deliberations more effectively than would be possible by inexperienced national representatives. It keeps and publishes records and in general performs those duties at conferences which its name implies. As the conference ends, following the signature by the delegates, the governments are called upon to ratify the treaty and thus make it a part of their national legal systems. When reluctance to ratify is shown, the interested officials of the Secretariat, as well as the Council, urge the governments to act.

The more recent League conferences in which the United States has participated are: the Conference on the Limitation of the Manufacture of Narcotic Drugs in 1931; the Disarmament Conference of 1932–34; the London Economic Conference in 1933; and a Conference on Drug Traffic in 1936. The United States has signed or ratified the following League treaties: International Opium Convention of 1925; Convention for the Supervision of the Traffic in Arms and Munitions of War, 1925; Prohibition of Poisonous Gases and Bacteriological Methods of Warfare, 1925; Slavery Convention, 1926; Convention for the Abolition of Import and Export Prohibitions and Restrictions, 1927; International Convention for the Suppression of Counterfeiting Currency, 1929; Protocol Relating to the Accession of the United States . . . to the Permanent Court of International Justice, 1929; Protocol Relating to Military Obligations in Certain Cases of Double Nationality, 1930; Convention for Limiting the Manufacture and Regulating the Distribution of Narcotic Drugs, 1931; Convention for the Regulation of Whaling, 1931; Final Act of the Conference of Wheat Exporting and Importing Countries and the Silver Agreement, 1933; Convention for Facilitating the International Circulation of Films of Educational Character, 1933; and a treaty relating to the Manufacture and Regulation of the Distribution of Narcotic Drugs, 1936. Numerous leading Americans have participated in the international conferences and in some instances very strong delegations have been sent to represent this country. The attitude of the Senate has undergone a marked change in advising ratification of League treaties.

The United States has also cooperated with the League in providing information about this country which may be of help in international planning. The answers to questionnaires cover a wide range of subjects in economic, social, humanitarian, and other fields. Since 1934 the United States has registered its treaties with the League, and they are published with all others in the League of Nations Treaty Series. Prior to that time, the Department of State felt "that in view of the fact that the United States is not a member of the League of Nations it would be inappropriate for this Government to register treaties with the Secretariat." Treaties are now registered with the understanding that the United States assumes no obligations under the Covenant and is not obliged to meet any of the expenses connected with this step. Article 18 of the Covenant obliges all members of the League to register treaties with the Secretariat with the provision that "no such treaty . . . shall be binding until so registered." This provision does not apply to the United States and our action in registering treaties is more a matter of convenience in making it possible to collect all treaties in a single depository. The compilation of treaties in a single series serves a useful purpose to scholars and statesmen who thus may find all inter-governmental agreements in a single publication.

The United States has been reluctant to cooperate with the League as regards to political questions, which proved a stumbling block to our membership. We looked askance upon any move that might entangle us in European politics. Thus in the first decade of the League's existence when many European disputes were settled at Geneva, the United States did not associate itself with them. Since 1930 the scene has shifted to include wars in Asia, Africa, and South America. In the Sino-Japanese imbroglio over Manchuria, the Leticia Boundary Dispute between Colombia and Peru, the war in the Chaco between Paraguay and Bolivia, and the Italo-Ethiopian dispute, the United States concerned itself, due to the fact that our traditional policy was different toward these three continents than toward Europe, and not because our interests were more vitally affected.

Our historic policy toward Europe has been negative in that we have not desired to meddle in political disputes, while in Asia we have assumed a positive role of helpful cooperation. In South America our policy has been one of active interference, predicated upon the Monroe Doctrine—too often to the annoyance of those republics. Our interest in Africa has been negative except in Liberia, which became the home of many freed slaves sent there by the American Colonization Society prior to the Civil War. The United States cooperated with the League in an investigation of reported slavery in this negro Republic in 1931–34, but due to American economic and financial interests little or no headway was made in abolishing it. Since the Firestone Plantations Company has extensive rubber plantations there and the Finance Corporation of America holds bonds payable by Liberia, the United States accepted the invitation of the Council that a Commission be appointed, one member by the United States, one by the Council, and a third by the Liberian Government to study conditions of labor in that country. The Commission found many abuses and recommended plans for their abolition, including a broad program of reform, but the United States could not see eye to eye with the League in these undertakings, as they were supposed to conflict with our interests, and therefore the collaboration between the United States and the League failed in this very necessary undertaking.

The invasion of Manchuria by Japan during the fall of 1931, claimed the attention of our State Department from the outset. The Council of the League also interested itself in this dispute and decided to forward all relevant documents to Washington, for as a signatory of the Pact of Paris and the Nine-Power Treaty, our Government had certain responsibilities to fulfill. Our Secretary of State expressed sympathy to the Council for its efforts to check hostilities. But the rapid military gains by the Japanese caused our State Department to sense the inefficacy of disjointed efforts by the United States and the League in exerting the necessary pressure to terminate this aggression. Secretary Henry L. Stimson indicated his willingness to have a representative of our Government sit as a neutral observer with the Council and to deliberate on questions relating to the treaties to which we were a signatory. The Council lost valuable time in considering the advisability of American participation in the discussions, as Japan strenuously opposed the extending of this privelege to a non-member state. The Council overruled the Japanese objections and Mr. Prentiss Gilbert, American Consul at Geneva, was formally invited to sit in with the Council. The time lost in the discussions of seating the American representative weakened the position of the Council, as the Japanese were thereby able to strengthen their military position during the early days of the invasion. The limited instructions to the American representative made it impossible for him to commit this country to a course of action that might restrain Japan. A later meeting of the Council at Paris found Ambassador Chas. G.

Dawes playing a rôle of still greater aloofness by remaining away from the Council sessions but waiting close by to consult with members of that body, should this prove to our advantage.

The unwillingness of our Government to take a strong stand against Japanese aggression was, of course, no different from the position taken by the member states of the League, as this dispute was far removed from the scenes that affected the immediate interests of most powers. The economic depression had also gripped the world and made the nations more reluctant to venture on untried paths. As a final step in the cooperation of the United States with the League in the Far East, the Secretary of State named one member of a neutral commission that journeyed to the scene of the trouble, where it was hoped that first-hand information would be obtained in fixing responsibility for the crisis and the recommending of a just settlement. During the prolonged discussions Japan advanced to a point where nothing short of complete military conquest of Manchuria would satisfy her. The cooperation of the United States with the League in the Far Eastern crisis appeared to be sufficiently close to lead the Council to believe that we could be counted upon for active support in affecting a just settlement. But, in reality, our middle of the road policy was detrimental to the League and did not enhance American prestige in the Far East. Either wholehearted cooperation or a "hands off" policy would at least have prevented the existing uncertainties.

Another instance of a hesitating policy of cooperation with the League was the interference in the Bolivia-Paraguay dispute over the Gran Chaco boundary. The matter was first called to the attention of the Council in 1928, but no active moves were then made by the League due to the danger of alienating the

United States. The Monroe Doctrine was still in force from the point of view of this country, and League interference in South America might, it was thought, precipitate trouble. The United States was in the meantime interested in settling the dispute, and thus began an independent move to achieve this end. As member states of the League, the two disputants brought their grievances before the League, and, under the Covenant, the Council could not well turn a deaf ear. Neutral countries of South America cooperated both with the United States and with the League, which meant not only a duplication of effort, but the apparent working at cross purposes to achieve the same end. The first active interference by the League in the Chaco dispute was in 1932 in the appointment of a Committee of the Council to follow the events and keep in touch with the Commission of Neutrals on which the United States was represented. The Commission appeared to welcome support from the Council so that the two bodies were drawn together in this work. The neighboring States of Argentina, Brazil, Chile, and Peru also sought to bring the warring sides together.

The attempts at mediation from three sources led to a discussion in the Council of the confusion that had resulted in having various agencies attempt a settlement instead of concentrating the matter in a single authority, the League. This was recognized by the Commission of Neutrals, of which Mr. Francis White, United States official, was Chairman, when it withdrew on June 24, 1933, with a statement that "if there is more than one center of negotiation, confusion and lack of agreement are the inevitable results." Mr. White further stated that the "negotiations can be centered in Geneva, if other peace agencies will take a similar attitude, allowing the League Committee to work with universal support for peace." Heavy fighting continued between Bolivia and Paraguay and the matter came before the Pan-American Conference at Montivedeo. Secretary of State Cordell Hull, leader of the United States delegation, urged the Conference to bring the utmost pressure on the warring parties to end hostilities. This again seems to have confused matters, and the League Commission gave up its task in March, 1934, although the Council continued the work of conciliation. It may be noted, that of the several Commissions seeking to end war in the Chaco, no one was definitely responsible for effecting reconciliation, but all had a part in temporarily bringing an end to the war in October, 1935. The Treaty terminating the war did not finally liquidate the dispute, as the Paraguayan army officers refused to heed a government order demanding the withdrawal of the army. Conciliation efforts were continued by neutral American countries, including the United States, but the warring parties continued their stubborn resistance until it appeared in the summer of 1937 that the deadly struggle would continue.

A dispute between Peru and Colombia over Leticia on the Amazon led to fighting in September, 1932. Thereupon the League and the American States, including this country, moved to settle it. Early in 1933 Colombia appealed to the Council but again there was hesitation in actively interfering in the dispute as it was feared that the United States might oppose this as an interference with the Monroe Doctrine. Our Department of State expressed a willingness to have the League attempt conciliation, whereupon a plan of settlement was immediately undertaken by the Council. The settlement did not prove as difficult as in the case of the Chaco. Colombia and Peru were willing to agree to the formula worked out by a League Commission. League officials supervised the evacuation of the territory with the aid of an international police force, and an agreement was signed by the two countries and ratifications exchanged in September, 1935, thus bringing an end to the dispute.

In the Italo-Ethiopian dispute that began in 1934, the United States was destined to come into contact with the League, not by way of cooperation, but through the conflict of world-wide economic interests. The League for the first time in its history imposed sanctions against an aggressor (in this case Italy) and our trade relations with that country had definite bearing upon League action. Italy had extensive trade relations with us, and to continue it would discourage the League powers in imposing sanctions. A neutrality law was in force in this country to stop the shipment of arms and munitions of war to belligerents, which the President promptly enforced when the Italian army invaded Ethiopia in October, 1935. This step gave little encouragement to the League as its members not only desired to embargo arms and munitions, but also materials that might be used in war. League embargoes covering materials not included on the American list would permit Italy to obtain them here and thus be able to carry out her objectives. The President could not, under existing laws, deprive Italy of the necessary supplies, and the League's efforts in that direction were paralyzed. In October, 1935, the Assembly voted to place an embargo on arms and munitions to Italy. The Committee also worked out measures to prohibit the exportation of raw materials and the granting of loans to Italy. The latter provision was effective as Italy could not float loans in this country due to a law that prohibited the nations that had defaulted in the payment of their public debts from borrowing money in the United States. The real issue was in our willingness to supply raw materials to Italy when fifty-two other countries were seeking to bar such shipments. They also refused to import goods from Italy which in turn made it very difficult for her to purchase greater quantities here for lack of gold and foreign exchange. Her gold stock dwindled rapidly as her purchases from us increased.

Secretary of State Cordell Hull issued a statement on November 15, 1935, which reads in part as follows: "The American people are entitled to know that there are certain commodities such as oil, copper, trucks, tractors, scrap iron and scrap steel which are essential war materials although not actually arms, ammunition, or implements of war, and that according to recent government trade reports, a considerably increased amount of these is being exported for war purposes. This class of trade is directly contrary to the policy of this government as announced in official statements of the President and Secretary of State, as it is also contrary to the general spirit of the recent neutrality act." As regards United States exports to Italian Africa, the Department of Commerce reports show an increase in monthly averages from $25,403 in the first ten months of 1934, to $359,702 in the corresponding period of 1935. American citizens were thus disposed to derive war profits at the expense of human lives, and this was possible due to the inadequacy of our neutrality law. Germany was not bound by League sanctions and was therefore also a factor in weakening its efforts. Although our Government insisted upon pursuing a neutral policy during the entire course of the Italo-Ethiopian dispute, it can hardly be said that this aim was achieved, for to supply a country with materials that will aid her in the prosecution of war hardly comes within the true conception of neutrality. Neutrality, as rightly conceived, does not consist in defeating the purposes of fifty-two nations, but rather in placing no obstacles in their paths to prevent them from restraining an aggressor. Our so-called neutrality aided Italy, as was indicated by Premier Mussolini when he declared that the American Congress had "rejected every proposal to enlarge the list of products at present under embargo and had not taken into the slightest account all Geneva's solicitations." He stated that "as Italians we cannot fail to receive with satisfaction this political direction on the part of the United States. . . ." The President and Secretary of State, in addition to millions of citizens throughout the country, were in sympathy with the League's efforts to stem Italian aggression, but under existing law no concrete expression could be given to this feeling. The occupation of Ethiopia by the Italian armies in the spring of 1936 led the League to abandon sanctions and also caused President Roosevelt to issue a proclamation revoking the embargo on arms and munitions of war.

On April 29, 1937, Congress enacted a permanent neutrality law which contains the essential provisions of previous legislation including the embargo on arms and ammunition and prohibits loans and credits, both of which apply to belligerents. The President is authorized to forbid American vessels from carrying "certain articles or materials" other than arms and ammunition and prohibit exportation of "articles or materials" until payment is made and ownership transferred to belligerents. The President may embargo more "implements of war" than was possible previously, but he may not include "raw materials" although they are essential in the conduct of war. The existing neutrality law of the United States would not operate to the advantage of the League should occasion arise when it again imposes sanctions.

Other occasions have arisen when America's course of action toward the coordinated efforts of the League was questioned. One such instance occurred in the discussions of the Disarmament Conference when certain countries were reluctant to agree to arms reduction unless they could know in advance what the position of the United States would be in case of international action to check an aggressor. In answer to this, Mr. Norman Davis, American delegate, read a carefully prepared speech before the Conference on May 22, 1933, in which he announced our position, stating that "we are ready not only to do our part toward the substantive reduction of armaments but, if this is effected by general international agreement, we are also prepared to contribute in other ways to the organization of peace. In particular, we are willing to consult the other states in case of a threat to peace, with a view to averting conflict. Further than that, in the event that the states, in conference, determine that a state has been guilty of a breach of the peace in violation of its international obligations and take measures against the violator, then if we concur in the judgment rendered as to the responsible and guilty party, we will refrain from any action tending to defeat such collective effort which these states may thus make to restore peace." This declaration, far-reaching as it then seemed, hinged upon the reduction of arms, and as this did not materialize, the pronouncement came to naught. A very interesting and logical position for the United States is here set forth as it is recognized that we will put no obstacles in the way of collective effort to maintain peace. This principle stands a chance of being tested under our present neutrality law. The possibility of not handicapping the League in its collective efforts may be all that can be hoped for so long as we, a non-member, do not actively cooperate in its work to maintain peace.

Until the United States became a member of the

International Labor Organization by a joint resolution of Congress on June 16, 1934, our Government had no official dealings with it. The Organization was set up at the Paris Conference of 1919 where leading Americans were active in its creation. But after the first Conference, which met at Washington, our only contact for fourteen years was by Americans appointed to commissions in a private capacity. The Organization maintained a branch office in Washington to collect information for studies relating to world-wide social and labor conditions. Our membership came about not as a result of prolonged agitation or even publicity, but in a rather unannounced manner when Congress authorized the President to accept membership on condition that "the President shall assume on behalf of the United States no obligation under the Covenant of the League of Nations." The public has scarcely been aware of this step and to publicize it might have led to the belief that we were entangled in a League agency. Since we became a member, the United States has been active in initiating labor legislation including three significant proposals that were accepted by the International Labor Conference in June, 1937. An International Textile Conference was held in Washington in April, 1937, at which more than twenty textile-producing countries were represented. Plans for the improvement of conditions in the textile industry, and especially for the modification of the hours of work were formulated. If American membership in this body proves to be distinctly beneficial, and political opposition is not directed against it, we may be encouraged to draw closer to the second great Institution at Geneva.

American attitude toward the Permanent Court of International Justice, commonly called the "World Court," has been more favorable than toward the

League, since it is legal and not political disputes that are settled by this body. The United States has for a long time been a leader in promoting arbitration, and it therefore seemed logical that, with the creation of the World Court at the close of the War, we should be a member. Like the League and the Labor Organization, the Court was created largely through the initiative of Americans. Having rejected membership in the League, the Harding Administration nevertheless took steps to obtain ratification of a Treaty that would make us a Court member. No definite action was taken by the Senate until January 27, 1926, when a membership Resolution was voted favorably, but with five reservations, the last of which would have given the United States a veto on advisory opinions "touching any dispute or question in which the United States has or claims an interest." No other country enjoyed what amounted to absolute veto power in submitting questions to the Court for advisory opinions, hence the other members would not agree to American membership with this reservation.

A Committee of Jurists met in Geneva in 1929, with Elihu Root as a member, to consider the revision of the World Court Statute, primarily in order to overcome the objections of the United States Senate. The Protocol embodying the changes was approved by most of the member states of the Court and was submitted to the Senate for approval in January, 1935. During the discussions in the Senate it appeared that the necessary two-thirds majority would vote favorably on the question, but the strong isolationist Senators began to make their influence felt by referring to the Court as an integral part of the League. This, in addition to strong opposition by certain isolationist newspapers and radio commentators, caused some Senators to become weak-kneed and when the vote was taken, on January 29, fifty-two Senators voted for and thirty-six against the proposal. The lack of the necessary two-thirds was above all else due to the fear of American entanglements in European affairs— a fear altogether groundless. Reference to the "World Court of the League of Nations" as propaganda against American membership caused widespread fear of commitments over which we would have no control in the future and indicated that a high percentage of the American public is ill-informed regarding the binding nature of such a treaty.

Under the existing rules of the World Court the United States may bring cases before that body for adjudication, but the seeming impropriety of this action would act as a deterrent. The United States is a member of the Permanent Court of International Arbitration, often referred to as the "Hague Court," but this is in no true sense a court, as its membership is not composed of a continuing panel of judges. The usefulness of the Hague Court has been largely destroyed with the advent of the World Court, for most nations turn to the latter body for the settlement of legal disputes. Leading jurists are elected to the World Court for a term of nine years. Their decisions are widely read by international lawyers, hence unfair judgments would quickly bring this body into disrepute. The record of the decisions of the World Court has received the commendation of legal specialists. The United States would most likely be in a better position to obtain just decisions before such a responsible Court, whereas decisions of the older Hague Court have been severely criticized for their unfairness to us. No valid arguments can be advanced for America's refusal to become a member of the World Court, and it is only due to an ill-informed public, swayed by isolationist propaganda, that prevents American entrance. Even as a member, our independence of action would be assured, as the United States would not be required to be a party to a dispute before the Court without its consent.

The same independence would not appear to exist if we were a member of the League, for under Article 10 of the Covenant the members are obliged to unite in preserving "the territorial integrity and existing political independence of all members of the League." While this obligation seems to be clear and definite, the same Article places upon the Council the responsibility of deciding "upon the means by which this obligation shall be fulfilled." American membership on the Council would make it possible for her to decide in each dispute what course should be pursued, and no move by that body could, under the rules of procedure, divert us from it. The history of League deliberations affecting international disputes reveals the interesting fact that members, other than the disputants, have in such instances made decisions of their own choosing. The effectiveness of sanctions as envisaged by the framers of the Covenant has not been fulfilled, and the peace machinery has been weakened. But this by no means destroys the usefulness of the League, as is attested by the record of its achievements. Too much concern has been given to political commitments, and not enough to the practical means of settling controversies by peaceful means.

The United States will not sign a political treaty which binds it in advance to a given course of action, wanting to preserve its freedom of decision in every contingency. Where such freedom exists, no danger can arise from consultation with other governments on questions relating to the furtherance of international peace. At times when peace is threatened in any part of the world there is a strong impulse to avoid war, and thus the first thought at such times is to declare our neutrality. The larger view of the dangers and economic repercussions involved in war does not sufficiently impress most persons. The best interest of our people, which should be kept uppermost in mind during such crises, may be best protected by cooperating with other nations to prevent their occurrence. It cannot be too strongly urged that the United States would be unable to ensure its safety by pursuing a policy of isolation. The alternative is to cooperate through the existing international organizations. One of the most important provisions in the Covenant is embodied in Article 19 which places a responsibility on member states to consider "international conditions whose continuance might endanger the peace of the world." Sufficient thought has not been given to the full implications of this Article in seeking to adjust the conditions that give rise to international rivalry. The United States can contribute much to international stability by working toward an adjustment of numerous economic, financial, and other matters affecting the well-being of all nations.

Closer American cooperation with other nations offers a degree of encouragement in that there has been a growing realization of the shortcomings of isolationism and an increasing interest in international affairs. The present Administration has pursued a positive foreign policy in seeking to cultivate the friendship of other nations, and more especially the South American Republics. But the Administration can go no further in this direction than public opinion will permit. At the Woodrow Wilson Foundation Dinner, December 28, 1933, President F. D. Roosevelt said "Today the United States is cooperating openly in the fuller utilization of the League of Nations machinery than ever before. I believe that I express the views of my countrymen when I state that the policies, the old alliances, the old combinations and balances of power, have proved themselves inadequate for the preservation of world peace. The League of Nations, encouraging as it does the extension of non-aggression pacts, of reduction of armaments agreements, is a prop in the world peace structure, and it must remain." While disavowing a desire to become a member, the President revealed the close relationship between the United States and the League in constructive undertakings.

The peace forces of the country are very strong but have not in the past been able to unite on the most effective means of preventing war. In so far as it went, the Pact of Paris, 1928, received universal support, as all agreed that the settlement of disputes should be brought about only by pacific means. Opinion has been divided as regards American membership in the League, with perhaps a larger number favoring this step than many realize. The political changes in some governments of Europe from democracies to dictatorships have discouraged many who looked upon the League as an effective peace Institution. Its very nature presupposes freedom of discussion and the formulation of public opinion which is not possible under dictatorial régimes. However with the popular interest in foreign affairs as expressed in this country the technique of League deliberations should make a strong appeal.

Polls have been conducted from time to time indicating the strong sentiment in favor of American membership in the League. In Massachusetts—where a "question of public policy" may be put on an official ballot when a sufficient number of petitioners request it—a popular referendum on American membership in the League was held in 1932 and in 1934. In each election two-thirds of all votes cast favored American membership in the League. It cannot be said that a similar vote in other parts of the country would show a like result, but other polls conducted by papers and church organizations indicate a very strong sentiment in favor of League membership. Organized effort to obtain American membership in the League is carried forward on a broad front. The organization having this as a definite objective is the League of Nations Association, 8 West 40th Street, New York City. Its purpose is "the cultivation of such public opinion as will influence the Government of the United States to cooperate to the fullest extent practicable in the activities of the League of Nations, and to enter the League of Nations at the earliest possible date." Aside from the immediate objective of working for America's entrance into the League, the Association has at present a broader program as follows: 1. United States cooperation with the League of Nations in the furtherance of political and economic justice and in its humanitarian activities; 2. Constructive efforts towards reducing trade restrictions and economic nationalism; 3. A "neutrality" policy for the United States consistent with the principles of the Pact of Paris; 4. The reduction of armament by international agreement; 5. A "good neighbor policy" consonant with the principle of collective security; and 6. Utilization of our membership in the International Labor Organization toward the achievement of social justice. This broader program is indicative of the part that the United States can perform in cooperation with other nations.

A very significant move of recent date was the acceptance by the National Peace Conference, 8 West 40th Street, New York City, of a statement of principle which favors American membership in the League. The National Peace Conference was organized to coordinate the activities of the leading peace organizations of the country, and forty such national organizations comprise its membership. To bring about the abolition of war the Conference included among other principles the statement that "The United States should join the League of Nations on terms of the 'Pope Resolution' which provides that the United States shall not be obliged to adopt measures which might involve the use of armed force; that the Kellogg-Briand Pact be regarded as the fundamental principle of the Covenant; and that the decision as to what action shall be taken by the United States in case the peace of nations is threatened, shall rest with the government of the United States acting according to the Constitution." This statement defines a safe course that may be pursued by the United States in accepting League membership. It is a very significant fact that so many leading peace organizations have accepted this statement of policy in their peace programs.

The Resolution referred to was introduced by Senator James P. Pope of Idaho in the Senate on May 7, 1935, calling for acceptance of League membership by the United States upon the terms and conditions as follows:

"WHEREAS, the United States is dedicated to the policy of the good neighbor, that is to say, to the mutual respect of the right and obligations of nations; and

WHEREAS, the recovery of economic prosperity can never be fully achieved without that stability of conditions which can only come through international peace and security; and

WHEREAS, it is to the manifest advantage of the United States to cooperate with other nations to this end; and

WHEREAS, the League of Nations, with 59 states as members, is an instrument of the creation of a world-wide economic stability, a permanent agency for mediation, the living symbol of the will to peace, and the only common meeting ground for the nations of the world; and

WHEREAS, the League of Nations has in the course of its history established the principle that its members assume no obligations to aid in the enforcement of peace without the consent of their respective governments, acting in accordance with their own constitutional methods and with due regard to their traditional policies and geographical situation; and

WHEREAS, it is therefore apparent that membership in the League of Nations upon these understood and agreed conditions would be consonant with and in furtherance of the vital interests of the United States: Now, therefore, be it

Resolved by the Senate and House of Representatives of the United States of America in Congress assembled, That the President is hereby authorized to notify the appropriate authority of the League of Nations that the United States accepts its membership in the League of Nations on the following terms and understandings:

(1) That the obligation of the Pact of Paris not to resort to war as an instrument of national policy is recognized as the fundamental and guiding principle of the Covenant: and

(2) That the provisions of the Covenant of the League of Nations relating to cooperation in the prevention of war shall

not be interpreted as obligating the United States to adopt measures which might involve the use of armed force; and that the decision as to what action shall be taken by the United States in case the peace of nations is threatened or violated shall rest with the Government of the United States acting according to the Constitution."

While the Resolution was not immediately pressed for action, it indicates a popular viewpoint as the basis on which the Government might accept membership. The reservations herein noted are necessary in view of the traditional mode of thinking that has developed in this country. In actual practice, no reservations are needed that will not oblige the United States to make decisions against its own choosing, as no League member does this, but as a double measure of safety the reservations may be beneficial to appease the overcautious. The task is clearly outlined for the next move by the United States in cultivating the friendly relations of other nations, and it is only a question as to whether the people are willing to measure up to these opportunities.

PART THREE

SEMI-LEAGUE ORGANIZATIONS

CHAPTER XIII

The International Labor Organization

The province of law in labor's behalf has now become well established. In this and other countries such policies have been moving steadily in the direction of greater benefits to labor. This has not always been true. At the beginning of the last century the general attitude of government toward labor was one of hostility. Various laws were enacted here and abroad which benefited the employer at the expense of labor. In 1799 and 1800, the English Parliament passed acts known as Combination Laws which declared labor unions and strikes illegal while a French Law of Coalitions (1791) had like aims. American courts early declared labor unions to be combinations engaged in criminal conspiracy and hence illegal.

Through prolonged agitation by workers and reformers a new stage was reached in the attitude of government toward labor. This was known as the laissez-faire or "hands off" policy. The British Parliament enacted laws in 1871 and 1875 which legalized picketing. A similar law was passed by the French Parliament in 1884. The position of government was definitely non-commital in such instances. This negative policy of government applied in general to all fields of economic activity. During the first half of the last century the idea gained acceptance that the function of government should be limited to that of maintaining order in society. Thomas Jefferson's dictum that "that government is best which governs least" very well expressed this view.

The policy of non-interference of government in labor problems could not continue in rapidly growing industrial countries. Labor was placed in an unfavorable position when bargaining with the employer. The result was low wages and deplorable working conditions. The workers in industrial countries won popular sympathy and awakened the social consciousness of the people, aided by a greater diffusion of education among the masses and the widening of the ballot which led to the enactment of labor laws. Especially was this true in the early part of the twentieth century which witnessed the growth of social legislation in France and England inspired, perhaps, by social reforms of Germany. These laws, of varying character, were designed to benefit the laboring classes. The re-entrance of government into business was now in behalf of labor, and against the employer. Earlier, when labor was unrestrained by government, the way was prepared for the formation of labor unions. These organizations grew rapidly, and proved effective in bringing about higher wages and better working conditions. The position of labor groups was therefore improved, first, by assistance from government in furthering their interest; and second, by the ability to organize and fight their own battles against the employer. The improved conditions of labor served to raise the standard of living of the masses and bring greater prosperity in those countries where the interests of labor were enhanced.

Some countries advanced more rapidly than others in the enactment of labor laws. These unequal conditions tended to create a sympathetic feeling between the laboring groups of one country and those of other countries, which cut across frontiers, in an effort to improve the status of labor on an international scale. Former national labor problems were destined to fall within the scope of inter-governmental action. This form of cooperation is quite recent, as is all international cooperation in non-political fields. The history of international labor legislation furnishes one of the best examples of a growing movement to transfer what was once considered a national problem into the international realm.

As previously stated, favorable national legislation in behalf of labor led to an effort to extend these benefits on an international scale. To achieve this aim the International Association for Labor Legislation was organized, which held annual congresses in various European cities from 1900 to the outbreak of the World War. The result of this private initiative was to stir up greater international interest in behalf of labor. It was largely due to the Association's effort that the Swiss Government was able to induce several European governments to send delegates to an International Conference on the Protection of Labor which met at Berne, September 1906. The Conference concerned itself particularly with the drawing up of treaties respecting the use of white phosphorus in the match industry and the employment of women in night work. White phosphorus, which is poisonous, proved highly injurious to the workers in the match industry. Red phosphorus, on the other hand, is not poisonous, but is more costly, and hence some countries continued to use the white product. The unequal costs placed the country using the white phosphorus in an advantageous position in the sale of matches in world markets, which discouraged all countries in the use of red phosphorus. Only through an agreement among all match manufacturing countries was it possible to induce each government to act and this was made possible by the signing of the treaty at Bern. This treaty as well as one relating to women employed in night work were put into force by a large number of governments. A beginning had now been made in the enactment of labor legislation through coordinated efforts by various governments.

Productive efforts by the governments working together in behalf of labor were interrupted by the World War. However, international labor organizations, conscious of their strength, commanded the attention of the governments during hostilities. The governments recognized the growing solidarity and were ready to lend a sympathetic ear to the demands of labor not only during the War but at the Peace Conference. The readiness of the governments to give organized labor a voice in the Peace Conference was no doubt furthered by a growing spirit of unrest and the threat of Communism among the workers of Europe. A strong revolt against all forms of war was making itself felt which led to a greater willingness on the part of governments to give labor a share in the building of a new social order. Demand for representation in the Peace Conference was made by various national labor bodies with the result that when the Conference met a Commission was appointed to "inquire into the conditions of employment from the international aspect, and to consider the means necessary to secure common action on matters affecting conditions of employment, and to recommend the form of a permanent agency to continue such inquiry and consideration in cooperation with and under the direction of the League of Nations." Samuel Gompers, then President of the American Federation of Labor, was appointed chairman of the Commission which drafted what finally became Part XIII of the Treaty of Versailles, which is the Charter of the now existing International Labor Organization.

The purpose of the International Labor Organization

is set forth in the Preamble of the Charter which states that: "Whereas the League of Nations has for its object the establishment of universal peace, and such a peace can be established only if it is based upon social justice; . . . whereas also the failure of any nation to adopt humane conditions of labor is an obstacle in the way of other nations which desire to improve the conditions in their own countries; the High Contracting Parties, moved by sentiments of justice and humanity as well as by the desire to secure the permanent peace of the world, agree to the following . . ." It will be noted that the purpose of the League is the establishment of peace whereas the Labor Organization goes beyond this and has for its aim the improvement of labor conditions which it considers the basis for universal peace. Part I of the Treaty of Versailles contains the Covenant of the former while Part XIII forms the Charter of the latter.

The Charter states that the membership of this Organization shall be the same as that of the League. While this rule generally holds, there have been and still are some, exceptions. Germany was admitted to membership, prior to her entrance into the League, and the United States became a member on August 20, 1934, without becoming a member of the League. Brazil withdrew from the League but retained membership in the Labor Organization. The membership of this Organization is greater than that of the League as the only country of importance outside is Germany. Sixty-one national governments were members in 1936.

The Charter provides for the setting up of a permanent organization to "be established at the seat of the League of Nations as part of the organization of the League." The Organization's budget is financed by funds out of the League's treasury. The annual appropriation amounts to $2,000,000 of which the United States Government contributes upward of

Keystone View Company

SAMUEL GOMPERS, CHAIRMAN OF THE COMMISSION WHICH CREATED THE INTERNATIONAL LABOR ORGANIZATION

$200,000. The dependence of the International Labor Organization on the League for funds does not in any way make it subservient to the League, for the two organizations are autonomous, each operating within its own field.

The International Labor Organization consists of: 1. the General Conference which is composed of the representatives of the member states, and may be compared to the Assembly of the League; 2. the Governing Body which in some ways corresponds to the League Council; and 3. the International Labor Office which is organized along similar lines as the Secretariat of the League.

The General Conference is composed of four representatives of each member state of whom two represent the government, one the organized workers, and the fourth the employer groups. Each country has four votes in the General Conference as delegates do not vote as a unit. The procedure of the General Conference presupposes a clash of interests between the representative of the workers and of the employers, thus affording the delegates representing the governments an opportunity to take sides with one or the other in deciding questions to the best interest of the general public. The responsibility for the choice of non-government delegates rests upon each member state and such choice is made in agreement with the most representative workers organization of the country where such exist, and the other in agreement with the most representative employers' organization. The American Federation of Labor nominates the workers' delegate (in 1937 the Committee on Industrial Organization did this) and the United States Chamber of Commerce the employers' delegate, the two non-government representatives from this country. Some difficulty has arisen in the General Conference over the seating of certain delegations as the employer-worker relation envisaged in the Charter does not exist in all countries. Italy has abolished trade unions and after prolonged discussion in the General Conference the Italian Government was permitted to seat delegates chosen by the Fascists corporations. Russia on the other hand has abolished the employer groups of that country and hence no clear line of demarcation can be drawn from divided groups interests in that country.

The General Conference meets at least once a year at Geneva and each session lasts about one month. It elects its own President and committees and adopts rules of procedure governing the sessions. The principal function of the Conference is the adoption of draft treaties and recommendations relating to the improvement of labor laws throughout the world. At these large gatherings opportunity is given for full discussions of all vital problems affecting labor. Extended debate on a proposed treaty or recommendation precedes final adoption. A majority of two-thirds vote cast by the delegates present is necessary before treaties are submitted to member states for ratification. The formality of signing a treaty differs from diplomatic conferences where it is customary for the head of each delegation to affix his signature in behalf of his government. Labor treaties or conventions, are authenticated by the signature of the President of the Conference and the Director of the International Labor Organization, and the treaties and recommendations are then deposited with the Secretary-General of the League. Copies are sent to each member state and they in turn communicate all ratifications to the Secretary-General. When sufficient ratifications are deposited (two will often suffice) a treaty goes into force in those countries which have forwarded their ratifications. Undue delay in these steps is avoided as each of the members is obliged to submit draft treaties or recommendations to the ratifying authorities for action within a period of eighteen months. Only if a member ratifies is an obligation assumed to enforce a labor treaty. Detailed provisions are made in the Charter whereby pressure may be brought against a member failing to execute a treaty thus ratified, but few such attempts have been made and they have met with little success.

Delay in the enactment of labor legislation was occasioned by a change in Conference procedure (1926) which permits full discussion of a proposed treaty in the first year and a formal vote the second year. This delay affords the members an opportunity to approve or disapprove a proposal in advance and thus avoid the danger of wholesale failures of ratifications. The full year period in the framing of a labor treaty permits the collecting of data to guide the delegates in their deliberations. This early expression of opinion by governments is also made possible by the practice of transmitting the agenda of the Conference to the members, to reach them four months before the session.

In federal states jurisdiction over labor legislation rests not with the central government but with the administrative subdivisions. Authorities are divided over the question of the power of the United States to ratify and enforce labor treaties. Precedent seems to favor the view that the national government may extend its jurisdiction into various fields under the treaty-making power of the Constitution where otherwise such exercise of authority would be unconstitutional. Whether the United States Government could, by ratifying labor treaties, supplant the states in the field of labor legislation is open to serious question. The Charter of the International Labor Organization stipulates that where federal states are thus limited in power the labor treaties are to be regarded as recommendations only and no action on ratification is necessary. The Congressional resolution which provided for membership by the United States in the International Labor Organization implies the lack of jurisdiction of the Federal Government over labor legislation through ratification of labor treaties. The Congressional resolution states that "special provision has been made in the Constitution of the International Labor Organization by which membership of the United States would not impose or be deemed to impose any obligation or agreement upon the United States to accept the proposals of that body as involving anything more than recommendations for its consideration. . . ." With this position taken by Congress the only obligation which rests upon the government of the United States is to bring such "recommendations" before the "authorities within whose competence the matter lies," which in this country are the states. The Federal Constitution clearly prohibits the states from entering into treaty relations with foreign powers, hence doubt may be cast upon the value which this country receives from membership in the Labor Organization. The value of membership may be found not so much in the effort to improve our labor laws as through cooperation with other member states in the improvement of labor conditions throughout the world, which will indirectly benefit this country.

While the General Conference formulates treaties and recommendations, the vast amount of preparatory work required for each conference is under the direction of a Governing Body, composed of thirty-two members of which sixteen represent governments and the rest the workers and employers. Of the sixteen government representatives eight are chosen by member states of chief industrial importance and the remaining eight by other government delegations at the Conference. As the organization and method of the General Conference has often been compared to that of the Assembly of the League so also has comparison been made with respect to the similar duties of the Governing Body and the Council of the League. While both bodies exercise executive functions, the comparison should not be carried too far. The Governing Body prepares the budget of the Labor Organization and submits it to the Assembly. The Governing Body supervises the work of the Labor Office, including the appointment of a Director. At least four meetings are held annually and the period of office of each member is three years. Decisions are taken by a majority vote. The duties of this Body are largely routine and thus do not come prominently before the public eye.

The International Labor Office consists of about four hundred international officials, who have duties similar to the Secretariat of the League. This staff is housed in an imposing building situated on the bank of Lake Geneva. Positions are open to men and women on the basis of competitive examinations with the result that highly skilled persons are chosen from all parts of the world to fill the staff. Much of the work is technical dealing with all phases of labor problems. The general duties of the International Labor Office are to collect and distribute information "on all subjects relating to the international adjustment of conditions of industrial life and labor, and particularly the examination of subjects which it is proposed to bring before the Conferences, with a view to the conclusion of international conventions, and the conduct of such special investigations as may be ordered by the Conference." A vast amount of research is carried on through the Labor Office, as collection of material on all phases of labor problems and the publication of numerous studies constitute an important part of its work. The Labor

Office contains a splendid library and press-cutting service which easily makes it the leading information center for the study of questions relating to labor. Direct contact, without diplomatic formalities, is maintained with various government departments, labor-employer organizations, cooperatives and so forth. A vast amount of work is required to translate the data collected from all parts of the world. The official languages of the Labor Office are English and French, and all publications appear in both languages. Branch offices are maintained in the capitols of all important countries including Washington, D. C.

The Labor Office is divided into four main divisions: Diplomatic, Research, Intelligence, and Administrative, over each of which there is a Chief of Division whose duties correspond to those of the Under-Secretariat General and Directors of the League Secretariat. Each of the four divisions is subdivided into sections with a Chief of Section. The detailed system of organization makes possible the expansion of work in numerous directions.

The Diplomatic Division is organized for the purpose of making the needed preparations for conferences; carrying on official correspondence with governments; acting as Secretariat of the Governing Body, the Conference and numerous committees. It reports on the ratification of labor treaties; keeps a record of official meetings; prepares the official bulletin, and undertakes the study of labor conditions in the Far East, the colonies, protectorates, and mandates. The Research Division takes in the bulk of the work undertaken at the Labor Office, which includes preparation of statistical studies relating to labor; the collection of statistics relating to prices, labor conditions, cost of living, wages, housing and so forth. This Division also collaborates with the statistical services of the League. The Research Division compiles studies relating to the labor legislation in force, by making a comparative study of existing labor laws. The methods of enforcement of such laws, with special reference to efficiency, come under the jurisdiction of this Division. Judicial decisions affecting labor as well as the varied legal systems come under the purview of this body. Studies

THE INTERNATIONAL LABOR OFFICE

relating to collective agreements, such as hours, wages, and conditions of labor are studied as are all efforts of conciliation and arbitration of labor disputes. Studies are made relating to working conditions of women and children, night work, leisure and technical training in scientific methods as applied to industries. The Research Division concerns itself with the study of emigration, the protection of foreign workers, the study of laws affecting immigrants, and prepares published material on these subjects. Studies are made relating to unemployment, relief, insurance, emergency works and methods used for finding employment. Extensive studies have been carried on during the years of the depression relating to unemployment. A study of the disabled on account of industrial accidents, and war as well as compensation relating to each is studied. Extended researches are carried on relating to agricultural labor in its many aspects. Close collaboration is maintained with the International Institute of Agriculture at Rome and with important agricultural organizations. The Health Service compiles studies concerning industrial hygiene, unhealthy occupations and laws governing them. Cooperation is maintained with the health organization of the League. The Safety Service prepares reports of factory inspection in industrial countries, accident prevention, and safety measures in force to prevent industrial accidents.

The Intelligence and Liaison Division maintains services relating to employers, workers and cooperative organizations in their relations with one another. General information and documentation service is maintained, and the library assists in the diffusion of information obtainable at the Labor Office. The fourth or Administrative Division deals with all questions relating to the staff finances, supplies, and the general office organization. This division examines, translates, and prepares for printing and distribution all publications of the Labor Office.

This array of undertakings by the Labor Office establishes it as an organization which fills a great need in the formulation of international standards of labor laws. The work of the Labor Office is designed to pave the way for the unification of labor legislation throughout the world. Governments hesitate to enact proper labor laws as they are thereby placed at a competitive disadvantage in world markets with states that permit the exploitation of labor, thereby lowering the costs of production. The problem is clearly one for international action which is brought about by labor treaties agreed to by the General Conference. The major share of the preparatory work which makes labor treaties possible is carried forward by the Labor Office. Hence it may be said that the successes in the achievement of international labor legislation is in no small measure due to the Labor Office itself.

The achievements thus far of the International Labor Organization are both encouraging and discouraging, depending upon one's viewpoint. A serious handicap is the failure of member states to ratify labor treaties or even submit them to national legislatures. Frequent violations of the labor Charter have been found in the failure of ratifying states to enforce such treaties although provisions are made in the Charter to bring pressure to bear upon defaulting states. Such measures, however, have frequently proved ineffective. Publicity and persuasion are employed, too often of no avail. The International Labor Organization has sometimes wasted efforts and incurred expenses not commensurate with results. While such criticisms are not groundless, it must be said in defense of the Labor Organization that all forms of international cooperation have suffered during the years of the economic depression. If future years hold out hope for better relations among nations, the Labor Organization will without doubt share these advantages.

The International Labor Organization was set up for the primary purpose of assisting labor. It does not occupy a neutral position between the employer and the worker but operates on the assumption that greater benefits must accrue to labor at the expense of the employer. It is quite natural that employer groups have generally looked askance upon these efforts. A strong feeling prevails that this is a socialistic organization. However, the orderly procedure of enacting laws to benefit labor is superior to the unending struggle of labor to seek its goal through strikes. A further ameliorating factor is to be found in the fact that government representatives at labor Conferences are quite as likely to favor employer groups as labor. The history of the Labor Organization would indicate that progress of socialism is little to be feared through the progress of legislation thus far attained. If, and when, labor becomes a stronger political factor in various countries we may anticipate marked progress in the international standards of labor legislation. Further retarding influences rest upon the impossible task of unifying labor laws in a world of varying conditions. The framers of the labor Charter recognized the differences of "climate, habits, and customs, economic opportunity, and industrial tradition" as barriers to the immediate attainment of uniform labor conditions which will no doubt continue to operate and thus prevent labor organizations from dominating international labor legislation. Indeed the general guiding principles which were laid down in Section II of the Charter were such as might readily be acceptable to the employer groups. The Labor Organization has not ventured sufficiently far into the labor field to threaten the control of industries by the employees. What the future holds in this respect no one knows, but it may safely be said that any change from the present slow method of advancing the interests of labor will depend upon a marked increase in the control of governments by labor. The struggle by labor in many countries to control government is ever present and the Labor Organization will be influenced by its successes or failures.

While political forces in various countries have retarded the Labor Organization, while differing conditions in every part of the globe have operated against international standards of labor legislation, and while the economic depression has weakened every form of international cooperation, the history of the Labor Organization has to date fully justified its existence. Up to and including 1937 the Labor Conference had adopted sixty international treaties or conventions affecting labor. Not all are yet in force but ratification by parliaments continues thus increasing the body of labor legislation. In approaching universality, the labor legislation thus far has tended to keep pace with changing industrial conditions. During the economic depression, when an effort was made to reduce the hours of work in industry, the Labor Organization undertook to formulate a treaty to bring about a forty-hour week, as against an earlier Treaty (1919), limiting the hours of work to forty-eight. A forty-hour week in the textile industry was adopted in 1937. The Organization has been carrying on a campaign of international economic planning in favor of national and international public works in an effort to combat the depression. In 1937 the Conference voted overwhelmingly in favor of this. Special effort has been made during the last six or seven years to formulate measures to hasten economic recovery. These efforts have included international planning of production and trade, as it is held that genuine economic recovery can only be attained by the coordinated efforts of all nations. As the economic depression was world-wide, so also must be the recovery. Hence it is not strange that the Labor Organization should concern itself with the larger problems vitally affecting labor. The various efforts to ameliorate labor conditions are secondary to the immediate problem of employment. While most of the treaties relate primarily to the improvement of general labor conditions, adverse factors affecting labor throughout the world during the depression have resulted in added stress on employment. In normal times it is to be expected that continued progress will be made to improve the general welfare of the workers in the matter of shorter hours, higher wages, and better working conditions.

CHAPTER XIV

The Permanent Court of International Justice

A HISTORY of the disputes dealt with by the League of Nations are, by their very nature, political. Various articles in the Covenant point to the nature of such disputes and outline the procedures to be followed in their settlement. The framers of the Covenant did not entrust the League bodies with the settlement of all disputes. Wisdom would dictate that the representatives at League meetings might effectively deal with political matters but that a court of law must, of necessity, settle legal controversies. With this in mind, the founders of the League incorporated Article 14 in the Covenant, which provides that "The Council shall formulate and submit to the members of the League for adoption plans for the establishment of a Permanent Court of International Justice." Broad powers are given to the Court to determine any dispute of an international nature which may be submitted to it. The Court is also empowered to give advisory opinions upon questions referred to it by the Council and Assembly.

Thus Article 14 obliged the Council to take the initiative in the organization of this Court. The creation of the Court differs from the League and Labor Organization in that the Covenant and Labor Charter are contained in the Treaty of Versailles while the Statute of the Court is not. Little time was lost by the Council in formulating plans for the execution of its

ELIHU ROOT, AMERICA'S FORMER DISTINGUISHED STATESMAN: "For these years the League in the political field and the Court in the judicial field have been rendering the best service to the cause of peace known to the history of civilization; incomparably the best."

mandate, and February, 1920, it appointed ten distinguished jurists including an American, Elihu Root, for that purpose. They met at the Hague a few months later and formulated a "Statute" or plan of organization which the Assembly adopted, with amendments, on December 13, 1920.

The Assembly then drew up an international Treaty creating the Permanent Court of International Justice which was agreed to by the Council, and ratified by the requisite number of States. The judges were elected in September, 1921, and the Court met for the first time on January 30, 1922. At the first meeting of what later became popularly known as the World Court, officers were elected, organization was effected and rules of procedure were adopted. The permanent place of meeting is at the Hague, in the Peace Palace erected by Andrew Carnegie.

The problem of selecting judges was, from the very outset, a difficult one. The Statute provided for the election of eleven judges and four deputies, but by an amendment of the Assembly of the League in 1930, the number of judges was increased to fifteen in addition to four deputy judges. The candidates are nominated by the national groups of the Permanent Court of International Arbitration at the Hague. (This Court of Arbitration was created at the first Hague Conference of 1899 and consists of a panel of judges four from each member state and from which arbitrators may be picked for each dispute. It does not meet collectively nor reside at The Hague hence is neither "permanent" nor a "court" in a true sense. In many instances this older Court proved useful, but did not meet the needs of a true court of international law. The Court has continued its existence, but its usefulness has been materially minimized by the newer Permanent Court of International Justice).

The election of the newer Court judges is made by the concurrent majority of the Council and the Assembly, each body voting independently of the other. They are elected for a term of nine years and may be re-elected. All member states of the League irrespective of size, have an equal voice in the election of judges. Nationality is not a factor in the election, for, according to the Statute of the Court, those elected must be "persons of high moral character, who possess the qualifications required in their respective countries for appointment to the highest judicial offices, or are juris consults of recognized competence in international law." Such eminent Americans as John Bassett Moore, Charles Evans Hughes, and Frank B. Kellogg have been judges of the Court. The Court meets once a year on June 15, and is therefore permanent, as its name implies. Many special sessions have been called to deal with urgent matters. Nine judges constitute a quorum. The judges are expected to devote their full time to the work of the Court, and the annual salary of each judge is $30,000 plus other allowances. The official languages are French and English.

Some sixty nations of the world are now members. The United States is one of the few remaining independent countries which is not a member, in spite of the expressed desire of each administration since the World War to accept membership and of the declaration in each of the major political platforms, since 1920, excluding those of 1936. The inability to obtain consent to ratification by the Senate has defeated American membership and this has been done in the face of favorable enlightened opinion. Non-membership does not preclude this country, however, from making use of the World Court, but up to the present no case has been tried in which the United States has been a party. So long as the United States remains out of the World

Court, there is little likelihood that the Government will feel free to turn to this body for the settlement of disputes.

A lingering opinion prevails in this country that no steps should be taken by our Government which will, in any way, involve us in foreign political commitments. Membership in the Court is thought by many to be a step committing us to a course in contravention to freedom of action. Extensive propaganda has been carried on since the War against all forms of international involvements which would obligate us to pursue a given course of action. The true nature of the Court has been little understood on this side of the Atlantic. This is a court of law where cases are settled on legal rather than political grounds. The United States has long favored the settlement of judicial questions by arbitration. It is only because of misrepresentation respecting the true nature of the Court that the United States is not a member. Its history to date clearly reveals a record of commendable decisions which have not operated to the detriment of the parties. A case before this judicial body is far more apt to be decided on the basis of law than it would be before some temporary tribunal of arbitration.

The jurisdiction of the Court may be either voluntary or compulsory. Article 36 of the Statute states that, "The jurisdiction of the Court comprises all cases which the parties refer to it and all matters specially provided for in treaties and conventions in force." This Article in time grew into what became known as an "optional clause" which some forty-two nations have voluntarily accepted. Acceptance of the "optional clause" gives the Court compulsory jurisdiction without any special arrangements by the parties to a dispute prior to settlement. A wide category of disputes are automatically submitted to the Court under these arrangements.

Where a state does not commit itself to accept the compulsory jurisdiction in advance, complete freedom is retained in the submission of disputes for legal settlement. It cannot be too strongly urged that nations have little to fear from the submission of legal disputes to this body. To be sure, the decisions cannot be favorable to all parties concerned, but the case would be the same in national courts. The justice of the decisions is the main objectives to be sought, rather than some advantage which might be obtained before an irresponsible body. This principle should be acknowledged in the consideration of American membership. Any dispute our Government may have with another country need not come before this Court without our consent. Complete freedom of action obtains in this respect and hence there should be no fear that American membership will obligate us to fulfill commitments contrary to our desires. Should the United States sign the "optional clause," which obligates the signatory to submit certain categories of disputes for settlement, our complete freedom of action in withholding cases from the Court would thus be voluntarily given up. This again is important in the consideration of American commitments as we may retain complete freedom of action as occasions arise if we choose to do so.

Elaborate rules of procedure have been drawn up for the Court in its deliberations. Under Article 30 of the Statute provision is made for the framing of rules of procedure by the Court itself; by virtue of this authority it has perfected the rules guiding it in its deliberations. These rules are similar to those that obtain in any court of law. The Court is petitioned to hear the dispute and the representatives of the two parties present both written and oral arguments and counter arguments, for which time limit is fixed. Decisions are made by a majority vote of the judges present at the hearing. The sessions have always been open to the public and all decisions reached by this body are announced in open court. The judgement is final and no appeal may be taken from it.

A criticism sometimes directed against the Court refers to the degree of partiality that may be shown in arriving at decisions. No legal body can be said to be completely free from impartial considerations, but the Court has a commendable record of fairness in deciding cases upon their merits. A small country is just as apt to get the decision as the more powerful one. The United States has lost more than one decision in arbitration tribunals where it is obvious that she should have won. Considerations other than legal dominated these temporary bodies. The present Court is a permanent continuing body whose members possess the highest legal education of their countries, and they can ill afford to endanger the prestige of the Court by deliberately placing expediency above law. The decisions including the grounds upon which they are based are presented in writing and become public records as are also dissenting opinions where such exist. These are widely studied and would cause grave criticisms if the best legal rules were not followed.

The Court has enjoyed an enviable record as regards the number of cases which have been submitted to it. Governments seem to have faith in the legal ability of the Court and naturally turn to it for the adjudication of disputes rather than to arbitration boards as was once the custom. The prestige of the Court has been such that nations submitting cases to it for settlement have been willing to carry out in good faith the judgements rendered. The long list of cases which have been handled by the Court is indicative of its value in international relationships. A brief summary of its judgements and orders follows:

Judgement No. 1. S.S. Wimbledon, On the Freedom of the Kiel Canal

On March 21, 1921, the German Government refused free access to the Kiel Canal to the British steamship "Wimbledon" which sailed under a French charter while

THE PEACE PALACE AT THE HAGUE

carrying munitions to Danzig, to be used by Poland in a war with Russia. Article 380 of the Treaty of Versailles states that "The Kiel Canal and its approaches shall be maintained free and open to the vessels of commerce and war of all nations at peace with Germany on terms of entire equality." By adhering to the Court Statute the German Government appointed one of its nationals to sit as a judge in this case. Oral arguments were heard by the Court between July 5 and July 10, 1923, and on August 17, 1923, a judgement was handed down which held "That the terms of Article 380 are categorical and give rise to no doubt." By this decision Germany was obliged to keep the Kiel Canal open, on a footing of equality to all vessels . . . but on one expressed condition, namely, that these vessels must belong to nations at peace with Germany." Germany was held responsible for the loss suffered by France and the amount to be awarded was fixed at 140,749 francs. Thus the first case before the Court was satisfactorily terminated.

Judgements Nos. 2, 5, and 10. The Mavrommatis Concessions in Palestine

Following the World War Palestine became a mandate of Great Britain. Upon assuming this rôle, the British Government refused to recognize certain public utility concessions in Jerusalem and Jaffa which Mavrommatis, a Greek, had obtained from Turkey. Under Article 26 of the mandate a provision is made for the submission of disputes to the Court by the mandatory and members of the League where settlements cannot otherwise be reached. On this basis the Greek Government filed claims in the Court against Great Britain for damages suffered by Mavrommatis. The British Government challenged the jurisdiction of the Court in this case.

The suit relating to the Jaffa concessions was dismissed as negotiations relating to the concessions had never been completed, but the Court held that the dispute relating to the Jerusalem concessions was, as a result of earlier Treaty arrangements, a matter to be settled under its compulsory jurisdiction. Great Britain accepted the judgement and later signed new contracts with Greece to replace the old ones. This settlement gave rise to a prolonged Court action and was successfully terminated. As a result, the Court was strengthened and its prestige enhanced.

Judgements Nos. 3 and 4. Interpretation of the Treaty of Neuilly

The Treaty of Neuilly of 1919, contained a provision authorizing the sale of properties belonging to Bulgarian nationals in any Allied country to pay claims of Allied nationals growing out of acts committed by the Bulgarian Government during the War. An arbitrator was appointed to settle the claims but Bulgaria disputed his competence. Greece and Bulgaria also disagreed over the scope of the claims. These questions were submitted to the World Court in August 25, 1924, which decided the types of claims falling under the provisions of the Treaty.

Greece and Bulgaria disagreed over the jurisdiction of the arbitrator in settlement of war claims, and sought the judgement of the Court. The Greek Government petitioned the Court for an interpretation of the law as to the extent to which Bulgarian property could be liquidated in Greece, and as to the distribution of the funds thus collected. The Court declined an interpretation as this request went beyond the limits of the disputes which was earlier settled by the Court.

Judgements Nos. 6, 7, 8, 11, and 13. Cases Relating to Polish Upper Silesia

Poland acquired part of Upper Silesia from Germany under a plebiscite in 1922. In that year a German-Polish Treaty was signed which related to details in the transfer of properties in this area. The Treaty exempted from seizure certain vested private property rights which were disregarded by Poland in enforcing an expropriation law passed in 1920. The German

THE PERMANENT COURT OF INTERNATIONAL JUSTICE

Government brought action before the World Court May 15, 1925, maintaining that Poland violated the German-Polish Treaty. Poland questioned the Court's jurisdiction but her plea was summarily dismissed.

The Polish Government had taken title to a nitrate factory acquired by two German companies. This was declared by the Court to be in violation of the German-Polish Treaty. The Court also held that rural estates "serving the needs of large industrial undertakings" could not by this Treaty be expropriated by Poland although she had declared her intention to do so. Other cases relating to the transfer of large rural estates were also settled by the Court as was the amount of the indemnity Poland was to pay to Germany for the seizure of the nitrate factory. This action by the Court led to an agreement between the German and Polish Governments which terminated the dispute.

Court Order. The Belgian-Chinese Case

On November 25, 1926, the Belgian Government filed with the World Court an application asking the Court to declare that the Chinese Government was not entitled to denounce a treaty signed at Peking November 2, 1865. China had not only abrogated the Treaty but refused to agree with Belgium to submit the case to the Court. The Court admitted the case, and indicated the protection which Belgian nationals in China were entitled to receive. Later the Belgian Government asked the Court to revoke the order as the dispute had been settled by the conclusion of a new treaty between the two countries. The Court formally complied with this request.

Judgement No. 9. The Lotus Case

On August 2, 1926, the French steamer "Lotus" and the Turkish collier "Boz-Kourt" collided on the high seas. The officer of the watch on the French steamer, and the captain of the Turkish collier were sentenced to serve prison terms by the Turkish authorities. The French Government protested against the imprisonment and fine of the French officer on the grounds that Turkish jurisdiction did not extend over the high seas and further that Turkey had agreed under the Lausanne Treaty to respect international law in her treatment of foreigners. The two governments agreed to submit the matter to the World Court for settlement. The Court held that Turkey was within her right in the exercise of such jurisdiction if this did not conflict with the rules of international law. The Court found no decisions of international tribunals which upheld the French contention, and concluded "that there is no rule of international law in regard to collision cases to the effect that criminal proceedings are exclusively within the jurisdiction of the state whose flag is flown." Turkey had, therefore, not acted contrary to the principle of international law or the Lausanne Treaty. The vote of the Court stood six to six with the President casting the deciding vote. Dissenting opinions were written which, in conjunction with the majority opinion, furnishes interesting and valuable material for students of international law.

Judgement No. 12. Rights of Minorities in Upper Silesia

On January 2, 1928, Germany applied to the World Court for a declaration against Poland based on a treaty (1922) which it was argued contained provisions permitting each individual of minority groups in Upper Silesia full liberty to declare his race, language, and religion and to choose the school for his child without interference by Polish authorities. Poland denied the jurisdiction of the Court over this case but was overruled. The Court held that the principle of minority rights permitted full exercise of freedom among non-Polish speaking groups which rights were to be based on facts and not on the intentions of individuals. The judgement limited the jurisdiction of the Polish authorities insofar as minority rights were respected in the German-Polish Treaty of 1922.

Judgement No. 14. The Payment of Serbian Loans Issued in in France

This dispute related to the monetary basis of certain bonds held by French citizens, which the Serb-Croat-Slovene Government was obligated to pay. Paper francs were offered in payment but the French contended that the holders should be paid in gold. By agreement of the two parties the dispute came before the Court on April 19, 1928. The question of the Court's jurisdiction arose, as one of the parties was a group of French bond-holders, and it was argued that only disputes between governments might come before it. The Court held that the case was the French Government's, thereby creating a dispute between the two states. The judgement of the Court on July 12, 1929, declared that the bonds contained stipulations for payment in gold, thus giving a favorable decision to France.

Judgement No. 15. The Payment of Brazilian Loans Issued in France

This case was similar to the previous one in that the Brazilian bonds were held by French citizens who instead of receiving payment in gold francs, as stated on the bonds, were offered French currency of lower value due to the devaluation of the franc. By special agreement the case came before the Court on August 27, 1927, and judgement was given July 12, 1929. The same legal principles applied here as in the case of the Serbian loans. The decision was favorable to France, and the Brazilian Government promptly complied with the Court's decision.

Judgement No. 16. Jurisdiction of The International Commission of the River Oder

The International Commission of the Oder was created under the terms of the Treaty of Versailles to regulate commerce of the Oder and its tributaries. The Polish Government challenged the jurisdiction of the Commission over the tributaries of the river in Poland. By agreement among the opposing parties the case came before the Court October 30, 1928, and it held on September 10, 1929, that the Commission's jurisdiction extended to all portions of the Oder River including tributaries in Poland insofar as they are navigable and provide more than one state with access to the sea.

Judgement No. 17. Free Zones of Upper Savoy and the District of Gex

A treaty of long standing gave the Swiss free custom zones in parts of France near Geneva. The Treaty of Versailles abrogated this but the Swiss Government refused to recognize an act to which she was not a party. A long dispute between France and Switzerland led to an agreement to submit it to the Court. The Court held August 19, 1929, that the treaty establishing the free zones was not abrogated by the Treaty of Versailles and the parties were given until May 1, 1930, to reach an agreement. As no agreement was reached, the Court again heard the case, confirmed the previous decision and set July 31, 1931, as a new agreement date. The failure of negotiations was followed by a final judgement by the Court on June 7, 1932, which confirmed the previous decisions and fixed January 1, 1934, as the date for France to forego the collection of customs duties on Swiss goods sent to Upper Savoy and Gex. France accepted this judgement and shortly thereafter negotiated a settlement with Switzerland.

Judgements Nos. 18 and 19. Interpretation of the Statute of the Memel Territory

This territory was transferred by the Allied Powers to Lithuania by treaty (1924) but was given a degree of local autonomy. The governor, appointed by the President of Lithuania, dismissed the President of the Directorate, which act was challenged by the Allied Powers. The Powers made application to the Court April 11, 1932, to determine whether this act and others performed by the President accorded with the treaty. Lithuania argued that the dispute should first come before the Council of the League but the Court found no ground for this contention. The judgement on August 11, 1932, was that the local autonomy was prescribed or limited by the treaty and the right to dismiss the President of the Directorate constituted a legitimate measure of protection to Lithuania and was not in violation of the Treaty. A successor might be appointed by the governor but the Court held that he had no right to dissolve the Diet on his own authority.

Judgement No. 20. Legal Status of Eastern Greenland

Denmark and Norway were united until 1814 when Norway was given to Sweden. Greenland, a dependency of Denmark and Norway, was not included in the transfer. The question of sovereignty over Greenland was not seriously raised until 1930 when Norway appointed officials in Eastern Greenland followed by a vigorous protest by Denmark. The dispute led to the occupation of a part of Eastern Greenland by

Norway under a Royal Proclamation of July 10, 1931. The Danish Government immediately applied to the Court for a judgement to have the proclamation declared "unlawful and invalid." After prolonged hearings the Court held, April 5, 1933, that the King of Denmark and Norway was sovereign over the whole of Greenland until 1814 but after that the sovereign was the King of Denmark. The Court also reasoned that the historical exercise of power over Greenland by the Danish Government had often been recognized by other powers. Denmark was declared to possess sovereignty over all Greenland. Both countries readily complied with this decision.

Court Order. The Administration of the Prince von Pless

The Court was asked by the German Government May 18, 1932, to declare that the Polish Government's attitude toward the adminstration of Prince von Pless in Polish Upper Selisia was in violation of a treaty binding Poland (1922), and an indemnity be paid to the Prince for losses sustained in the payment of excessive taxes. The Polish Government objected to the application on the ground that redress had not been exhausted in the Polish courts. This was sustained, whereupon Germany asked the Court for measures to protect the property of the Prince until the final decision. The Polish Government assented to this and during the delay of settlement Germany announced her withdrawal from membership in the World Court and the League of Nations. She also notified the Court that she did not intend to proceed with the suit.

Judgement No. 21. The Royal Hungarian Peter Pazmany University

In 1775 Queen Maria Theresa gave certain large estates to this University as a perpetual endowment.

Upon becoming an independent state in 1918 Czechoslavakia acquired certain of these properties. A Czechoslavak-Hungarian mixed arbitral tribunal set up to settle all property claims, ordered the property to be returned to the University. Czechoslavakia appealed to the Court to have this decision set aside on the ground that the University was a state institution and its properties belonged to the state, whereas the tribunal's power covered only private property. The Court held, December 15, 1933, that the University had the capacity in private law to receive legacies and own property which gave it a distinct personality apart from the state. The decision of the arbitral Tribunal was upheld and Czechoslavakia was ordered to restore the property to the University.

Judgement No. 22. The Lighthouses

In 1860 the Ottoman Empire granted a French firm concessions to erect lighthouses on its coast and collect lighthouse dues as remuneration. In April, 1913, a new agreement was reached but soon thereafter a treaty, concluded at the close of the second Balkan War, November, 1913, ceded some Turkish territory, including lighthouses, to Greece. The 1913 contract, insofar as it related to these lighthouses, was revoked by the Greek Government which also refused to satisfy claims for losses by the French firm. The French and Greek Governments agreed to submit the case to the Court, 1931, in order to determine the validity of the 1913 contract. The Court decided the case in favor of France on March 17, 1934, by stating that the contract was "duly entered into" and hence valid.

Judgement No. 23. The Oscar Chinn Case

Under a Treaty (1919) the Belgian Government was obliged to maintain commercial freedom and equality to all nations on the Congo River. In 1925 a Belgian transport company was organized which charged rates fixed by the Government. The rates were materially reduced in 1931 with the resulting losses to the company which were to be borne by the Government. Equal

Keystone View Company

PERMANENT COURT OF INTERNATIONAL JUSTICE IN SESSION UNDER THE PRESIDENCY OF FRANK B. KELLOGG OF THE U. S. TO SETTLE THE LEGALITY OF AUSTRO-GERMAN CUSTOMS PACT

terms were refused to other shippers with the result that Oscar Chinn, a British shipper in the Congo, was unable to continue his business. The British Government contended that the action taken by the Belgian Government (1931) was in conflict with treaty obligations and demanded damages for Mr. Chinn. The Court held, December 12, 1934, that Belgium was required to maintain freedom of navigation for all vessels on the Congo but was not obliged under the treaty to insure equality of commercial opportunity, hence the Belgian Government had not violated her treaty obligations.

In addition to the Judgements and Orders, the Court has given twenty-seven advisory opinions (December 1935) dealing with the interpretation of international law. Space does not permit a summary of these but they vary widely in nature and importance. Two nations engaged in a dispute may prefer to obtain the Court's opinion rather than judgement, as the way is thus prepared for wider latitude in settlement. The records show that compliance with its opinions has been most commendable. Requests for them come from the Assembly and Council of the League. A dispute involving legal points may come before the Council and in the course of negotiations be submitted to the Court for an opinion as an aid to settlement. This does not mean that the Court acts as legal advisor to the League, which is a function of the legal section of the Secretariat. A resolution by the Council or Assembly requesting an advisory opinion must be of great importance and undertaken only when there are parties to a dispute.

In case of litigation the parties to the dispute assume a legal obligation to comply with the award. The Court has a legal obligation to hear a case if it has jurisdiction, but it is free to decline a request for an advisory opinion, which it has already done. Only independent states may have access to the Court. If an individual has a grievance against a foreign power he may prevail upon his government to act as a party in the case. Some cases of this nature are recorded. The criticism is sometimes advanced that the Court possesses no machinery to enforce its judgements. Against this it may be said that certain well established practices have grown up which take it for granted that the decisions will be executed. The practices apply not alone to the World Court but also to national courts.

Taking a parallel case, the judgments of the United States Supreme Court have not always been executed, but this in no way detracts from its present effectiveness. Complete confidence in the ability and fairness of the World Court decisions suffices as an enforcement agency. Provision is made in Article 13 of the League Covenant for steps to be taken by the Council against a League member that fails to carry out an award or decision of the Court. The pressure method, as inferred in this Article, is, however, of doubtful value and contrary to experience in the execution of decisions. The fact that the decisions are enforced is their best evidence of effectiveness. It is highly important that the prestige of the Court be maintained if respect for advisory opinions and judgements is to continue.

The relation of the Court to the League of Nations should also be clearly noted. The two are closely related as regards the election of judges, finances, and the admitting of new states on the invitation of the members of the League who act on behalf of the members of the Court. The League bodies may not, however, remove the judges nor enact measures binding upon the Court. Neither can they revise the Statutes or procedure of the Court. Sitting at the Hague, the Court is removed from the Geneva influences, and its work is carried forward in complete independence of League bodies. While the League may not restrain the Court's action, the states, members of the Court, may do so. Their consent was required for the ratification of the Treaty which gave it being and also for the amending of the Statute or constitution which governs the Court's actions. Most of the members of the Court are also League members, a fact which may operate to protect its interests in its relations with the Court. An understanding of these points of contact between the League and the Court is especially important in this country because of insistent agitation that American membership in the Court would closely associate it with the League. This fear is unfounded in view of the highly independent position which the Court occupies.

The judgements and opinions of the Court serve to build up a series of precedents for the future. They result in the development of a body of international law in the same way as national court decisions create case law which serve as precedents within a nation's legal system. While Article 59 of the Statute conforms to the Continental system of law by declaring that "the decision of the Court has no binding force except between the parties and in respect of that particular case," nevertheless the previous judgements are cited by the Court in arriving at decisions. Attempts have been made in international conferences to codify existing legal principles which may become the accepted laws of the nations, but these efforts have only met with partial success. The legal principles enunciated by the Court offer a more promising method of developing a universal code by growth of law through judicial interpretation in serving to guide the nations in their relations with one another.

The importance of the Court is further enhanced by clauses customarily contained in treaties which provide that disputes arising out of their interpretation or execution shall be settled by the Court. There are close to five hundred such treaties now in existence. The agreements entered into in advance by the treaty making states places them under "compulsory jurisdiction" to submit these disputes to the Court. Such agreements are not to be confused with the "optional clause" previously referred to where member states agree in advance to summit all legal disputes to the Court for settlement. The rapid development of treaty-making since the War takes cognizance of the Court as the accepted judicial body in their interpretation. The continued usefulness of the Court will be recognized in this field.

While various forms of international cooperation have suffered a serious set-back during recent years the standing and usefulness of the Court have not experienced a like decline. The years of its existence have made it a firmly established organization filling a distinct world need. What is needed to bring about closer working relations among nations is not a more effective judicial tribunal for the settlement of controversies but the devising of methods for the settlement of political disputes. The effective settlement of justiciable disputes in the post-war period marks a distinct advance in the rule of law. These successes should serve to point the way to greater amity among nations in other realms of cooperation.

CHAPTER XV

Evaluation and Future of the League

The League is not now the institution that it was designed to be by the framers of the Covenant. President Wilson and his collaborators postulated an organization that would be universal in membership and would exercise the necessary authority to check an aggressor state. The League was weak in the first years of its existence, but new members were added and a remarkable record of achievement was witnessed in the settlement of disputes. At the end of the first decade of the League's history it appeared that the purposes of the founders would be fulfilled. The turning point came in 1931 when the member states of the League failed to check Japanese aggression in Manchuria. But the more serious blow came in 1935 in the failure of economic sanctions instituted against Italy in her aggression in Ethiopia. These were severe blows to the League and many believed that collective security was at an end. The apprehension was heightened by the withdrawal of Japan and Germany from the League and the indifferent attitude displayed by Italy toward it. Still greater danger to collective security was the rapid rearmament by the same Powers. Russia's acceptance of League membership partly offset these discouraging trends and the remaining states continued to look to Geneva as the center of international collaboration. Encouragement was also found in a move by Great Britain to greatly increase her armaments as this would add force to League decisions. A strong British navy is widely regarded as a stabilizer and not a disturber of world peace.

Following the defeat of the League in applying economic sanctions against Italy, an elaborate discussion took place regarding Covenant revision to make it more

Keystone View Company

RUSSIA ENTERS THE LEAGUE

effective in future crises. This was not new, for the Covenant had been revised before, and necessarily so, as the founders could not create an organization that would meet all future contingencies in a changing world. Article 26 provides that the Covenant may be amended when agreed upon by the members of the Council and a majority of the members of the Assembly. Hence, while the framers of the Covenant planned the best organization that could then be contemplated, they clearly saw that changes would be necessary. The

League has to some degree been prevented from undergoing change to meet new conditions by having thrust upon it the task of executing certain provisions of the Treaty of Versailles and nations particularly satisfied with the international settlement following the War have favored the status quo in international planning. Nor did the League keep pace with the rapid shift in the political scene. The need for an organization that would function more effectively came sharply to the fore and serious discussions took place as to how the League might be reorganized to avoid new pitfalls.

At a meeting of the Assembly in July, 1936, it was decided to invite the member states to submit plans on how to "improve . . . the application of the principles of the Covenant" to be discussed in the September meeting. Numerous plans were submitted but no one wished to abandon the League. All agreed that it should be made a more effective institution. Broadly speaking, the League members were divided into two camps, the one favoring a restricted membership definitely committed to a firm stand on security against aggression in a limited area, and the other group favoring a universal organization, the task of which should be confined largely to consultation, conciliation, and international planning with no political commitments to bind members to a definite course of action. There is much to be said for each of these views as well as a possible compromise plan. As discussions of Covenant revision proceeded in the Assembly, it became increasingly clear that no immediate steps would be taken to bring this about. Instead of formal amendments, which would have been difficult in the light of divergent views, a tendency has since developed to permit each member state to decide for itself the extent to which it is willing to fulfill Covenant obligations. In other words, there is a growing recognition of individual freedom by each member in critical times. This open recognition would be an acceptance of a *fait accompli*.

The member states advocating limited membership, but an effective League, have many strong points in their favor. They desire to retain Articles 10 and 16—the very essence of the Covenant—and to bind themselves in what amounts to a defensive military alliance. The conception presupposes a League based on force, and with this backing it is believed that the nations on the outside would be more hesitant to act against its members. The collective assurance against war requires, under this plan, quick action against an aggressor and hence a favorable attitude is taken toward a simplification of the rules of procedure. Obligations under the Covenant would be limited to Europe as it is recognized by the sanctionists that wars in other parts of the world would most likely be localized. It is simple enough to point to the failures of the League when effective military guarantees are lacking, and hence the members should bind themselves to the coercive clauses of the Covenant and have a militarized organization to be used against aggressors. Some even advocate the creation of an international army or police force. It is maintained that had Mussolini known in advance of his invasion in Africa that more than fifty nations would have brought effective measures to bear against him, he would have taken a different course. Thus the prospect of being confronted with an overwhelming force would make a nation shun the attempt to use force. Those opposing limited liability point to its weakness as one of the reasons why the danger in Europe has greatly increased during the last few years.

Over against the advocates of a League with strong military sanctions is a group of nations who, in 1936, also desired an effective organization for the maintenance of peace, but differed as to the method of achieving it. These nations oppose commitments that will bind them in advance to a course of military action, admitting that it may be necessary, but holding that decisions should be reached as occasions arise. This, in their opinion, has been the procedure in past disputes, and the League has been measurably successful as a peace institution. Many believe that it is too much to hope for the League to develop into a full-fledged guardian of world peace in the short period of its existence. The development of some form of a world federation may, it is believed, eventually come, but the process cannot be hastened. In the view of many, the League can best be strengthened for the present by reducing rather than extending its obligations in the employment of force. The anti-sanctionists maintain that the automatic obligations to go to war against an aggressor have caused nations to leave the League, as well as prevent others from joining it. Its usefulness without the coercive clauses might still be maintained, as representatives of nations can meet periodically at a round table to settle their problems. This would make the League a creator of peace rather than an enforcer of it. By repealing Articles 10 and 16 of the Covenant, the League would still operate as the accepted agency in promoting world peace, continuing as a recognized institution for the furtherance of international planning.

Those who advocate a universal League with limited liability hope that Germany and Japan will return to its membership, and the United States will join it. With this larger membership there would also be the free discussion of the best means of maintaining peace, primarily by moral suasion. Under this plan, it might even be possible for member states to unite in joint action against an aggressor, but it is held that, as sanctions cannot be made decisive and automatic, they should be abandoned as a treaty commitment. To agree to the binding provisions of Articles 10 and 16 without living up to the obligations, is said to destroy not only the binding force of these Articles, but to weaken respect for all treaties. It is agreed that the prestige of the League would be greatly lessened if it bound the member states to obligations that are not fulfilled. It is suggested that only those liabilities should be assumed which could be carried out. In answer to this, it may be said that if the League gives up its intention to employ force against an aggressor the countries of Europe would go back to the old system of military alliances as guarantees of security. In reply to this, again, it may be countered that a League backed by force which is ineffective would not prevent separate military treaties. To strip the League of sanctions would also deprive it of its ability to stand up against a disturber of world peace. As a purely consultative and legislative body, the League would, of course, lose much of the glamour that has hitherto surrounded it. But the magnitude of international planning is sufficiently great to keep the organization intact and active.

The above discussion sets forth the positions of two divergent views as regards the future effectiveness of the League, namely the sanctionists countries, headed by France, that favor the retention of the military guarantees of the Covenant, and the others, under the leadership of Great Britain, that desire to forego commitments involving military action in advance of a crisis. A possible middle course might be the retention of the present enforcement Articles of the Covenant, leaving the responsibility of their fulfillment to each member state as it deems fit. This has, to a large extent, been the history of League sanctions especially in the Italo-Ethiopian dispute, when each member decided upon its own course of action. This by all odds is the easier course in view of the divergent positions of the two camps. Reluctance to tackle the problem of revision following the discussions in the Assembly of July, 1936, indicates the possibility of the final acceptance of this position. Instead of formal revision of the Covenant, each member state may, in the future, place more emphasis upon its own interpretations of the military provisions of the Covenant. The weakness of the middle course, which is the status quo, is the uncertainty as to what the likelihood of concerted action would be. On the other hand, if there is desire to maintain the membership intact, as was strongly shown in the discussions of reorganization, the uncertain nature of the binding clauses must be continued. A hopeful augury may be found in the nations' genuine wish to cooperate under a given condition, regardless of the non-committal attitude of some members.

Mr. Paul-Boncour of France spoke before the Disarmament Conference at Geneva of a gradation of responsibility by the nations in the maintenance of peace. An inference was drawn from the abyss of Dante's Inferno, shaped in concentric circles, applied to some nations engulfed in the dangers of war, and those on the outer rim enjoying comparative freedom from danger. The hell, or war, here pictured has definite application to western Europe. Hence those nations, according to Mr. Paul-Boncour, that are the most deeply engulfed in the abyss should bind themselves to definite commitments to take military action in case of aggression, while the nations farthest removed, such as the United States, would necessarily refrain from doing this. The position of the United States in this system of progressive responsibility for the maintenance of peace is ably discussed in a book entitled "On the Rim of the Abyss" by James T. Shotwell. He points out that it is "useless to expect nations 'on the outer rim' to assume or to perform" the duty of taking military action in case of aggression in remote parts of the world. The universality of the sanction Articles of the Covenant has been its weakness, and it is believed that if such responsibility is made regional, greater effectiveness would ensue. Under this proposal the League would continue to operate as a universal institution in the many fields of international planning. Experience has shown that nations will only act in accordance with their own self-interest, and if a war occurs in a remote region that does not endanger or vitally affect a nation, there is the inevitable desire to remain neutral. There is much to be said in favor of this proposal as it not only provides a practical basis for binding groups of nations together for peace, but also makes possible a universal membership in the League. A drawback may again be found in the unwillingness of the members to revise the Covenant and agree upon the responsibility each nation should shoulder.

Responsibilities have been scaled down in the regional treaties that obligate the signatories to come to the aid of one another in case of attack. Typical of these are the Locarno Treaties, the Little Entente, the Balkan Pact, and the Treaties of the Pan-American Union. There are also numerous bilateral pacts designed to prevent war. Between these treaties and the League Covenant there is no conflict, as they merely supplement one another. They have in fact been encouraged by the League.

A practical proposal for the reorganization of the League has been made by the League of Nations Association of the United States along the following principles:

"1. acceptance of the Kellogg Pact as the fundamental and guiding principle of a universal league; 2. establishment within the orbit of this universal league of arrangements for peaceful modification of the status quo and for the advancement of social and economic justice; 3. gradation of obligations for maintaining collective security in accordance with the geographical position and special situation of states; and 4. separation of the Covenant of the League of Nations from the Treaty of Versailles." These proposals are in accord with general League trends, and if fulfilled there should be no reason why the United States should not join it, since no risks are involved, and no diplomatic "entanglements" could be feared. Not least of all, it could not only do us no harm, but there would be much to be gained by being represented at the gatherings.

Continued increase in political uncertainty throughout the world makes the United States hesitant to adopt a vigorous international policy. It is not enough that assurance may be found in definite understandings with other nations relieving us of political obligations, but the strong urge is ever present to remain aloof from the cross currents of world trouble. Justification for this may be found in the continuous threat of war in various parts of the world. A popular view prevails that war is inevitable and we must bend every effort to keep out. Against this view, many far-sighted observers hold that our interests may be best served by active cooperation with other nations in the development of alternatives to war. By taking our place with other nations in the meetings of the League the opportunity would be provided to plan a world society by peaceful processes. The Assembly meets annually, the Council at least four times a year, and numerous League conferences assemble, giving a certain continuity to its technique to deal with the multifarous problems. The

United States may well serve its best interests and those of the world by meeting with representatives of other governments in these assemblies.

The present attitude of doubt toward the future of the League, in addition to a widespread hostile feeling, may in time change, as the League not only survives, but grows in importance. The time may come when the people of the United States may no longer take the attitude that the successful operation of the League depends merely upon our support, but rather that the League, as the accepted organization in world society, is the only means of cooperating with other nations. No government can rely upon its armed forces to maintain its power and prestige among other nations where they are organized in a common purpose. Thus far we have looked upon the League as weak and disorganized, but the time may come when the organized strength of its members may embarrass us. In this eventuality, we may more advantageously unite and work together with other states than against them.

The future success of the League may be enhanced through our efforts first, by the non-recognition of territorial changes brought about in disregard of Covenant obligations, as in the cases of Manchuria and Ethiopia, the conquests of both of which have not received our official recognition; second, by our taking no steps that may weaken League efforts to deal with an aggressor. If the members of the League institute a boycott or take other forceful measures against a state, we should by no means render these efforts void through trade, credit or other forms of encouragement. We should be willing to consult with other nations on various matters likely to lead to war. The extent of the above forms of cooperation are by no means far-reaching, but would do much to improve the existing peace machinery.

As a matter of fact there is no reason why international conferences may not assemble more frequently in the future than in the past to collaborate on common matters even without the definite aim of reaching tangible agreements. In certain circles it is felt that if a treaty is not made at an international conference, a terrible catastrophe has occurred. This feeling was especially marked after the London Economic Con-

THE LEAGUE OF NATIONS BUILDINGS, GENEVA

ference and the World Disarmament Conference, both of which met under League auspices. These failures should not cause the nations to despair of making progress in these respective fields, but should rather lead to frequent meetings in the hope of arriving at definite results. No harm and much good may come from frequent planning. The conference habit is a splendid fashioner of international life.

A factor that may not seem important in the creation of international solidarity but is nevertheless of great moment, is the impressive new palace that has recently been erected at Geneva to house all League activities. It stands today as perhaps the greatest edifice built anywhere in the world during the depression, and is one of the greatest monumental structures of all time. An air of permanence prevails at Geneva and the member states look upon this international seat with a sense of pride. There the members of the Secretariat are permanently occupied with the duties placed upon them.

The conference system developed at Geneva follows well defined lines of accepted procedure. Thus not only do the periodic international gatherings lend weight to League prestige, but the manner of conducting the meetings has enhanced its influence. This technique is far superior to the haphazard conference structure that existed before the World War. Pre-War conferences were not correlated, adequate preparation was not made, and no accepted rules of procedure obtained. No Secretariat existed as a continuing body to carry out the details in connection with the meetings. The League is a great improvement over the conference system of the pre-War era. As the nations learn to work together in a recognized manner for the conduct of business there is greater possibility of achieving results. The same efficient manner of performing international functions is found in the organization and procedure of the Permanent Court of International Justice and the International Labor Organization. Most persons are interested in what is accomplished and not so much in how results are brought about. But the manner of transacting international negotiations often goes far in affecting the results. There have in the past been great injustices wrought in conference deliberations due to the lack of preparation, organization, and the follow-up work which accompanies the making of treaties. The League has overcome these obstacles and promises to unite the world in a standardized conference system.

The League has become not only an effective organization of international planning, but a tremendously active center of varied activities in all fields of international endeavor. Even though political cooperation breaks down, the nations will nevertheless find this an indispensable agency in world undertakings. As the nations become more closely united through the expansion of common interests the League will increase in usefulness. What the future will bring, and what the League may eventually become no one can tell. There are, however, some considerations to be noted that may serve as a guide in evaluating the future of the League. Is it not reasonable to suppose that the nations will utilize the League because it is needed now more than ever before as an agency to which they can turn for the solution of their numerous problems? The very fact that this organization exists and that the nations have access to it will suffice to draw them together.

An assurance of the future usefulness of the League may be found in its successful efforts to preserve peace in the disputes that have arisen during its short history. An account of the League's achievements in preventing wars as well as putting an end to others which were already in progress, has been given. The record reveals the interesting fact that upward of thirty international disputes have been settled at Geneva. The three glaring examples of the League's failures are, of course, the Sino-Japanese controversy, the Chaco Boundary Dispute in South America, and the Italo-Ethiopian War. These failures have caused many to look upon the League as a failure, but this indictment is unjust as one must weigh achievements against failures. If the League had succeeded in settling only half of the disputes which have come before it, its value as a peace organization would be established. The record is even better, as all disputes dealt with except those mentioned have been successfully adjusted.

No institution in our imperfect world is faultless either in organization or operation. There are laws in every country to restrain the aggressor yet they are not always obeyed or enforced. All governments experience successes and failures but that does not necessarily lead to a desire to overthrow them. Thus if various governments continue to experience imperfection after long years of development, can it then be expected that the League will, during the short years of its existence, function with an unblemished record? To organize the world on the basis of law and order is in many respects more difficult than to organize the people of a particular area under a government. While many obstacles present themselves in international cooperation, yet the League is becoming increasingly well established and will be better able to cope with an ever-increasing number of international problems. The world has become so interdependent that some centralized agency for discussion and decision of policy is now indispensable. Should the League not survive, due to some fearful cataclysm, some similar institution would in time be built upon the same structure and serving the same needs. In other words the League has become an indispensable organization in a world community.

While the need for the League is well recognized and its continuance may be assured, it may not necessarily be able to prevent all wars. But with the passing of time new means will no doubt be devised for strengthening the existing peace machinery, and as lessons are learned from the successes and failures of the past, new methods will be formulated for perfecting it. Thus far the most successful approach to the settlement of international disputes has been by consultation and the consent of the disputing parties to utilize the League in reaching compromises. The future holds out still greater possibilities for conciliation, as improved technique is developed through experience.

Greater emphasis should in the future be placed upon the promotion of peace and less upon the prevention of war. The two are closely related, for if the nations work for peace, less need will be felt for the prevention of war. This is obviously the more rational and safer form of cooperation. Not that the League should give up the available machinery for ensuring peace by restraining an aggressor, but such restraint should only be exercised when it is directed against unwarranted aggression. Conditions must be created that will make it unnecessary for nations to resort to force in order to continue their normal existence. Much has been said about peaceful change but very little done about it. The Assembly may, under Article 19, give consideration to the revision of treaties that are no longer applicable or that operate to endanger the peace of the world. While this Article opens avenues of potential possibilities for promoting peace among nations it has hardly been utilized by the League members. Some treaty clauses are still legally binding but have fallen into disuse, due to changed conditions. Among these is the Treaty of Versailles which on several occasions has been modified, but only by flagrant violations. Such changes might far better have been made by orderly processes through common consent. The League members may justly be criticized for stressing the war-prevention clauses of the Covenant in an effort to maintain political stability, while disregarding the same document as an instrument of change. This was not President Wilson's conception of the purposes of the League, as he clearly envisaged a changing world and anticipated an institution that would be sufficiently flexible to meet the changes as they occurred. The League cannot hope to succeed and maintain the support of a preponderant majority of nations if in its sessions undue emphasis is placed upon the status quo. The world is moving rapidly, and political, economic, and social changes occur with greater frequency. Hence, the nations should be ready to adapt themselves to changes.

The United States may logically cooperate with other nations in their efforts to promote peace. This has been and still is a serious concern of the American people. Great interest has been taken in the movement to "outlaw" war and much literature has been disseminated depicting its horrors. The effort to promote peace, as emphasized in this country, may well be carried by us into League assemblies. The United States, as one of the most powerful nations on earth, is in a position to exert a tremendous moral influence in shaping world events. This may call for sacrifices in such matters as tariffs, war debts, currencies, movements of people; but the cost is trivial, as compared to the larger benefits that may be realized. The intense popular desire in this country to prevent war can be made to fit perfectly into the future pattern of the League. The similarity of purpose has failed to result in co-operation because of a bias against the ultimate goal of the League. We would do well to assist in rectifying the mistakes of the League rather than remaining on the side-line and offering criticisms. The interests of the United States are too wide-spread for us to continue a policy of aloofness in shaping the destinies of the world. As our Government takes a more active part in international planning, we may expect to find the League fulfilling, to an increasing degree, the original intentions conceived by the founders.

PART FOUR
APPENDICES

APPENDIX I

The Covenant of the League of Nations [1]

The High Contracting Parties

In order to promote international co-operation and to achieve international peace and security

by the acceptance of obligations not to resort to war,
by the prescription of open, just and honourable relations between nations,
by the firm establishment of the understandings of international law as the actual rule of conduct among Governments,
and by the maintenance of justice and a scrupulous respect for all treaty obligations in the dealings of organised peoples with one another,

Agree to this Covenant of the League of Nations.

Article 1

1. The original Members of the League of Nations shall be those of the Signatories which are named in the Annex to this Covenant and also such of those other States named in the Annex as shall accede without reservation to this Covenant. Such accession shall be effected by a Declaration deposited with the Secretariat within two months of the coming into force of the Cove-

---

[1] Text numbered in conformity with the resolution adopted by the seventh ordinary session of the Assembly on September 16th, 1926, and containing Article 6 as amended, in force since August 13th, 1924, Articles 12, 13 and 15 as amended, in force since September 26th, 1924, and Article 4 as amended, in force since July 29th, 1926. The texts printed in italics indicate the amendments.

nant. Notice thereof shall be sent to all other Members of the League.

2. Any fully self-governing State, Dominion or Colony not named in the Annex may become a Member of the League if its admission is agreed to by two-thirds of the Assembly, provided that it shall give effective guarantees of its sincere intention to observe its international obligations, and shall accept such regulations as may be prescribed by the League in regard to its military, naval and air forces and armaments.

3. Any Member of the League may, after two years' notice of its intention so to do, withdraw from the League, provided that all its international obligations and all its obligations under this Covenant shall have been fulfilled at the time of its withdrawal.

Article 2

The action of the League under this Covenant shall be effected through the instrumentality of an Assembly and of a Council, with a permanent Secretariat.

Article 3

1. The Assembly shall consist of Representatives of the Members of the League.

2. The Assembly shall meet at stated intervals and from time to time as occasion may require at the Seat of the League or at such other place as may be decided upon.

3. The Assembly may deal at its meetings with any matter within the sphere of action of the League or affecting the peace of the world.

4. At meetings of the Assembly, each Member of the League shall have one vote, and may have not more than three Representatives.

Article 4

1. The Council shall consist of Representatives of the Principal Allied and Associated Powers, together with Representatives of four other Members of the League. These four Members of the League shall be selected by the Assembly from time to time in its discretion. Until the appointment of the Representatives of the four Members of the League first selected by the Assembly, Representatives of Belgium, Brazil, Spain and Greece shall be members of the Council.

2. With the approval of the majority of the Assembly, the Council may name additional Members of the League whose Representatives shall always be Members of the Council; the Council with like approval may increase the number of Members of the League to be selected by the Assembly for representation on the Council.

2bis. *The Assembly shall fix by a two-thirds majority the rules dealing with the election of the non-permanent Members of the Council, and particularly such regulations as relate to their term of office and the conditions of re-eligibility.*

3. The Council shall meet from time to time as occasion may require, and at least once a year, at the Seat of the League, or at such other place as may be decided upon.

4. The Council may deal at its meetings with any matter within the sphere of action of the League or affecting the peace of the world.

5. Any Member of the League not represented on the Council shall be invited to send a Representative to sit as a member at any meeting of the Council during the cousideration of matters specially affecting the interests of that Member of the League.

6. At meetings of the Council, each Member of the League represented on the Council shall have one vote, and may have not more than one Representative.

ARTICLE 5

1. Except where otherwise expressly provided in this Covenant or by the terms of the present Treaty, decisions at any meeting of the Assembly or of the Council shall require the agreement of all the Members of the League represented at the meeting.

2. All matters of procedure at meetings of the Assembly or of the Council, including the appointment of Committees to investigate particular matters, shall be regulated by the Assembly or by the Council and may be decided by a majority of the Members of the League represented at the meeting.

3. The first meeting of the Assembly and the first meeting of the Council shall be summoned by the President of the United States of America.

ARTICLE 6

1. The permanent Secretariat shall be established at the Seat of the League. The Secretariat shall comprise a Secretary-General and such secretaries and staff as may be required.

2. The first Secretary-General shall be the person named in the Annex; thereafter the Secretary-General shall be appointed by the Council with the approval of the majority of the Assembly.

3. The secretaries and staff of the Secretariat shall be appointed by the Secretary-General with the approval of the Council.

4. The Secretary-General shall act in that capacity at all meetings of the Assembly and of the Council.

5. *The expenses of the League shall be borne by the Members of the League in the proportion decided by the Assembly.*

Article 7

1. The Seat of the League is established at Geneva.
2. The Council may at any time decide that the Seat of the League shall be established elsewhere.
3. All positions under or in connection with the League, including the Secretariat, shall be open equally to men and women.
4. Representatives of the Members of the League and officials of the League when engaged on the business of the League shall enjoy diplomatic privileges and immunities.
5. The buildings and other property occupied by the League or its officials or by Representatives attending its meetings shall be inviolable.

Article 8

1. The Members of the League recognize that the maintenance of peace requires the reduction of national armaments to the lowest point consistent with national safety and the enforcement by common action of international obligations.
2. The Council, taking account of the geographical situation and circumstances of each State, shall formulate plans for such reduction for the consideration and action of the several Governments.
3. Such plans shall be subject to reconsideration and revision at least every ten years.
4. After these plans have been adopted by the several Governments, the limits of armaments therein fixed shall not be exceeded without the concurrence of the Council.

5. The Members of the League agree that the manufacture by private enterprise of munitions and implements of war is open to grave objections. The Council shall advise how the evil effects attendant upon such manufacture can be prevented, due regard being had to the necessities of those Members of the League which are not able to manufacture the munitions and implements of war necessary for their safety.

6. The Members of the League undertake to interchange full and frank information as to the scale of their armaments, their military, naval and air programmes and the condition of such of their industries as are adaptable to warlike purposes.

ARTICLE 9

A permanent Commission shall be constituted to advise the Council on the execution of the provisions of Articles 1 and 8 and on military, naval and air questions generally.

ARTICLE 10

The Members of the League undertake to respect and preserve as against external aggression the territorial integrity and existing political independence of all Members of the League. In case of any such aggression or in case of any threat or danger of such aggression, the Council shall advise upon the means by which this obligation shall be fulfilled.

ARTICLE 11

1. Any war or threat of war, whether immediately affecting any of the Members of the League or not, is hereby declared a matter of concern to the whole League, and the League shall take any action that may be deemed wise and effectual to safeguard the peace of nations. In case any such emergency should arise,

the Secretary-General shall, on the request of any Member of the League, forthwith summon a meeting of the Council.

2. It is also declared to be the friendly right of each Member of the League to bring to the attention of the Assembly or of the Council any circumstance whatever affecting international relations which threatens to disturb international peace or the good understanding between nations upon which peace depends.

ARTICLE 12

1. The Members of the League agree that if there should arise between them any dispute likely to lead to a rupture they will submit the matter either to arbitration *or judicial settlement* or to enquiry by the Council, and they agree in no case to resort to war until three months after the award by the arbitrators *or the judicial decision* or the report by the Council.

2. In any case under this article the award of the arbitrators *or the judicial decision* shall be made within a reasonable time, and the report of the Council shall be made within six months after the submission of the dispute.

ARTICLE 13

1. The Members of the League agree that whenever any dispute shall arise between them which they recognise to be suitable for submission to arbitration *or judicial settlement*, and which cannot be satisfactorily settled by diplomacy, they will submit the whole subject-matter to arbitration *or judicial settlement*.

2. Disputes as to the interpretation of a treaty, as to any question of international law, as to the existence of any fact which, if established, would constitute a breach of any international obligation, or as to the extent and nature of the reparation to be made for any

such breach, are declared to be among those which are generally suitable for submission to arbitration *or judicial settlement.*

3. *For the consideration of any such dispute, the court to which the case is referred shall be the Permament Court of International Justice, established in accordance with Article 14, or any tribunal agreed on by the parties to the dispute or stipulated in any Convention existing between them.*

4. The Members of the League agree that they will carry out in full good faith any award *or decision* that may be rendered, and that they will not resort to war against a Member of the League which complies therewith. In the event of any failure to carry out such an award *or decision*, the Council shall propose what steps should be taken to give effect thereto.

ARTICLE 14

The Council shall formulate and submit to the Members of the League for adoption plans for the establishment of a Permanent Court of International Justice. The Court shall be competent to hear and determine any dispute of an international character which the parties thereto submit to it. The Court may also give an advisory opinion upon any dispute or question referred to it by the Council or by the Assembly.

ARTICLE 15

1. If there should arise between Members of the League any dispute likely to lead to a rupture, which is not submitted to arbitration *or judicial settlement* in accordance with Article 13, the Members of the League agree that they will submit the matter to the Council. Any party to the dispute may effect such submission by giving notice of the existence of the dispute to the

Secretary-General, who will make all necessary arrangements for a full investigation and consideration thereof.

2. For this purpose, the parties to the dispute will communicate to the Secretary-General, as promptly as possible, statements of their case with all the relevant facts and papers, and the Council may forthwith direct the publication thereof.

3. The Council shall endeavour to effect a settlement of the dispute, and if such efforts are successful, a statement shall be made public giving such facts and explanations regarding the dispute and the terms of settlement thereof as the Council may deem appropriate.

4. If the dispute is not thus settled, the Council either unanimously or by a majority vote shall make and publish a report containing a statement of the facts of the dispute and the recommendations which are deemed just and proper in regard thereto.

5. Any Member of the League represented on the Council may make public a statement of the facts of the dispute and of its conclusions regarding the same.

6. If a report by the Council is unanimously agreed to by the members thereof other than the Representatives of one or more of the parties to the dispute, the Members of the League agree that they will not go to war with any party to the dispute which complies with the recommendations of the report.

7. If the Council fails to reach a report which is unanimously agreed to by the members thereof, other than the Representatives of one or more of the parties to the dispute, the Members of the League reserve to themselves the right to take such action as they shall consider necessary for the maintenance of right and justice.

8. If the dispute between the parties is claimed by one of them, and is found by the Council, to arise out of a matter which by international law is solely within the domestic jurisdiction of that party, the Council shall so report, and shall make no recommendation as to its settlement.

9. The Council may in any case under this article refer the dispute to the Assembly. The dispute shall be so referred at the request of either party to the dispute provided that such request be made within fourteen days after the submission of the dispute to the Council.

10. In any case referred to the Assembly, all the provisions of this article and of Article 12 relating to the action and powers of the Council shall apply to the action and powers of the Assembly, provided that a report made by the Assembly, if concurred in by the Representatives of those Members of the League represented on the Council and of a majority of the other Members of the League, exclusive in each case of the Representatives of the parties to the dispute, shall have the same force as a report by the Council concurred in by all the members thereof other than the Representatives of one or more of the parties to the dispute.

ARTICLE 16

1. Should any Member of the League resort to war in disregard of its covenants under Articles 12, 13 or 15, it shall, *ipso facto*, be deemed to have committed an act of war against all other Members of the League, which hereby undertake immediately to subject it to the severance of all trade or financial relations, the prohibition of all intercourse between their nationals

and the nationals of the Covenant-breaking State, and the prevention of all financial, commercial or personal intercourse between the nationals of the covenant-breaking State and the nationals of any other State, whether a Member of the League or not.

2. It shall be the duty of the Council in such case to recommend to the several Governments concerned what effective military, naval or air force the Members of the League shall severally contribute to the armed forces to be used to protect the covenants of the League.

3. The Members of the League agree, further, that they will mutually support one another in the financial and economic measures which are taken under this article, in order to minimise the loss and inconvenience resulting from the above measures, and that they will mutually support one another in resisting any special measures aimed at one of their number by the covenant-breaking State, and that they will take the necessary steps to afford passage through their territory to the forces of any of the Members of the League which are co-operating to protect the covenants of the League.

4. Any Member of the League which has violated any covenant of the League may be declared to be no longer a Member of the League by a vote of the Council concurred in by the Representatives of all the other Members of the League represented thereon.

ARTICLE 17

1. In the event of a dispute between a Member of the League and a State which is not a member of the League or between States not members of the League, the State or States not members of the League shall be invited to accept the obligations of membership in the League for the purposes of such dispute, upon such conditions

as the Council may deem just. If such invitation is accepted, the provisions of Articles 12 to 16 inclusive shall be applied with such modifications as may be deemed necessary by the Council.

2. Upon such invitation being given, the Council shall immediately institute an enquiry into the circumstances of the dispute and recommend such action as may seem best and most effectual in the circumstances.

3. If a State so invited shall refuse to accept the obligations of membership in the League for the purposes of such dispute, and shall resort to war against a Member of the League, the provisions of Article 16 shall be applicable as against the State taking such action.

4. If both parties to the dispute when so invited refuse to accept the obligations of membership in the League for the purposes of such dispute, the Council may take such measures and make such recommendations as will prevent hostilities and will result in the settlement of the dispute.

ARTICLE 18

Every treaty or international engagement entered into hereafter by any Member of the League shall be forthwith registered with the Secretariat and shall, as soon as possible, be published by it. No such treaty or international engagement shall be binding until so registered.

ARTICLE 19

The Assembly may from time to time advise the reconsideration by Members of the League of treaties which have become inapplicable and the consideration of international conditions whose continuance might endanger the peace of the world.

Article 20

1. The Members of the League severally agree that this Covenant is accepted as abrogating all obligations or under standings *inter se* which are inconsistent with the terms thereof, and solemnly undertake that they will not hereafter enter into any engagements inconsistent with the terms thereof.

2. In case any Member of the League shall, before becoming a Member of the League, have undertaken any obligations inconsistent with the terms of this Covenant, it shall be the duty of such Member to take immediate steps to procure its release from such obligations.

Article 21

Nothing in this Covenant shall be deemed to affect the validity of international engagements, such as treaties of arbitration or regional understandings like the Monroe doctrine, for securing the maintenance of peace.

Article 22

1. To those colonies and territories which as a consequence of the late war have ceased to be under the sovereignty of the States which formerly governed them and which are inhabited by peoples not yet able to stand by themselves under the strenuous conditions of the modern world, there should be applied the principle that the well-being and development of such peoples form a sacred trust of civilisation and that securities for the performance of this trust should be embodied in this Covenant.

2. The best method of giving practical effect to this principle is that the tutelage of such peoples should be entrusted to advanced nations who, by reason of their resources, their experience or their geographical

position, can best undertake this responsibility, and who are willing to accept it, and that this tutelage should be exercised by them as Mandatories on behalf of the League.

3. The character of the mandate must differ according to the stage of the development of the people, the geographical situation of the territory, its economic conditions and other similar circumstances.

4. Certain communities formerly belonging to the Turkish Empire have reached a stage of development where their existence as independent nations can be provisionally recognised subject to the rendering of administrative advice and assistance by a Mandatory until such time as they are able to stand alone. The wishes of these communities must be a principal consideration in the selection of the Mandatory.

5. Other peoples, especially those of Central Africa, are at such a stage that the Mandatory must be responsible for the administration of the territory under conditions which will guarantee freedom of conscience and religion, subject only to the maintenance of public order and morals, the prohibition of abuses such as the slave trade, the arms traffic and the liquor traffic, and the prevention of the establishment of fortifications or military and naval bases and of military training of the natives for other than police purposes and the defence of territory, and will also secure equal opportunities for the trade and commerce of other Members of the League.

6. There are territories, such as South West Africa and certain of the South Pacific Islands, which, owing to the sparseness of their population, or their small size, or their remoteness from the centres of civilisation, of their geographical contiguity to the territory of the Mandatory, and other circumstances, can be best

administered under the laws of the Mandatory as integral portions of its territory, subject to the safeguards above mentioned in the interests of the indigenous population.

7. In every case of mandate, the Mandatory shall render to the Council an annual report in reference to the territory committed to its charge.

8. The degree of authority, control or administration to be exercised by the Mandatory shall, if not previously agreed upon by the Members of the League, be explicitly defined in each case by the Council.

9. A permanent Commission shall be constituted to receive and examine the annual reports of the Mandatories and to advise the Council on all matters relating to the observance of the mandates.

Article 23

Subject to and in accordance with the provisions of international Conventions existing or hereafter to be agreed upon, the Members of the League:

(a) will endeavour to secure and maintain fair and humane conditions of labour for men, women and children, both in their own countries and in all countries to which their commercial and industrial relations extend, and for that purpose will establish and maintain the necessary international organisations;

(b) undertake to secure just treatment of the native inhabitants of territories under their control;

(c) will entrust the League with the general supervision over the execution of agreements with regard to the traffic in women and children, and the traffic in opium and other dangerous drugs;

(d) will entrust the League with the general supervision of the trade in arms and ammunition with the countries in which the control of this traffic is necessary in the common interest;

(e) will make provision to secure and maintain freedom of communications and of transit and equitable treatment for the commerce of all Members of the League. In this connection, the special necessities of the regions devastated during the war of 1914–1918 shall be borne in mind;

(f) will endeavour to take steps in matters of international concern for the prevention and control of disease.

ARTICLE 24

1. There shall be placed under the direction of the League all international bureaux already established by general treaties if the parties to such treaties consent. All such international bureaux and all commissions for the regulation of matters of international interest hereafter constituted shall be placed under the direction of the League.

2. In all matters of international interest which are regulated by general Conventions but which are not placed under the control of international bureaux or commissions, the Secretariat of the League shall, subject to the consent of the Council and if desired by the parties, collect and distribute all relevant information and shall render any other assistance which may be necessary or desirable.

3. The Council may include as part of the expenses of the Secretariat the expenses of any bureau or commission which is placed under the direction of the League.

ARTICLE 25.

The Members of the League agree to encourage and promote the establishment and co-operation of duly authorised voluntary national Red Cross organisations having as purposes the improvement of health, the prevention of disease and the mitigation of suffering throughout the world.

ARTICLE 26

1. Amendments to this Covenant will take effect when ratified by the Members of the League whose Representatives compose the Council and by a majority of the Members of the League whose Representatives compose the Assembly.

2. No such amendments shall bind any Member of the League which signifies its dissent therefrom, but in that case it shall cease to be a Member of the League.

APPENDIX II

Rules of Procedure Adopted by the First Assembly of the League

Rule 1.—1. The Assembly shall meet every year, at the seat of the League of Nations, commencing on the first Monday in September.

2. Sessions may also be held at such times as the Assembly at a previous meeting decides, and at such times as the Council, by a majority vote, decides.

3. If a Member of the League considers a Session to be desirable, it may request the Secretary-General to summon a special session of the Assembly. The Secretary-General shall thereupon inform the other Members of the League of the request, and inquire whether they concur in it. If within a period of one month from the date of such communication of the Secretary-General, a majority of the Members concur in the request, a Special Session shall be summoned.

Rule 2. The Sessions of the Assembly shall be held at the seat of the League, or, in exceptional circumstances, at such other place as is designated by the Assembly or by a majority of the Council, or by a majority of the Members of the League.

Rule 3.—1. The Sessions of the Assembly shall be summoned by the President of the Council, acting through the Secretary-General.

2. The summons shall be addressed to the Members of the League not less than four months before the date fixed for the opening of the Session. In exceptional

circumstances, however, the Council, by a majority vote, may sanction a shorter period.

3. Nothing contained in paragraph 2 of this Rule shall affect the provisions concerning special cases contained in the Covenant.

Rule 4.—1. The agenda shall be drawn up by the Secretary-General with the approval of the President of the Council. The complete agenda shall be circulated as nearly as possible four months before the date fixed for the opening of the Session.

2. The agenda of a General Session shall include:

(*a*) A report upon the work of the Council since the last Session;

(*b*) A report by the Secretary-General upon the work of the Secretariat and upon the measures taken to execute the decisions of the Assembly;

(*c*) All items whose inclusion has been ordered by the Assembly at a previous session;

(*d*) All items proposed by the Council;

(*e*) All items proposed by any Member of the League; and

(*f*) The budget for the next fiscal period and the report on the accounts of the last fiscal period.

3. Any Member of the League may, at least one month before the date fixed for the opening of the Session, request the inclusion of additional items in the agenda. Such items shall be placed on a supplementary list, which shall be circulated to the Members of the League at least three weeks before the date fixed for the opening of the Session. The Assembly shall decide whether items on the supplementary list shall be included in the agenda of the Session.

4. The Assembly may in exceptional circumstances place additional items on the agenda; but all consideration of such items shall, unless otherwise ordered by a two-thirds majority of the Assembly, be postponed until

four days after they have been placed on the agenda, and until a committee has reported upon them.

Rule 5.—1. Each Member shall communicate to the Secretary-General, if possible before the opening of the Session, the names of its Representatives, of whom there shall be not more than three. The names of Substitute-Representatives may be added.

2. Each Representative shall, as soon as possible, and preferably before the opening of the Session, present his credentials to the Secretary-General.

3. A committee of eight members for the examination of the credentials shall be elected by the Assembly by secret ballot. The committee shall report without delay.

4. Any Representative to whose admission objection has been made shall sit provisionally, with the same rights as other Representatives unless the Assembly decides otherwise.

Rule 6.—1. In addition to the Substitute-Representatives mentioned in paragraph 1 of Rule 5, the Representatives of a Member of the League attending the Assembly, acting together as a Delegation, may appoint substitutes. Any such appointment shall be communicated in writing to the President.

2. A Substitute-Representative appointed by a Member of the League may take the place of a Representative without having been nominated by the Representatives.

3. A Substitute-Representative or substitute may take the place of a Representative who is absent from a meeting of the Assembly, or is temporarily prevented from taking part in its deliberations, but if the Representative is present at the meeting the Substitute-Representative or substitute is only entitled to assist him.

4. A delegation may appoint for service on a com-

mittee a deputy or technical adviser other than those referred to in the above paragraphs of this Rule; but a deputy or adviser so appointed shall not be eligible for appointment as Chairman or Rapporteur, or for a seat in the Assembly.

Rule 7.—1. The officers of the Assembly shall consist of a President and of six Vice-Presidents, together with the Chairman of the main Committees of the Assembly, who shall be ex-officio Vice-Presidents of the Assembly. These officers shall form the General Committee.

2. The President and the six Vice-Presidents shall be elected at the beginning of each Session.

3. Until the election of the President, the President of the Council shall act as President of the Assembly.

Rule 8.—1. The President shall announce the opening, suspension, and adjournment of the meetings of the Assembly, direct the work of the Assembly, insure the observance of the Rules of Procedure, accord the right to address the Assembly, declare the debates to be closed, put questions to the vote, and announce the result of the voting.

2. In the general directions of the work of the Assembly, in the constitution of such committees as the Assembly decides to create, in deciding on the communications to be made to the Assembly, in the framing of the agenda for each meeting, and the determination of the order of priority for its various items, the President shall be assisted by the General Committee.

Rule 9.—1. The Secretary-General shall be responsible for the organization of the Secretariat of the Assembly and of the Secretariat of any committees set up by the Assembly.

2. The Secretary-General may be assisted or replaced at the meeting of the Assembly by a deputy or deputies. The Secretary-General, or one of his deputies, may at

any time, on the invitation of the President, bring before the Assembly reports concerning any question which is being considered by the Assembly, and may be invited by the President to make verbal communications concerning any question under consideration.

Rule 10.—1. It shall be the duty of the Secretariat, *inter alia*, to receive, print, circulate, and translate documents, reports, and resolutions; to translate speeches made at the meetings; to draft, print and circulate the Minutes of the Session; to have the custody and proper preservation of the documents in the archives of the Assembly; to publish the reports of the meetings; and generally, to perform all other work which the Assembly thinks fit to intrust to it.

2. All documents emanating from the Assembly shall be circulated to the Governments of the Members of the League.

Rule 11.—1. The public shall be admitted to the plenary meetings of the Assembly, by cards distributed by the Secretary-General.

2. The Assembly may decide that particular meetings shall be private.

3. All decisions of the Assembly upon items on the agenda which have been taken at a private meeting, shall be announced at a public meeting of the Assembly.

Rule 12.—A list of the attendance at each meeting of the Assembly shall be kept by the Secretariat.

Rule 13.—At the beginning of each meeting the President shall present to the Assembly all communications addressed to the Assembly or to the League, the importance of which appears to him to warrant such action.

Rule 14.—1. The Assembly shall establish such committees as it thinks fit for the consideration of the items on the agenda. Items of the same nature will be referred to the committee.

2. The Assembly shall not decide items on the agenda in full meeting until the report of the committee upon them has been presented and circulated, unless the Assembly itself, by a two-thirds majority, determines otherwise.

3. Each Delegation may designate one member, and may nominate technical advisers for each committee.

4. Each committee shall appoint its Chairman and Rapporteur.

5. Each committee may appoint subcommittees, which shall elect their own officers.

6. Each committee shall meet in private unless it decides otherwise. It shall keep a Register of its discussions, and Minutes, which shall be published at the earliest possible date, but not until they have been approved by the committee. They may at any time be consulted by any member of the Assembly.

7. Every Representative shall have the right to place before any committee any communication which he considers should be made to it, but no Representative may, without special leave from the Chairman, speak at a meeting of any committee of which he is not a member.

8. The Secretary-General or his deputies may make to any committee or subcommittee any report or verbal communication which he or they may consider desirable.

Rule 15.—1. No Representative may address the Assembly without having previously obtained the permission of the President.

2. Speakers shall be called upon in the order in which they have signified their desire to speak. The Chairman and the Rapporteur of a committee may be accorded precedence for the purpose of defending or explaining the conclusions arrived at by their committee. The

same principle shall apply to any member of the Council.

3. The President may call a speaker to order if his remarks are not relevant to the subject under discussion. If necessary he may direct the speaker to resume his seat.

4. When a motion is under discussion, a Representative may rise to a point of order, and such point of order shall be immediately decided by the President in accordance with the Rules of Prodecure.

5. The Assembly may limit the time allowed to each speaker.

Rule 16.—1. Speeches in French shall be summarized in English, and vice versa, by an interpreter belonging to the Secretariat.

2. A Representative speaking in another language shall provide for the translation of his speech into one of these two languages.

3. All documents, resolutions, and reports circulated by the President or the Secretariat shall be rendered in both French and English.

4. Any Representative may have documents circulated in a language other than French and English, but the Secretariat will not be responsible for their translation or printing.

5. Any Member of the League, or any group of Members, may require that all documents and publications of the League shall be regularly translated into and printed and circulated in a language other than French or English; but shall in such case defray all the necessary expenses.

Rule 17.—1. Resolutions, amendments, and motions must be introduced in writing and handed to the President. The President shall cause copies to be distributed to the Representatives.

2. As a general rule, no proposal shall be discussed or put to a vote at any meeting of the Assembly unless

copies of it have been circulated to all Representatives not later than the day preceding the meeting.

3. The President may, however, permit the discussion and consideration of amendments, or of motions as to procedure, without previous circulation of copies.

Rule 18.—1. During the discussion of any question, any Representative may move the previous question or the adjournment. Any such motion shall have priority in the debate. In addition to the proposer of the motion, two Representatives may speak in favor of, and two against, the motion.

2. Parts of a proposal shall be voted on separately, if a Representative requests that the proposal be divided.

3. A Representative may at any time move the closure of the debate whether any other Representative has signified his wish to speak or not. If application is made for permission to speak against the closure, it may be accorded only to not more than two speakers.

4. The President shall take the sense of the Assembly on a motion for closure. If the Assembly decides in favor of the closure, the President shall declare the closure of the debate.

5. When a number of proposals are before the Assembly, the proposal furthest removed in substance from the principal one shall be voted on first.

6. If an amendment striking out part of a proposal is moved, the Assembly shall first vote on whether the words in question shall stand as part of the proposal. If the decision is in the negative, the amendment shall then be put to the vote.

7. When an amendment adds to a proposal, it shall be voted on first, and if it is adopted the amended proposal shall then be voted on.

Rule 19.—1. Except where otherwise expressly provided in the Covenant or by the terms of a treaty, decisions of the Assembly shall be taken by a unanimous vote of the Members of the League represented at the meeting.

2. All matters of procedure at a meeting of the Assembly, including the appointment of committees to investigate particular matters, shall be decided by a majority of the Members of the League represented at the meeting.

3. All decisions taken in virtue of these Rules shall be considered as matters of procedure.

4. A majority decision requires the affirmative votes of more than half of the Members of the League represented at the meeting.

5. For the purposes of this Rule, Representatives who abstain from voting shall be considered as not present.

Rule 20.—1. The Assembly shall vote by "Appel Nominal," except when the Members of the League represented at the meeting agree that the method of voting shall be by heads of Delegations rising in their seats, and except in the cases provided for in Rule 21. The "Appel Nominal" shall be taken in the following manner.

The Delegation of each Member of the League represented at the meeting shall be provided with two voting tickets, on which the name of the country is written, one red and one blue, the former being "Aye," the latter, "No." The voting tickets shall be deposited in an urn placed near the President's platform. When all the votes have been collected, the President shall declare the ballot closed and the General Committee shall proceed to count the votes. The individual votes shall be communicated to the Assembly and the result shall be announced to the President.

Rule 21.—1. All decisions relating to individuals shall be taken by a secret ballot.

2. If, when one person only is to be elected, no one

person obtains at the first ballot an absolute majority of votes, an entirely new ballot shall be taken; but on this occasion the voting shall be confined to the two candidates who obtained the largest number of votes at the first ballot. If there is at this ballot an equality of votes for the two candidates, the elder candidate shall be declared elected.

3. When a number of elective places of the same nature are to be filled at one time, those persons who obtain an absolute majority at the first ballot shall be elected. If the number of persons obtaining such majority is less than the number of persons to be elected, there shall be a second ballot to fill the remaining places, the voting being restricted to the unsuccessful candidates who obtained the greatest number of votes at the first ballot, not more than double in number the places remaining to be filled. Those candidates, to the number required to be elected, who receive the greatest number of votes at the second ballot shall be declared elected.

Rule 22.—In case of equality in any voting other than that referred to in Rule 21, in which a majority is required, a second vote shall be taken in the course of the next meeting; this meeting shall be held within forty-eight hours from the date on which the first vote was taken, and it shall be expressly mentioned on the agenda that a second vote will be taken on the matter in question. Unless there is at this subsequent meeting a majority in favor of the proposal, it shall be considered as lost.

Rule 23.—1. The President may declare a meeting to be adjourned or suspended, if a proposal for adjournment or suspension made by him does not meet with objection from the Assembly.

2. The President shall declare an adjournment or suspension of the meeting upon a vote to this effect by the Assembly.

Rule 24.—The General Committee, in cases where it deems it necessary, may revise the resolutions adopted by the Assembly, changing their form but not their substance. Any such changes shall be reported to the Assembly.

Rule 25.—The verbatim report of each meeting shall be drawn up by the Secretariat and submitted to the Assembly after approval by the President.

Rule 26.—The resolutions adopted by the Assembly shall be circulated by the Secretary-General to the Members of the League within fifteen days after the termination of the Session.

Rule 27.—These Rules of Procedure shall apply to the proceedings of committees of the Assembly.

Rule 28.—These Rules of Procedure may be altered by a decision of the Assembly; but no such alteration shall be made except upon a majority vote of the Assembly taken after a committee has reported upon the proposed alteration.

APPENDIX III

Constitution of the International Labour Organisation [1]

SECTION I

ORGANISATION OF LABOUR

Whereas the League of Nations has for its object the establishment of universal peace, and such a peace can be established only if it is based upon social justice;

And whereas conditions of labour exist involving such injustice, hardship and privation to large numbers of people as to produce unrest so great that the peace and harmony of the world are imperilled; and an improvement of those conditions is urgently required: as, for example, by the regulation of the hours of work, including the establishment of a maximum working day and week, the regulation of the labour supply, the prevention of unemployment, the provision of an adequate living wage, the protection of the worker against sickness, disease and injury arising out of his employment, the protection of children, young persons and women, provision for old age and injury, protection of the interests of workers when employed in countries other than their own, recognition of the principle of freedom of association, the organisation of vocational and technical education and other measures;

Whereas also the failure of any nation to adopt

---

[1] Part XIII, Labour, of the Treaty of Peace with Germany, Versailles, June 28, 1919.

humane conditions of labour is an obstacle in the way of other nations which desire to improve the conditions in their own countries;

The HIGH CONTRACTING PARTIES, moved by sentiments of justice and humanity as well as by the desire to secure the permanent peace of the world, agree to the following:

CHAPTER I

Organisation

ARTICLE 387

A permanent organisation is hereby established for the promotion of the objects set forth in the Preamble.

The original Members of the League of Nations shall be the original Members of this organisation, and hereafter membership of the League of Nations shall carry with it membership of the said organisation.

ARTICLE 388

The permanent organisation shall consist of:
(1) a General Conference of Representatives of the Members and,
(2) an International Labour Office controlled by the Governing Body described in Article 393.

ARTICLE 389

The meetings of the General Conference of Representatives of the Members shall be held from time to time as occasion may require, and at least once in every year. It shall be composed of four Representatives of each of the Members, of whom two shall be Government Delegates and the two others shall be Delegates representing respectively the employers and the workpeople of each of the Members.

Each Delegate may be accompanied by advisers,

who shall not exceed two in number for each item on the agenda of the meeting. When questions specially affecting women are to be considered by the Conference, one at least of the advisers should be a woman.

The Members undertake to nominate non-Government Delegates and advisers chosen in agreement with the industrial organisations, if such organisations exist, which are most representative of employers or workpeople, as the case may be, in their respective countries.

Advisers shall not speak except on a request made by the Delegate whom they accompany and by the special authorisation of the President of the Conference, and may not vote.

A Delegate may by notice in writing addressed to the President appoint one of his advisers to act as his deputy, and the adviser, while so acting, shall be allowed to speak and vote.

The names of the Delegates and their advisers will be communicated to the International Labour Office by the Government of each of the Members.

The credentials of Delegates and their advisers shall be subject to scrutiny by the Conference, which may, by two-thirds of the votes cast by the Delegates present, refuse to admit any Delegate or adviser whom it deems not to have been nominated in accordance with this article.

Article 390

Every Delegate shall be entitled to vote individually on all matters which are taken into consideration by the Conference.

If one of the Members fails to nominate one of the non-Government Delegates whom it is entitled to nominate, the other non-Government Delegate shall be allowed to sit and speak at the Conference, but not to vote.

If in accordance with Article 389 the Conference refuses admission to a Delegate of one of the Members, the provisions of the present article shall apply as if that Delegate had not been nominated.

Article 391

The meetings of the Conference shall be held at the seat of the League of Nations, or at such other place as may be decided by the Conference at a previous meeting by two-thirds of the votes cast by the Delegates present.

Article 392

The International Labour Office shall be established at the seat of the League of Nations as part of the organisation of the League.

Article 393 [2]

The International Labour Office shall be under the control of a Governing Body consisting of twenty-four persons, appointed in accordance with the following provisions:

---

[2] The Conference on October 18, 1922, adopted the following amendment to Article 393, which has entered into force as prescribed in Article 422:

"*The International Labour Office shall be under the control of a Governing Body consisting of 32 persons:*

"*Sixteen representing Governments,*
"*Eight representing the Employers, and*
"*Eight representing the Workers.*

"*Of the 16 persons representing Governments, eight shall be appointed by the members of chief industrial importance, and eight shall be appointed by the members selected for that purpose by the Government delegates to the Conference excluding the delegates of the eight members mentioned above. Of the 16 members represented six shall be non-European states.*

"*Any question as to which are the members of chief industrial importance shall be decided by the Council of the League of Nations.*

"*The persons representing the Employers and the persons representing the Workers shall be elected respectively by the Employers' delegates and the Workers' delegates to the Conference. Two Employers' representatives and two Workers' representatives shall belong to non-European states.*

"*The period of office of the Governing Body shall be three years.*

"*The method of filling vacancies and of appointing substitutes, and other similar questions, may be decided by the Governing Body subject to the approval of the Conference.*

The Governing Body of the International Labour Office shall be constituted as follows:

Twelve persons representing the Governments;

Six persons elected by the Delegates to the Conference representing the employers;

Six persons elected by the Delegates to the Conference representing the workers.

Of the twelve persons representing the Governments eight shall be nominated by the Members which are of the chief industrial importance, and four shall be nominated by the Members selected for the purpose by the Government Delegates to the Conference, excluding the Delegates of the eight Members mentioned above.

Any questions as to which are the Members of the chief industrial importance shall be decided by the Council of the League of Nations.

The period of office of the Members of the Governing Body will be three years. The method of filling vacancies and other similar questions may be determined by the Governing Body subject to the approval of the Conference.

The Governing Body shall, from time to time, elect one of its members to act as its Chairman, shall regulate its own procedure and shall fix its own times of meeting. A special meeting shall be held if a written request to that effect is made by at least ten members of the Governing Body.

Article 394

There shall be a Director of the International Labour Office, who shall be appointed by the Governing Body, and, subject to the instructions of the Governing

---

"*The Governing Body shall, from time to time, elect one of its number to act as its Chairman, shall regulate its own procedure, and shall fix its own times of meeting. A special meeting shall be held if a written request to that effect is made by at least 12 of the representatives on the Governing Body.*"

Body, shall be responsible for the efficient conduct of the International Labour Office and for such other duties as may be assigned to him.

The Director or his deputy shall attend all meetings of the Governing Body.

Article 395

The staff of the International Labour Office shall be appointed by the Director, who shall, so far as is possible with due regard to the efficiency of the work of the Office, select persons of different nationalities. A certain number of these persons shall be women.

Article 396

The functions of the International Labour Office shall include the collection and distribution of information on all subjects relating to the international adjustment of conditions of industrial life and labour, and particularly the examination of subjects which it is proposed to bring before the Conference with a view to the conclusion of international conventions, and the conduct of such special investigations as may be ordered by the Conference.

It will prepare the agenda for the meetings of the Conference.

It will carry out the duties required of it by the provisions of this Part of the present treaty in connection with international disputes.

It will edit and publish in French and English, and in such other languages as the Governing Body may think desirable, a periodical paper dealing with problems of industry and employment of international interest.

Generally, in addition to the functions set out on this article, it shall have such other powers and duties as may be assigned to it by the Conference.

Article 397

The Government Departments of any of the Members which deal with questions of industry and employment may communicate directly with the Director through the Representative of their Government on the Governing Body of the International Labour Office, or failing any such Representative, through such other qualified officials as the Government may nominate for the purpose.

Article 398

The International Labour Office shall be entitled to the assistance of the Secretary-General of the League of Nations in any matter in which it can be given.

Article 399

Each of the Members will pay the traveling and subsistence expenses of its Delegates and their advisers and of its Representatives attending the meetings of the Conference or Governing Body, as the case may be.

All the other expenses of the International Labour Office and of the meetings of the Conference or Governing Body shall be paid to the Director by the Secretary-General of the League of Nations out of the general funds of the League.

The Director shall be responsible to the Secretary-General of the League for the proper expenditure of all moneys paid to him in pursuance of this article.

Chapter II

Procedure

Article 400

The agenda for all meetings of the Conference will be settled by the Governing Body, who shall consider any suggestion as to the agenda that may be made by the Government of any of the Members or by any representative organisation recognised for the purpose of Article 389.

Article 401

The Director shall act as the Secretary of the Conference, and shall transmit the agenda so as to reach the Members four months before the meeting of the Conference, and, through them, the non-Government Delegates when appointed.

Article 402

Any of the Governments of the Members may formally object to the inclusion of any item or items in the agenda. The grounds for such objection shall be set forth in a reasoned statement addressed to the Director, who shall circulate it to all the Members of the Permanent Organisation.

Items to which such objection has been made shall not, however, be excluded from the agenda, if at the Conference a majority of two-thirds of the votes cast by the Delegates present is in favor of considering them.

If the Conference decides (otherwise than under the preceding paragraph) by two-thirds of the votes cast by the Delegates present that any subject shall be considered by the Conference, that subject shall be included in the agenda for the following meeting.

Article 403

The Conference shall regulate its own procedure, shall elect its own President, and may appoint committees to consider and report on any matter.

Except as otherwise expressly provided in this Part of the present Treaty, all matters shall be decided by a simple majority of the votes cast by the Delegates present.

The voting is void unless the total number of votes cast is equal to half the number of the Delegates attending the Conference.

Article 404

The Conference may add to any committees which it appoints technical experts, who shall be assessors without power to vote.

Article 405

When the Conference has decided on the adoption of proposals with regard to an item in the agenda, it will rest with the Conference to determine whether these proposals should take the form: (*a*) of a recommendation to be submitted to the Members for consideration with a view to effect being given to it by national legislation or otherwise, or (*b*) of a draft international convention for ratification by the Members.

In either case a majority of two-thirds of the votes cast by the Delegates present shall be necessary on the final vote for the adoption of the recommendation or draft convention, as the case may be, by the Conference.

In framing any recommendation or draft convention of general application the Conference shall have due regard to those countries in which climatic conditions, the imperfect development of industrial organisation or other special circumstances make the industrial conditions substantially different and shall suggest the modifications, if any, which it considers may be required to meet the case of such countries.

A copy of the recommendation or draft convention shall be authenticated by the signature of the President of the Conference and of the Director and shall be deposited with the Secretary-General of the League of Nations. The Secretary-General will communicate a certified copy of the recommendation or draft convention to each of the Members.

Each of the Members undertakes that it will, within the period of one year at most from the closing of the session of the Conference, or if it is impossible owing to exceptional circumstances to do so within the period of one year, then at the earliest practicable moment and in no case later than eighteen months from the closing of the session of the Conference, bring the recommendation or draft convention before the authority or authorities within whose competence the matter lies, for the enactment of legislation or other action.

In the case of a recommendation, the Members will inform the Secretary-General of the action taken.

In the case of a draft convention, the Member will, if it obtains the consent of the authority or authorities within whose competence the matter lies, communicate the formal ratification of the convention to the Secretary-General and will take such action as may be necessary to make effective the provisions of such convention.

If on a recommendation no legislative or other action is taken to make a recommendation effective, or if the draft convention fails to obtain the consent of the authority or authorities within whose competence the matter lies, no further obligation shall rest upon the Member.

In the case of a federal state, the power of which to enter into conventions on labour matters is subject to limitations, it shall be in the discretion of that Government to treat a draft convention to which such limitations apply as a recommendation only, and the provisions of this article with respect to recommendations shall apply in such case.

The above article shall be interpreted in accordance with the following principle:

In no case shall any Member be asked or required, as a result of the adoption of any recommendation or draft convention by the Conference, to lessen the protection afforded by its existing legislation to the workers concerned.

Article 406

Any convention so ratified shall be registered by the Secretary-General of the League of Nations, but shall only be binding upon the Members which ratify it.

Article 407

If any convention coming before the Conference for final consideration fails to secure the support of two-thirds of the votes cast by the Delegates present, it shall nevertheless be within the right of any of the Members of the Permanent Organisation to agree to such convention among themselves.

Any convention so agreed to shall be communicated by the Governments concerned to the Secretary-General of the League of Nations, who shall register it.

Article 408

Each of the Members agrees to make an annual report to the International Labour Office on the measures which it has taken to give effect to the provisions of conventions to which it is a party. These reports shall be made in such form and shall contain such particulars as the Governing Body may request. The Director shall lay a summary of these reports before the next meeting of the Conference.

Article 409

In the event of any representation being made to the International Labour Office by an industrial association of employers or of workers that any of the Members has failed to secure in any respect the effective observance within its jurisdiction of any convention to which it is a party, the Governing Body may communicate this representation to the Government against which it is made and may invite that Government to make such statement on the subject as it may think fit.

Article 410

If no statement is received within a reasonable time from the Government in question, or if the statement when received is not deemed to be satisfactory by the Governing Body, the latter shall have the right to publish the representation and the statement, if any, made in reply to it.

Article 411

Any of the Members shall have the right to file a complaint with the International Labour Office if it is not satisfied that any other Member is securing the effective observance of any convention which both have ratified in accordance with the foregoing articles.

The Governing Body may, if it thinks fit, before referring such a complaint to a Commission of Inquiry, as hereinafter provided for, communicate with the Government in question in the manner described in Article 409.

If the Governing Body does not think it necessary to communicate the complaint to the Government in question, or if, when they have made such communication, no statement in reply has been received within a reasonable time which the Governing Body considers to be satisfactory, the Governing Body may apply for the appointment of a Commission of Inquiry to consider the complaint and to report thereon.

The Governing Body may adopt the same procedure

either of its own motion or on receipt of a complaint from a Delegate to the Conference.

When any matter arising out of Articles 410 or 411 is being considered by the Governing Body, the Government in question shall, if not already represented thereon, be entitled to send a representative to take part in the proceedings of the Governing Body while the matter is under consideration. Adequate notice of the date on which the matter will be considered shall be given to the Government in question.

Article 412

The Commission of Inquiry shall be constituted in accordance with the following provisions:

Each of the Members agrees to nominate within six months of the date on which the present Treaty comes into force three persons of industrial experience, of whom one shall be a representative of employers, one a representative of workers, and one a person of independent standing, who shall together form a panel from which the Members of the Commission of Inquiry shall be drawn.

The qualifications of the persons so nominated shall be subject to scrutiny by the Governing Body, which may by two-thirds of the votes cast by the representatives present refuse to accept the nomination of any person whose qualifications do not in its opinion comply with the requirements of the present article.

Upon the application of the Governing Body, the Secretary-General of the League of Nations shall nominate three persons, one from each section of this panel, to constitute the Commission of Inquiry, and shall designate one of them as the President of the Commission. None of these three persons shall be a person nominated to the panel by any Member directly concerned in the complaint.

Article 413

The Members agree that, in the event of the reference of a complaint to a Commission of Inquiry under Article 411 they will each, whether directly concerned in the complaint or not, place at the disposal of the commission all the information in their possession which bears upon the subject-matter of the complaint.

Article 414

When the Commission of Inquiry has fully considered the complaint, it shall prepare a report embodying its findings on all questions of fact relevant to determining the issue between the parties and containing such recommendations as it may think proper as to the steps which should be taken to meet the complaint and the time within which they should be taken.

It shall also indicate in this report the measures, if any, of an economic character against a defaulting Government which it considers to be appropriate, and which it considers other Governments would be justified in adopting.

Article 415

The Secretary-General of the League of Nations shall communicate the report of the Commission of Inquiry to each of the Governments concerned in the complaint, and shall cause it to be published.

Each of these Governments shall within one month inform the Secretary-General of the League of Nations whether or not it accepts the recommendations contained in the report of the commission; and if not, whether it proposes to refer the complaint to the Permanent Court of International Justice of the League of Nations.

Article 416

In the event of any Member failing to take the action required by Article 405 with regard to a recommendation or draft convention, any other Member shall be entitled to refer the matter to the Permanent Court of International Justice.

Article 417

The decision of the Permanent Court of International Justice in regard to a complaint or matter which has been referred to it in pursuance of Article 415 or Article 416 shall be final.

Article 418

The Permanent Court of International Justice may affirm, vary or reverse any of the findings or recommendations of the Commission of Inquiry, if any, and shall in its decision indicate the measures, if any, of an economic character which it considers to be appropriate, and which other Governments would be justified in adopting against a defaulting Government.

Article 419

In the event of any Member failing to carry out within the time specified the recommendations, if any, contained in the report of the Commission of Inquiry, or in the decision of the Permanent Court of International Justice, as the case may be, any other Member may take against that Member the measures of an economic character indicated in the report of the commission or in the decision of the Court as appropriate in the case.

Article 420

The defaulting Government may at any time inform the Governing Body that it has taken the steps necessary to comply with the recommendations of the Commission of Inquiry or with those in the decision of the Permanent Court of International Justice, as the case may be, and may request it to apply to the Secretary-General of the League to constitute a Commission of Inquiry to verify its contention. In this case the provisions of Articles 412, 413, 414, 415, 417 and 418 shall apply, and if the report of the Commission of Inquiry or the decision of the Permanent Court of International Justice is in favor of the defaulting Government, the other Governments shall forthwith discontinue the measures of an economic character that they have taken against the defaulting Government.

Chapter III
General
Article 421

The Members engage to apply conventions which they have ratified in accordance with the provisions of this Part of the present Treaty to their colonies, protectorates and possessions which are not fully self-governing:

(1) Except where owing to the local conditions the convention is inapplicable, or

(2) Subject to such modifications as may be necessary to adapt the convention to local conditions.

And each of the Members shall notify to the International Labour Office the action taken in respect of each of its colonies, protectorates and possessions which are not fully self-governing.

Article 422

Amendments to this Part of the present Treaty which are adopted by the Conference by a majority of two-thirds of the votes cast by the Delegates present shall take effect when ratified by the states whose representatives compose the Council of the League of Nations and by three-fourths of the Members.

Article 423

Any question or dispute relating to the interpretation of this Part of the present Treaty or of any subsequent convention concluded by the Members in pursuance of the provisions of this Part of the present treaty shall be referred for decision to the Permanent Court of International Justice.

Chapter IV
Transitory Provisions
Article 424

The first meeting of the Conference shall take place in October, 1919. The place and agenda for this meeting shall be as specified in the Annex hereto.

Arrangements for the convening and the organization of the first meeting of the Conference will be made by the Government designated for the purpose in the said Annex. That Government shall be assisted in the preparation of the documents for submission to the Conference by an International Committee constituted as provided in the said Annex.

The expenses of the first meeting and of all subsequent meetings held before the League of Nations has been able to establish a general fund, other than the expenses of Delegates and their advisers, will be borne by the Members in accordance with the apportionment of the expenses of the International Bureau of the Universal Postal Union.

Article 425

Until the League of Nations has been constituted all communications which under the provisions of the foregoing articles should be addressed to the Secretary-General of the League will be preserved by the Director of the International Labour Office, who will transmit them to the Secretary-General of the League.

Article 426

Pending the creation of a Permanent Court of International Justice disputes which in accordance with this Part of the present Treaty would be submitted to it for decision will be referred to a tribunal of three persons appointed by the Council of the League of Nations.

ANNEX

First Meeting of Annual Labour Conference, 1919

The place of meeting will be Washington.

The Government of the United States of America is requested to convene the Conference.

The International Organising Committee will consist of seven Members, appointed by the United States of America, Great Britain, France, Italy, Japan, Belgium and Switzerland. The committee may, if it thinks necessary, invite other Members to appoint representatives.

Agenda:

(1) Application of principle of the 8-hours day or of the 48-hours week.

(2) Question of preventing or providing against unemployment.

(3) Women's employment:
    (*a*) Before and after child-birth, including the question of maternity benefit;
    (*b*) During the night;
    (*c*) In unhealthy processes.

(4) Employment of children:
    (*a*) Minimum age of employment;

(b) During the night;
(c) In unhealthy processes.

(5) Extension and application of the international conventions adopted at Berne in 1906 on the prohibition of night work for women employed in industry and the prohibition of the use of white phosphorus in the manufacture of matches.

SECTION II

GENERAL PRINCIPLES

ARTICLE 427

The High Contracting Parties, recognising that the well-being, physical, moral and intellectual, of industrial wage-earners is of supreme international importance, have framed, in order to further this great end, the permanent machinery provided for in Section I and associated with that of the League of Nations.

They recognise that differences of climate, habits and customs, of economic opportunity and industrial tradition, make strict uniformity in the conditions of labour difficult of immediate attainment. But, holding as they do, that labour should not be regarded merely as an article of commerce, they think that there are methods and principles for regulating labour conditions which all industrial communities should endeavor to apply, so far as their special circumstances will permit.

Among these methods and principles, the following seem to the High Contracting Parties to be of special and urgent importance:

First.—The guiding principle above enunciated that labour should not be regarded merely as a commodity or article of commerce.

Second.—The right of association for all lawful purposes by the employed as well as by the employers.

Third.—The payment to the employed of a wage adequate to maintain a reasonable standard of life as this is understood in their time and country.

Fourth.—The adoption of an eight hours day or a forty-eight hours week as the standard to be aimed at where it has not already been attained.

Fifth.—The adoption of a weekly rest of at least twenty-four hours, which should include Sunday wherever practicable.

Sixth.—The abolition of child labour and the imposition of such limitations on the labour of young persons as shall permit the continuation of their education and assure their proper physical development.

Seventh.—The principle that men and women should receive equal remuneration for work of equal value.

Eighth.—The standard set by law in each country with respect to the conditions of labour should have due regard to the equitable economic treatment of all workers lawfully resident therein.

Ninth.—Each state should make provision for a system of inspection in which women should take part, in order to insure the enforcement of the laws and regulations for the protection of the employed.

Without claiming that these methods and principles are either complete or final, the High Contracting Parties are of opinion that they are well fitted to guide the policy of the League of Nations; and that, if adopted by the industrial communities who are Members of the League, and safeguarded in practice by an adequate system of such inspection, they will confer lasting benefits upon the wage-earners of the world.

APPENDIX IV

The Statute for the Permanent Court of International Justice [1]

PROVIDED FOR BY ARTICLE XIV OF THE COVENANT OF THE LEAGUE OF NATIONS

Article 1. A Permanent Court of International Justice is hereby established, in accordance with Article 14 of the Covenant of the League of Nations. This Court shall be in addition to the Court of Arbitration organized by the Conventions of The Hague of 1899 and 1907, and to the special Tribunals of Arbitration to which States are always at liberty to submit their disputes for settlement.

Chapter I. Organisation of the Court

Art. 2. The Permanent Court of International Justice shall be composed of a body of independent judges elected regardless of their nationality from amongst persons of high moral character, who possess the qualifitions required in their respective countries for appointment to the highest judicial offices, or are jurisconsults of recognized competence in international law.

*Art. 3. The Court shall consist of fifteen members: eleven judges and four deputy-judges. The number of judges and deputy-judges may hereafter be increased by the Assembly, upon the proposal of the Council of the League of Nations, to a total of fifteen judges and six deputy-judges.

---

[1] The articles marked with an asterisk are those which will be amended if the Protocol for the Revision of the Statute of September 14, 1929 comes into force.

*Art. 4. The members of the Court shall be elected by the Assembly and by the Council from a list of persons nominated by the national groups in the Court of Arbitration, in accordance with the following provisions.

In the case of Members of the League of Nations not represented in the Permanent Court of Arbitration, the lists of candidates shall be drawn up by national groups appointed for this purpose by their Governments under the same conditions as those prescribed for members of the Permanent Court of Arbitration by Article 44 of the Convention of The Hague of 1907 for the Pacific Settlement of International Disputes.

Art. 5. At least three months before the date of the election, the Secretary-General of the League of Nations shall address a written request to the Members of the Court of Arbitration belonging to the States mentioned in the Annex to the Covenant or to the States which join the League subsequently, and to the persons appointed under paragraph 2 of Article 4, inviting them to undertake, within a given time, by national groups, the nomination of persons in a position to accept the duties of a member of the Court.

No group may nominate more than four persons, not more than two of whom shall be of their own nationality. In no case must the number of candidates nominated be more than double the number of seats to be filled.

Art. 6. Before making these nominations, each national group is recommended to consult its Highest Court of Justice, its Legal Faculties and Schools of Law, and its National Academies and national sections of International Academies devoted to the study of Law.

Art. 7. The Secretary-General of the League of Nations shall prepare a list in alphabetical order of all the persons thus nominated. Save as provided in Article 12, paragraph 2, these shall be the only persons eligible for appointment.

The Secretary-General shall submit this list to the Assembly and to the Council.

*Art. 8. The Assembly and the Council shall proceed independently of one another to elect, firstly the judges, then the deputy-judges.

Art. 9. At every election, the electors shall bear in mind that not only should all the persons appointed as members of the Court possess the qualifications required, but the whole body also should represent the main forms of civilization and the principal legal systems of the world.

Art. 10. Those candidates who obtain an absolute majority of votes in the Assembly and in the Council shall be considered as elected.

In the event of more than one national of the same Member of the League being elected by the votes of both the Assembly and the Council, the eldest of these only shall be considered as elected.

Art. 11. If, after the first meeting held for the purpose of the election, one or more seats remain to be filled, a second and, if necessary, a third meeting shall take place.

Art. 12. If, after the third meeting, one or more seats still remain unfilled, a joint conference consisting of six members, three appointed by the Assembly and three by the Council, may be formed, at any time, at the request of either the Assembly or the Council, for the purpose of choosing one name for each seat still vacant, to submit to the Assembly and the Council for their respective acceptance.

If the Conference is unanimously agreed upon any person who fulfils the required conditions, he may be included in its list, even though he was not included in the list of nominations referred to in Articles 4 and 5.

If the joint conference is satisfied that it will not be successful in procuring an election, those members of the

Court who have already been appointed shall, within a period to be fixed by the Council, proceed to fill the vacant seats by selection from amongst those candidates who have obtained votes either in the Assembly or in the Council.

In the event of an equality of votes among the judges, the eldest judge shall have a casting vote.

*Art. 13. The members of the Court shall be elected for nine years.

They may be re-elected.

They shall continue to discharge their duties until their places have been filled. Though replaced, they shall finish any cases which they may have begun.

*Art. 14. Vacancies which may occur shall be filled by the same method as that laid down for the first election. A member of the Court elected to replace a member whose period of appointment had not expired will hold the appointment for the remainder of his predecessor's term.

*Art. 15. Deputy-judges shall be called upon to sit in the order laid down in a list.

This list shall be prepared by the Court and shall have regard firstly to priority of election and secondly to age.

*Art. 16. The ordinary members of the Court may not exercise any political or administrative function. This provision does not apply to the deputy-judges except when performing their duties on the Court.

Any doubt on this point is settled by the decision of the Court.

*Art. 17. No member of the Court can act as agent, counsel or advocate in any case of an international nature. This provision only applies to the deputy-judges as regards cases in which they are called upon to exercise their functions on the Court.

No member may participate in the decision of any case in which he has previously taken an active part, as agent, counsel or advocate for one of the contesting parties, or as a member of a national or international court, or of a commission of inquiry, or in any other capacity.

Any doubt on this point is settled by the decision of the Court.

Art. 18. A member of the Court can not be dismissed unless, in the unanimous opinion of the other members, he has ceased to fulfil the required conditions.

Formal notification thereof shall be made to the Secretary-General of the League of Nations, by the Registrar.

This notification makes the place vacant.

Art. 19. The members of the Court, when engaged on the business of the Court, shall enjoy diplomatic privileges and immunities.

Art. 20. Every member of the Court shall, before taking up his duties, make a solemn declaration in open Court that he will exercise his powers impartially and conscientiously.

Art. 21. The Court shall elect its President and Vice-President for three years; they may be re-elected.

It shall appoint its Registrar.

The duties of Registrar of the Court shall not be deemed incompatible with those of Secretary-General of the Permanent Court of Arbitration.

Art. 22. The seat of the Court shall be established at The Hague.

The President and Registrar shall reside at the seat of the Court.

*Art. 23. A session of the Court shall be held every year.

Unless otherwise provided by Rules of Court, this

session shall begin on the 15th of June, and shall continue for so long as may be deemed necessary to finish the cases on the list.

The President may summon an extraordinary session of the court whenever necessary.

Art. 24. If, for some special reason, a member of the Court considers that he should not take part in the decision of a particular case, he shall so inform the President.

If the President considers that for some special reason one of the members of the Court should not sit on a particular case, he shall give him notice accordingly.

If in any such case the member of the Court and the President disagree, the matter shall be settled by the decision of the Court.

*Art. 25. The full Court shall sit except when it is expressly provided otherwise.

If eleven judges can not be present, the number shall be made up by calling on deputy-judges to sit.

If, however, eleven judges are not available, a quorum of nine judges shall suffice to constitute the Court.

*Art. 26. Labor cases, particularly cases referred to in Part XIII (Labor) of the Treaty of Versailles and the corresponding portion of the other Treaties of Peace, shall be heard and determined by the Court under the following conditions:

The Court will appoint every three years a special chamber of five judges, selected so far as possible with due regard to the provisions of Article 9. In addition, two judges shall be selected for the purpose of replacing a judge who finds it impossible to sit. If the parties so demand, cases will be heard and determined by this Chamber. In the absence of any such demand, the Court will sit with the number of judges provided for in Article 25. On all occasions the judges will be assisted by four technical assessors sitting with them, but without the right to vote, and chosen with a view to ensuring a just representation of the competing interests.

If there is a national of one only of the parties sitting as a judge in the Chamber referred to in the preceding paragraph, the President will invite one of the other judges to retire in favor of a judge chosen by the other party in accordance with Article 31.

The technical assessors shall be chosen for each particular case in accordance with rules of procedure under Article 30 from a list of "Assessors for Labor cases" composed of two persons nominated by each Member of the League of Nations and an equivalent number nominated by the Governing Body of the Labor Office. The Governing Body will nominate, as to one-half, representatives of the workers, and as to one-half, representatives of employers from the list referred to in Article 412 of the Treaty of Versailles and the corresponding articles of the other Treaties of Peace.

In Labor cases the International Labor Office shall be at liberty to furnish the Court with all relevant information, and for this purpose the Director of that Office shall receive copies of all the written proceedings.

*Art. 27. Cases relating to transit and communications, particularly cases referred to in Part XII (Ports, Waterways and Railways) of the Treaty of Versailles and the corresponding portions of the other Treaties of Peace shall be heard and determined by the Court under the following conditions:

The Court will appoint every three years a special chamber of five judges, selected so far as possible with due regard to the provisions of Article 9. In addition, two judges shall be selected for the purpose of replacing a judge who finds it impossible to sit. If the parties so demand, cases will be heard and determined by this chamber. In the absence of any such demand, the Court will sit with the number of judges provided for in

Article 25. When desired by the parties or decided by the Court, the judges will be assisted by four technical assessors sitting with them, but without the right to vote.

If there is a national of one only of the parties sitting as a judge in the chamber referred to in the preceding paragraph, the President will invite one of the other judges to retire in favor of a judge chosen by the other party in accordance with Article 31.

The technical assessors shall be chosen for each particular case in accordance with rules of procedure under Article 30 from a list of "Assessors for Transit and Communications cases" composed of two persons nominated by each Member of the League of Nations.

Art. 28. The special chambers provided for in Articles 26 and 27 may, with the consent of the parties to the dispute, sit elsewhere than at The Hague.

*Art. 29. With a view to the speedy dispatch of business, the Court shall form annually a chamber composed of three judges who, at the request of the contesting parties, may hear and determine cases by summary procedure.

Art. 30. The Court shall frame rules for regulating its procedure. In particular, it shall lay down rules for summary procedure.

*Art. 31. Judges of the nationality of each contesting party shall retain their right to sit in the case before the Court.

If the Court includes upon the Bench a judge of the nationality of one of the parties only, the other party may select from among the deputy-judges a judge of its nationality, if there be one. If there should not be one, the party may choose a judge, preferably from among those persons who have been nominated as candidates as provided in Articles 4 and 5.

If the Court includes upon the Bench no judge of the nationality of the contesting parties, each of these may proceed to select or choose a judge as provided in the preceding paragraph.

Should there be several parties in the same interest, they shall, for the purpose of the preceding provisions, be reckoned as one party only. Any doubt upon this point is settled by the decision of the Court.

Judges selected or chosen as laid down in paragraphs 2 and 3 of this Article shall fulfil the conditions required by Articles 2, 16, 17, 20, 24 of this Statute. They shall take part in the decision on an equal footing with their colleagues.

*Art. 32. The judges shall receive an annual indemnity to be determined by the Assembly of the League of Nations upon the proposal of the Council. This indemnity must not be decreased during the period of a judge's appointment.

The President shall receive a special grant for his period of office, to be fixed in the same way.

The Vice-President, judges and deputy-judges, shall receive a grant for the actual performance of their duties, to be fixed in the same way.

Traveling expenses incurred in the performance of their duties shall be refunded to judges and deputy-judges who do not reside at the seat of the Court.

Grants due to judges selected or chosen as provided in Article 31 shall be determined in the same way.

The salary of the Registrar shall be decided by the Council upon the proposal of the Court.

The Assembly of the League of Nations shall lay down, on the proposal of the Council, a special regulation fixing the conditions under which retiring pensions may be given to the personnel of the Court.

Art. 33. The expenses of the Court shall be borne

by the League of Nations, in such a manner as shall be decided by the Assembly upon the proposal of the Council.

Chapter II. Competence of the Court

Art. 34. Only States or Members of the League of Nations can be parties in cases before the Court.

*Art. 35. The Court shall be open to the Members of the League and also to States mentioned in the Annex to the Covenant.

The conditions under which the Court shall be open to other States shall, subject to the special provisions contained in treaties in force, be laid down by the Council, but in no case shall such provisions place the parties in a position of inequality before the Court.

When a State which is not a Member of the League of Nations is a party to a dispute, the Court will fix the amount which that party is to contribute towards the expenses of the Court.

Art. 36. The jurisdiction of the Court comprises all cases which the parties refer to it and all matters specially provided for in Treaties and Conventions in force.

The Members of the League of Nations and the States mentioned in the Annex to the Covenant may, either when signing or ratifying the Protocol to which the present Statute is adjoined, or at a later moment, declare that they recognize as compulsory *ipso facto* and without special agreement, in relation to any other Member or State accepting the same obligation, the jurisdiction of the Court in all or any of the classes of legal disputes concerning:

    (*a*) the interpretation of a treaty;
    (*b*) any question of international law;

(c) the existence of any fact which, if established, would constitute a breach of an international obligation;
(d) the nature or extent of the reparation to be made for the breach of an international obligation.

The declaration referred to above may be made unconditionally or on condition of reciprocity on the part of several or certain Members or States, or for a certain time.

In the event of a dispute as to whether the Court has jurisdiction, the matter shall be settled by the decision of the Court.

Art. 37. When a treaty or convention in force provides for the reference of a matter to a tribunal to be instituted by the League of Nations, the Court will be such tribunal.

Art. 38. The Court shall apply:
1. International conventions, whether general or particular, establishing rules expressly recognized by the contesting States;
2. International custom, as evidence of a general practice accepted as law;
3. The general principles of law recognized by civilized nations;
4. Subject to the provisions of Article 59, judicial decisions and the teachings of the most highly qualified publicists of the various nations, as subsidiary means for the determination of rules of law.

This provision shall not prejudice the power of the Court to decide a case *ex aequo et bono*, if the parties agree thereto.

Chapter III. Procedure

*Art. 39. The official languages of the Court shall be French and English. If the parties agree that the case shall be conducted in French, the judgment will be delivered in French. If the parties agree that the case shall be conducted in English, the judgment will be delivered in English.

In the absence of an agreement as to which language shall be employed, each party may, in the pleadings, use the language which it prefers; the decision of the Court will be given in French and English. In this case the Court will at the same time determine which of the two texts shall be considered as authoritative.

The Court may, at the request of the parties, authorize a language other than French or English to be used.

*Art. 40. Cases are brought before the Court, as the case may be, either by the notification of the special agreement, or by a written application addressed to the Registrar. In either case the subject of the dispute and the contesting parties must be indicated.

The Registrar shall forthwith communicate the application to all concerned.

He shall also notify the Members of the League of Nations through the Secretary-General.

Art. 41. The Court shall have the power to indicate, if it considers that circumstances so require, any provisional measures which ought to be taken to reserve the respective rights of either party.

Pending the final decision, notice of the measures suggested shall forthwith be given to the parties and the Council.

Art. 42. The parties shall be represented by agents. They may have the assistance of counsel or advocates before the Court.

Art. 43. The procedure shall consist of two parts: written and oral.

The written proceedings shall consist of the communication to the judges and to the parties of Cases, Counter-Cases and, if necessary, Replies; also all papers and documents in support.

These communications shall be made through the Registrar, to the order and within the time fixed by the Court.

A certified copy of every document produced by one party shall be communicated to the other party.

The oral proceedings shall consist of the hearing by the Court of witnesses, experts, agents, counsel and advocates.

Art. 44. For the service of all notices upon persons other than the agents, counsel and advocates, the Court shall apply direct to the government of the State upon whose territory the notice has to be served.

The same provision shall apply whenever steps are to be taken to procure evidence on the spot.

*Art. 45. The hearing shall be under the control of the President or, in his absence, of the Vice-President; if both are absent, the senior judge shall preside.

Art. 46. The hearing in Court shall be public, unless the Court shall decide otherwise, or unless the parties demand that the public be not admitted.

Art. 47. Minutes shall be made at each hearing, and signed by the Registrar and the President.

These minutes shall be the only authentic record.

Art. 48. The Court shall make orders for the conduct of the case, shall decide the form and time in which each party must conclude its arguments, and make all arrangements connected with the taking of evidence.

Art. 49. The Court may, even before the hearing begins, call upon the agents to produce any document, or to supply any explanations. Formal note shall be taken of any refusal.

Art. 50. The Court may, at any time, entrust any individual, body, bureau, commission or other organization that it may select, with the task of carrying out an enquiry or giving an expert opinion.

Art. 51. During the hearing, any relevant questions are to be put to the witnesses and experts under the conditions laid down by the Court in the rules of procedure referred to in Article 30.

Art. 52. After the Court has received the proofs and evidence within the time specified for the purpose, it may refuse to accept any further oral or written evidence that one party may desire to present unless the other side consents.

Art. 53. Whenever one of the parties shall not appear before the Court, or shall fail to defend his case, the other party may call upon the Court to decide in favor of his claim.

The Court must, before doing so, satisfy itself, not only that it has jurisdiction in accordance with Articles 36 and 37, but also that the claim is well founded in fact and law.

Art. 54. When, subject to the control of the Court, the agents, advocates and counsel have completed their presentation of the case, the President shall declare the hearing closed.

The Court shall withdraw to consider the judgment.

The deliberations of the Court shall take place in private and remain secret.

Art. 55. All questions shall be decided by a majority of the judges present at the hearing.

In the event of an equality of votes, the President or his deputy shall have a casting vote.

Art. 56. The judgment shall state the reasons on which it is based.

It shall contain the names of the judges who have taken part in the decision.

Art. 57. If the judgment does not represent in whole or in part the unanimous opinion of the judges, dissenting judges are entitled to deliver a separate opinion.

Art. 58. The judgment shall be signed by the President and by the Registrar. It shall be read in open Court, due notice having been given to the agents.

Art. 59. The decision of the Court has no binding force except between the parties and in respect of that particular case.

Art. 60. The judgment is final and without appeal. In the event of dispute as to the meaning or scope of the judgment, the Court shall construe it upon the request of any party.

Art. 61. An application for revision of a judgment can be made only when it is based upon the discovery of some fact of such a nature as to be a decisive factor, which fact was, when the judgment was given, unknown to the Court and also to the party claiming revision, always provided that such ignorance was not due to negligence.

The proceedings for revision will be opened by a judgment of the Court expressly recording the existence of the new fact, recognizing that it has such a character as to lay the case open to revision, and declaring the application admissible on this ground.

The Court may require previous compliance with the terms of the judgment before it admits proceedings in revision.

The application for revision must be made at latest within six months of the discovery of the new fact.

No application for revision may be made after the lapse of ten years from the date of the sentence.

Art. 62. Should a State consider that it has an interest of a legal nature which may be affected by the decision in the case, it may submit a request to the Court to be permitted to intervene as a third party.

It will be for the Court to decide upon this request.

Art. 63. Whenever the construction of a convention to which States other than those concerned in the case are parties is in question, the Registrar shall notify all such States forthwith.

Every State so notified has the right to intervene in the proceedings; but if it uses this right, the construction given by the judgment will be equally binding upon it.

Art. 64. Unless otherwise decided by the Court, each party shall bear its own costs.

BIBLIOGRAPHY

BAKER, P. J. N., *Disarmament*, London, 1926
BAKER, R. S., *Woodrow Wilson and World Settlement*, New York, 1922
BOECKEL, F. B., *Between War and Peace*, New York, 1928
BUTLER, SIR G., *Handbook to the League of Nations*, 2d ed., London, 1925
BUSTAMANTE, A. S. DE, *World Court*, New York, 1925

CONWELL-EVANS, T. P., *The League Council in Action*, London, 1929
COOPER, RUSSEL M., *American Consultation in World Affairs*, New York, 1934

DUNN, FREDERICK S., *The Practice and Procedure of International Conferences*, Baltimore, 1929

EAGLETON, CLYDE, *International Government*, New York, 1932

FITE, E. D., *Government by Cooperation*, New York, 1932

GREAVES, H. G. R., *The League Committees and World Order*, Oxford, 1931

HEDGES, R. YORKE, *International Organization*, London, 1935
HILL, NORMAN L., *International Administration*, New York, 1931
HILL, NORMAN L., *The Public International Conference*, Stanford, 1929
HOWARD-ELLIS, C., *The Origin, Structure and Working of the League of Nations*, London, 1928
HUBBARD, URSULA P., *The Cooperation of the United States with the League of Nations*, New York, 1937
HUDSON, MANLEY O., *International Legislation (Texts of Treaties, 1919–1931)* Vol. 1–5, Washington
HUDSON, MANLEY O., *The Permanent Court of International Justice*, New York, 1934

HUDSON, MANLEY O., *By Pacific Means*, New Haven, 1935
HUNT, E. E., *Conferences, Committees, Conventions*, New York, 1925

International Labour Office, *Report of the Director*, Annual

JESSUP, PHILIP C., *International Security*, New York, 1935

KNUDSON, JOHN I., *Methods of International Legislation*, Geneva, 1928

League of Nations, Secretariat, *Ten Years of World Cooperation*, Geneva, 1930
League of Nations Information Section, *Essential Facts About the League of Nations*, 1937
League of Nations, *Handbook of International Organizations*, Geneva, 1937
League of Nations, *Monthly Summary*
League of Nations, *Official Journal*
League of Nations, *Report of the Secretary-General*, Annual
League of Nations, *Treaty Series*
League of Nations, Labor Office, *The First Decade*, Geneva, 1931

MADARIAGA, S. DE, *Disarmament*, Oxford, 1929
MARBURG, T., *Development of the League of Nations Idea*, New York, 1932
MILLER, D. H., *Drafting of the Covenant*, New York, 1928
MITRANY, D., *Problem of International Sanctions*, London, 1925
MORLEY, FELIX, *The Society of Nations*, Washington, 1932
MOWER, E. C., *International Government*, Boston, 1931
MYERS, DENYS P., *Handbook of the League of Nations*, Boston, 1935

PARKES, J. W., *International Conferences*, Geneva, 1933
POOLE, D. C., *Conduct of Foreign Relations under Modern Democratic Conditions*, New Haven, 1924
PORRITT, A., ED., *The Causes of War*, London, 1932
POTTER, PITMAN B., *An Introduction to the Study of International Organization*, New York, 1935

RAPPARD, W. E., *International Relations as Viewed from Geneva*, New Haven, 1925
REINSCH, P. S., *Public International Unions*, Boston, 1911
Report on the Work of the League (Official Publications), Annual

SATOW, SIR E., *International Congresses*, London, 1920
SAYRE, F. B., *Experiments in International Administration*, New York, 1919
SCHUMAN, FREDERICK L., *International Politics*, New York, 1937
SHOTWELL, JAMES T., *On the Rim of the Abyss*, New York, 1936

TEMPERLEY, H. W. V., ED., *History of the Peace Conference of Paris*, London, 1920
The League Year to Year (Information Section), Annual
The Future of the League of Nations (Royal Institute of International Affairs), London, 1936

VINACKE, H. M., *International Organization*, New York, 1934

WEBSTER, C. K., *League of Nations in Theory and Practice*, London, 1933
WHITE, L. C., *Structure of Private International Organization*, Philadelphia, 1933
WILLIAMS, BENJAMIN H., *American Diplomacy*, 1936
WILLIAMS, JOHN F., *Some Aspects of the Covenant of the League of Nations*, London, 1934
WILSON, F., *Origins of the League Covenant*, London, 1928
WILSON, F. G., *The International Labor Organization*, New York, 1932
WOOLF, L. S., *International Government*, New York, 1916
WRIGHT, Q., *Mandates under the League of Nations*, Chicago, 1930

INDEX

A

Aerial transportation, 239, 240
Alexander I, Assassination of, 93
Alexandretta dispute, 106, 163
Angell, Norman, 23
Anglo-French Agreement (1935), 128
Arbitration, 63ff
Arms competition, 151ff
Arts and Letters, Comm. of, 283
Asquith, Prime Minister, 23
Assembly of the League, Committees, 46–47; Convoking Conferences, 247, 250, 254; Covenant revision, 356ff; Disputes, settlement of, 67, 68, 85, 86; Jurisdiction, 42, 52, 56, 59, 60, 335; Legislation, 47, 200, 201; Membership, 46; Minorities, 171, 172
Auxiliary Organs of the League, 60ff
Avenol, M. Joseph, 54

B

Balfour, A. J., 23
Bank for International Settlements, 180
Bannerman, Sir Henry C., 23
Barthou, Louis, 93
Bentham, Jeremy, 21
"Big Four," 29
Borah, William E., 40
Boycott, economic, 72
Bryce, Lord, 23
Budget of the League, 60

C

Calendar Reform, 242
Carnegie Endowment for International Peace, 22

Cecil, Lord Robert, 25, 32
Central Organization for the Durable Peace, 23
Chaco Dispute, 84–86, 296ff, 367
Chamber of Commerce, International 242
Chamberlain, William H., 117
Child welfare, 59, 251ff
Cinematographic Institute, 275
Clemenceau, Georges, 29, 153
Commission, Permanent Mandates, 161ff
Committee of Eighteen, 98–99
Communication and Transit Section, 59, 201, 202, 230ff
Conferences, Armaments (1932), 147ff; Barcelona, 231, 233, 237; Brussels, 207; Customs Formalities, 210; Definition, 203; Imports and Exports, 210, 211; Labor, 321ff; Lisbon (1930), 238; Opium, 247
Congress of Vienna (1815), 226, 237, 261
Corfu Incident, 76, 77
Council of the League, Administration, 161, 179, 180; Disputes, settlement of, 65ff, 295; Executive duties, 52, 290; Jurisdiction, 46, 49ff, 333; Meetings, 51ff; Membership, 48–49; Minorities, 169ff
Covenant of the League, Article 1; 44; Article 3; 47; Article 5; 38, 47; Article 8; 138, 149; Article 10; 36, 81, 85, 136, 287, 306, 358ff; Article 11; 65ff, 108ff; Article 12; 81, 89, 98, 110, 111; Article 13; 352; Article 14; 82, 333;

[441]

INDEX

Covenant of the League (*cont.*)
Article 15; 70, 86, 89, 91, 96, 97, 136;
Article 16; 11, 44, 50, 111, 136, 358ff;
Article 18; 57, 58, 119, 293; Article 19; 42, 70, 71, 307, 369; Article 22; 159, 160; Article 23; 206, 230, 245, 246, 250, 262, 265; Article 24; 59, 229, 230, 265; Article 26; 50, 356; Amendment of, 356ff
Cox, Jas. M., 41
Crucé, Emeric, 21

D

Danzig, Administration, 182; Background, 181; High Commissioner, 50; Recent disturbances, 183, 184
Davis, Norman, 79, 185, 302
Dawes, Chas. G., 295, 296
Disarmament Conference (1932), 58, 121, 147ff, 277, 302, 361, 365
Drummond, Sir James Eric, 37, 54
Dubois, Pierre, 21

E

Economic Committee, 209ff
Economic Conference (1933), 121, 202, 215ff, 365
Economic nationalism, 218ff
Eden, Anthony, 125, 131
Experts, 202, 203, 207, 216ff, 231ff

F

Fellowship of Reconciliation, 22
Financial Section, 58, 208, 209
Foreign Affairs, control of, 114ff
"Fourteen Points," 27, 37, 118, 119, 167, 168
Franco, Francisco, 107

G

Garibaldi, G., 22
Geneva Protocol (1924), 146
Geneva, seat of League, 121ff

Germany, Rearmament, 102, 103; Rhineland occupation, 103, 104
Gilbert, Prentiss, 295
Gompers, Samuel, 318
Governing Body of Labor, 321, 324ff
Graham, Frank P., 18
Grey, Sir Edward, 23, 137
Grotius, Hugo, 21

H

Hague Peace Conference (1899), 64, 140, 196; (1907), 140
Harding, Warren G., 40, 41, 287
Health Section, 59, 201, 263ff
Henderson, Arthur, 148
Highway Traffic Control, 235, 236
Hitler, Adolf, 102, 149
Hoare, Sir Samuel, 100, 128ff
Holt, Hamilton, 24
Holy Alliance, 20
Hoover, Herbert, 143
Howland, Chas. P., 256
Howland, William, 24
Hubbard, Ursula P., 18
Hudson, Manley O., 18
Hughes, Charles E., 33, 142, 336
Hugo, Victor, 22
Hull, Cordell, 7, 9, 99, 213, 298, 300
Hurst, Sir Cecil, 32, 33

I

Information Section, 58, 121, 123
Institute of Intellectual Cooperation, 274
Intellectual Cooperation, 59, 230, 272ff
International Bureaus, 59
International Disputes, Albanian Boundary, 71; Alexandretta, 106, Anglo-Persian Oil Dispute, 90; Bulgarian Armed Bands, 75; Chaco Dispute, 84–86; Civil War in Spain, 107; Columbia and Peru, 91–92; Corfu Incident, 76; Eastern Carelia, 74;

[442]

INDEX

International Disputes (*cont.*)
Finland and Sweden, 68; Finland and the United Kingdom, 95; Greco-Bulgarian Incident, 81; Greco-Turkish Frontier, 82; Hungarian-Czechoslovakian Frontier, 75; Hungarian Property in Rumania, 76; Hungarian-Yugoslav Frontier, 92–94; Italo-Ethiopian Conflict, 96–102; Memel, 79; Moslems of Albanian Origin in Greece, 83; Mosul Boundary Dispute, 80; Oecumenical Patriarch, Expulsion of, 80; Persia and Soviet Russia, 68; Poland and Lithuania, 69; Polish Czechoslovakian Frontier, 78; Rearmament of Germany, 102–3; Remilitarization of the Rhineland, 103–5; Sino-Japanese Conflict, 86–90; Tacna-Arica, 70; Upper Silesia, 73; Uruguay and Russia, 105; War Losses of Swiss Nationals, 94–5
International Financial Conference, 51
International League for Peace and Freedom (1867), 22
International Legislation, Extent of, 199ff, 245ff; History of, 194ff, 225ff; Methods of, 291ff; Procedure, 197, 366
"International Passports," 257
International Peace Congress (1830), 22
International Red Cross, 260
International Relief Union, 260ff
International Women's Peace Society (1896), 22
Italo-Ethiopian Conflict, 96–102, 126, 127ff, 150, 299ff, 367

J
Johnson, Hiram W., 40

K
Kant, Immanuel, 21
Kellogg-Briand Pact, 87, 91, 139, 154, 308, 310, 363

Kellogg, Frank B., 336
Knox, Philander C., 40

L
Labor Organization, International, General Conference, 321ff; Governing Body, 324ff; Labor Office, 325ff; Membership, 319; Objectives, 329ff; Origin, 318ff; United States and, 303
Lausanne, Treaty of, 80, 81, 83
Laval, Premier Pierre, 100, 127ff
League to Enforce Peace, 23–5, 40
League of Nations Assn., 309, 362–363
League of Nations' Society, 22
League of Nations Union, 126
Legal Section of the League, 57
Lemonnier, A., 22
Lengyel, Emil, 18
Leticia, 91, 92, 298
Lloyd George, David, 29, 30
Locarno Treaties (1926), 104, 146–7, 150, 362
Lodge, Senator H. C., 33, 39
Lowell, A. Lawrence, 24
Lytton Report, 88

M
MacDonald, Ramsay, 143
Mandates, 58, 61; Change in status, 164; Commission, 161ff; Extension of, 165; Territories, 160
Marburg, Theodore, 24
Marsiglio of Padua, 21
McDonald, Jas. G., 258
Mediation, 63ff
Membership in the League, 43, 44ff
Memel, 79, 185ff
Meyers, Denys P., 18
Miller, David Hunter, 32, 33
Minorities, 58; Background, 165ff; Extension of, 172, 173; Successes, 174, 175; Treaties, 168ff; Weaknesses, 177
Monetary and Economic Conference (1933), 215–217

[443]

INDEX

Monroe Doctrine, 33, 35, 36, 294, 298
Montevideo Conference, 85
Moore, John Basset, 64, 336
Mussolini, Premier, 125ff, 301, 358

N

Nansen, Dr. Fridtjof, 256
National Peace Conference, 309
Neutrality, American, 300, 301
New York Peace Society, 22
"Nine Power" Treaty, 9, 10, 295
Nobel Peace Foundation, 22

O

Obscene Publications, 253ff
"Official Journal," 62, 170, 179
Opium, Traffic in, 59, 61, 246ff
"Optional Clause," 337, 338
Organizations, Private International, 117ff
Orlando, Signor, 29

P

Pan-American Conference, 84, 85
Pan-American Union, 264, 362
Paris Peace Conference (1919), 27ff, 37, 198, 200, 318
Passport Facilities, 232ff
Paul-Boncour, J., 361
"Peace ballot" in England, 125, 126
Penn, William, 21
Permanent Court of International Justice, Advisory Opinions, 74, 78, 80, 81, 95, 351, 171; Belgian-Chinese Case, 343; Brazilian Loans, 345–6; Eastern Greenland, 347, 348; Election of Judges, 336; Judgements, 340; Jurisdiction 337ff; Lighthouses, 349; Lotus Case, 343, 344; Mavrommatis Concession, 341; Membership, 336; Memel Territory, 347; Minorities in Upper Silesia, 344, 345, Oder River Commission, 346; Organization of,

Permanent Court (cont.)
47, 333ff; Oscar Chinn Case, 349, 350; Peter Pazmany University, 348–9; Polish Upper Silesia, 342, 343; Prince von Pless, 348; Procedure, 338, 339, 366; Relation to the League, 50, 352, 353; Serbian Loans, 345; S. S. Wimbledon, 340, 341; Statutes, 335; Treaty of Neuilly, 342; United States and, 303ff, 336ff; Upper Savoy, 346
Permanent Health Organization, 265ff
Phillimore, Sir Walter, 25
Political Section of the League, 57
Pope, Senator James P., 310
Ports and Maritime Navigation, 236–239
Postal Union, Universal, 227–229
Power Transmission, 240, 241
Private Law, unification of, 277
Public Opinion, influence of, 118ff, 127ff, 134ff
Public Unions, 59
Public Works Projects, 242

R

Radio, Control of, 228, 278
Railway Transportation, 234, 235
Reed, Jas. A., 40
Refugees, 255ff
Rockefeller Foundation, 22, 271, 288
Rockefeller, John D. Jr., 57
Roosevelt, Pres. Franklin D., 8, 11, 15, 301, 307, 308
Roosevelt, Theodore, 24
Root, Elihu, 33, 40, 154, 288, 304, 335
Rush-Bagot Agreement, 139

S

Saar Basin, Administration, 177ff; Commission, 50, 179; Plebiscite, 180; Territory, 179
St. Germain, Treaty (1919), 78
Saint-Pierre, A., 21

INDEX

Secretariat, Duties, 53, 56, 57, 61, 266, 291ff; Officials, 57; Staff regulations, 54
Secretary-General of the League, Appointment of, 54; Duties, 55, 56, 65, 202, 203
Senate of U. S., 6, 25, 33, 34, 38, 40, 45, 119, 120, 304ff
Shotwell, James T., 281, 283, 362
Sino-Japanese Conflict, 86–90, 295ff, 367
Slavery, Traffic in, 260ff
Smuts, General, 32, 158
Society of Friends, 22
Spain, Civil War, 107ff
Stead, W. B., 23
"Stimson Doctrine," 89
Stimson, Henry L., 295
Studies Conference, 282ff
Supreme War Council, 28, 73, 198

T

Tacna-Arica Dispute, 70
Taft, William H., 24, 25, 33, 40
Telegraphic Union, International, 227, 229
Trade Union Congress, 126
Transit Organization, 230ff
Treasury Section, 59
Treaty, Mutual Assistance (1923), 146
Treaties of Peace, 30, 31, 37–43, 141
Treaties, Registration of, 58, 203, 204, 293

U

Union of Democratic Control, 22
United States, Abstention from League, 286ff, 364; Council sessions, 87, Economic Conf., 215, 216; Foreign policy, 294, 309ff, 363; Foreign trade, 220ff; Italo-Ethiopian Dispute, 299ff; Labor Organization, 303, 319, 323, 324; League Conferences, 289ff, 364ff, 370; Minorities, 175ff; Sanctions, 99, 100, 299ff; Trade treaties, 224; World Court, 303ff
"Unofficial observers," 288, 289
Upper Silesia, 73, 187ff

W

Wallace, Henry A., 223
"Walwal incident," 96
Washington Conference (1922), 141, 142
White, Francis, 297
Wilson, Woodrow, "Fourteen Points," 27, 167; League to Enforce Peace, 25; Mandates, 158; Meeting of Council, 38; Minorities, 167ff; Peace Conference, 28ff, 34, 35; Senate of U. S., 40; Territorial Administration, 178, 181, 184
Women and Children, Traffic in, 59, 249ff
World Peace Foundation, 22
World Union of Women for International Concord, 23

AUGSBURG COLLEGE AND SEMINARY
LIBRARY - MINNEAPOLIS 4, MINN.